# Nottinghamshire's Lost Railways

Neil Burgess

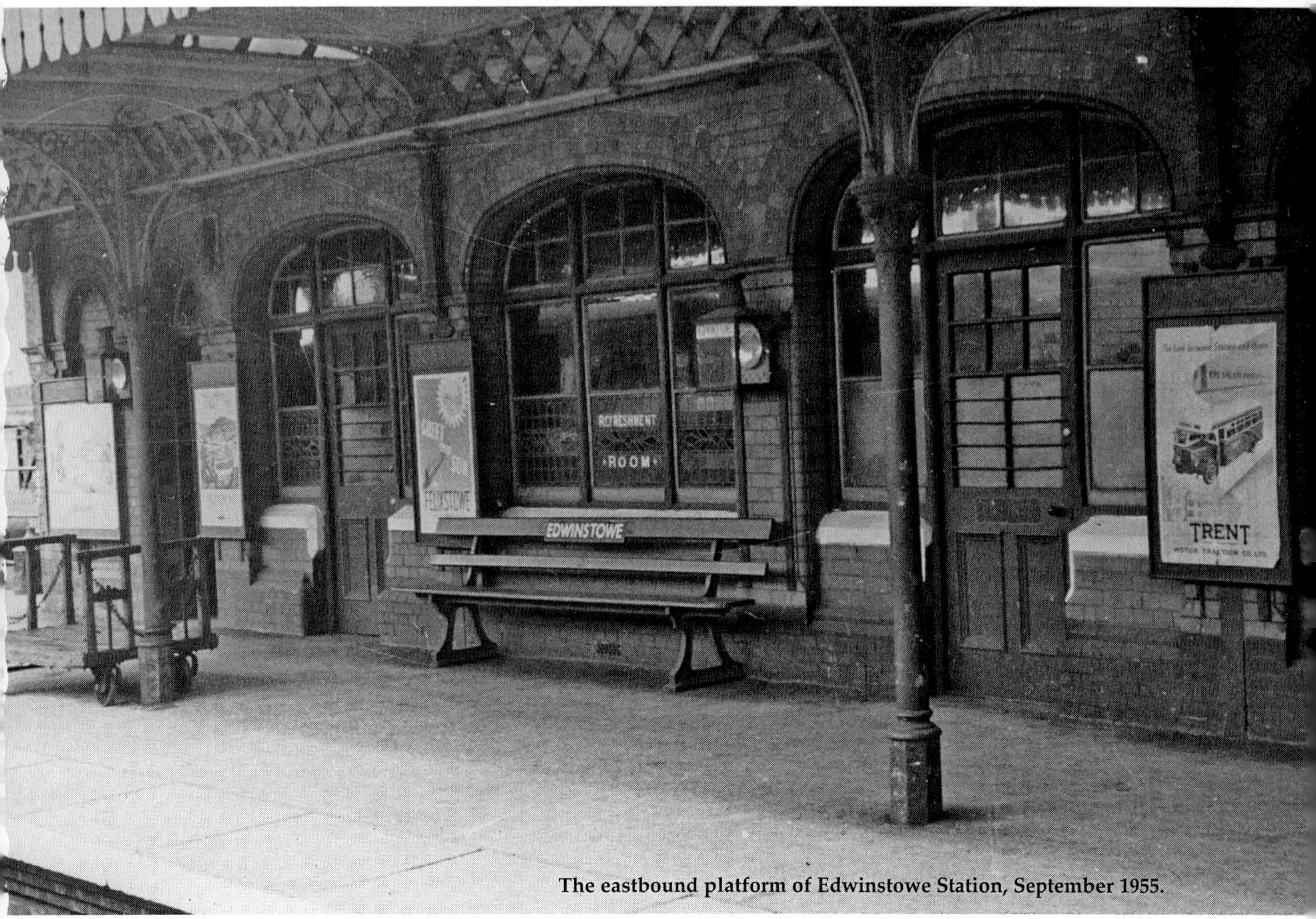


The eastbound platform of Edwinstowe Station, September 1955.

Stenlake Publishing Ltd

Text © Neil Burgess, 2017
First Published in the United Kingdom, 2017
Stenlake Publishing Limited
54–58 Mill Square, Catrine, KA5 6RD
www.stenlake.co.uk

ISBN 9781840337747

*Printed by*
Blissetts,
Roslin Road
Acton
W3 8DH

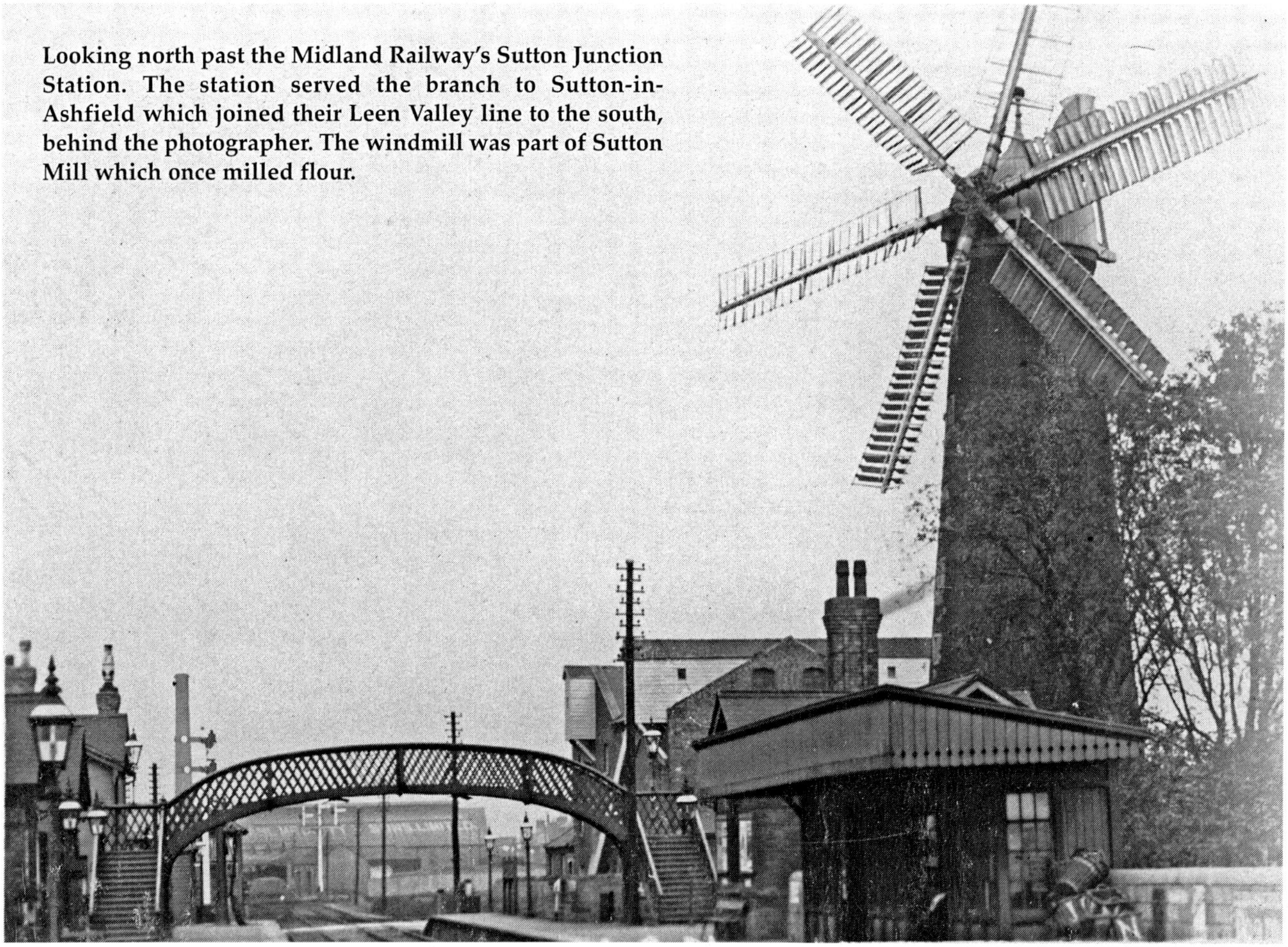

**Looking north past the Midland Railway's Sutton Junction Station. The station served the branch to Sutton-in-Ashfield which joined their Leen Valley line to the south, behind the photographer. The windmill was part of Sutton Mill which once milled flour.**

## Closure Dates

This book lists dates when stations and lines were closed to regular scheduled passenger traffic. Readers should recognise that sources vary in deciding closure dates, some giving the last day on which regular services operated, and others the first day when closure was effected and no passenger traffic operated. Especially on lines with no regular Sunday service, this might yield a discrepancy of two days, depending on the method used.

In some cases, particularly before the mid-1960s, stations along closed lines might have been left substantially intact and periodically excursion trains would call to pick up or set down passengers. Where sources indicate that this happened it may be noted in the text, but it does not affect the official closure date.

## Acknowledgements

I am again grateful to my friend and fellow railway historian Richard Morton for his meticulous proof-reading and for checking the information in this book. He has, as ever, drawn my attention to various points and inaccuracies and I am indebted to him for his diligence. The publishers wish to thank the following for contributing photographs to this book: John Alsop for the back cover, and the inside front and back covers (both) as well as pages 2, 5, 6 (both), 7, 8,) 10 (upper), 12, 14 (lower), 16 (upper), 24 (upper), 27 (lower), 28 (upper), 35 (upper), 36 (both), 42 (upper), 43 (lower), 44 (both), 46 (upper), 50 (both), 51, 52, 53 (both), 55 (both), 57, 60 (lower), 61 (upper), 62, 63 (both), 64 (upper), 65 (both), 71 (both), 72 (both), 76 (lower), 77, 78 and 80 (both); Richard Casserley for the front cover, as well as pages 1, 4, 9 (both), 10 (lower), 11 (both), 14 (upper), 15 (upper), 16 (lower), 17 (both), 18, (both), 19 (both), 21 (both), 22 (both), 23, 24 (lower), 25, 26 (both), 27 (upper), 32 (lower), 33 (both), 34, 35 (lower), 37 (both), 38 (both), 40, 41 (both), 43 (upper), 45, 46 (lower), 47, 48 (both), 49, 54 (both), 60 (upper), 61 (lower), 64 (lower), 66, 68 (both), 69, 73, 74, 76 (upper); and Richard Stenlake for pages 28 (lower), 29 (both), 30 (both), 31 (both), 32 (upper), 42 (lower) and 56.

# Introduction

Nottingham is the largest city in the east midlands and the county has a particular place within the popular history of England, for who has not heard of Robin Hood and his old adversary, the Sheriff of Nottingham? Robin's stronghold, the royal Forest of Sherwood, covered not only most of the county but spread across the Trent almost to Lincoln. Charles I surrendered to the forces of Parliament at Newark in 1647 and that ancient borough was one of the staging points on the Great North Road between London and Scotland. Until the coming of the industrial age in the nineteenth century Nottinghamshire was a largely rural county and the east and south still have a pastoral feel, even if some of their villages have become suburbanised by the outward spread of Nottingham. Waterways like the Trent, and the canals which were developed through the second half of the eighteenth century, allowed industry to grow, including textiles and the lace-making which made Nottingham famous. But it was coal which transformed the western side of the county, the coalfield crossing the River Erewash into Derbyshire and taking in ancient Nottinghamshire towns like Mansfield and Worksop, as well as transforming many of the villages into mining communities. It was here, in Eastwood just north of Nottingham, that David Herbert Lawrence was born and grew up, the novels which later made him famous reflecting the often harsh realities of life in the coalfield. Not far down the road from Eastwood, at Newstead, lived another of Nottinghamshire's literary sons, Lord Byron; though in truth he spent little of his time actually in residence at Newstead Abbey, which he inherited along with his title in 1810.

As a railway centre, Nottingham is significant as one of the terminal points for the Midland main line from St Pancras and also deals with a healthy volume of cross-country passenger traffic: indeed the Midland Railway itself grew out of an amalgamation of three companies, one of which, the Midland Counties Railway, was formed in 1832 at a meeting at the Sun Inn in Eastwood. Long before its ambitions took it to the capital, the Midland developed a network of lines through Nottinghamshire, radiating out from the city in search of coal and the wealth that traffic brought. Coal was the attraction for a rival, in the form of the Great Northern Railway, its line cutting across the county from Grantham to Derby, going on eventually – and slowly – to Stafford and throwing off a variety of branch lines through the valleys of the Leen and the Erewash. Coal even brought the Midland's arch-rival, the London & North Western Railway, into the heart of Nottingham, but only at the end of a long and straggling line through the Leicestershire uplands.

Nottingham also housed the showpiece of the northern end of the last long-distance main line to be constructed in Britain. The Manchester, Sheffield & Lincolnshire Railway promoted its route to London through Nottingham during the 1890s, transforming itself into the Great Central in the process and constructing the vast and splendid Victoria Station – a far more impressive structure than its London terminus at Marylebone – in the very heart of the city. The Great Central was a truly visionary project, a line built to

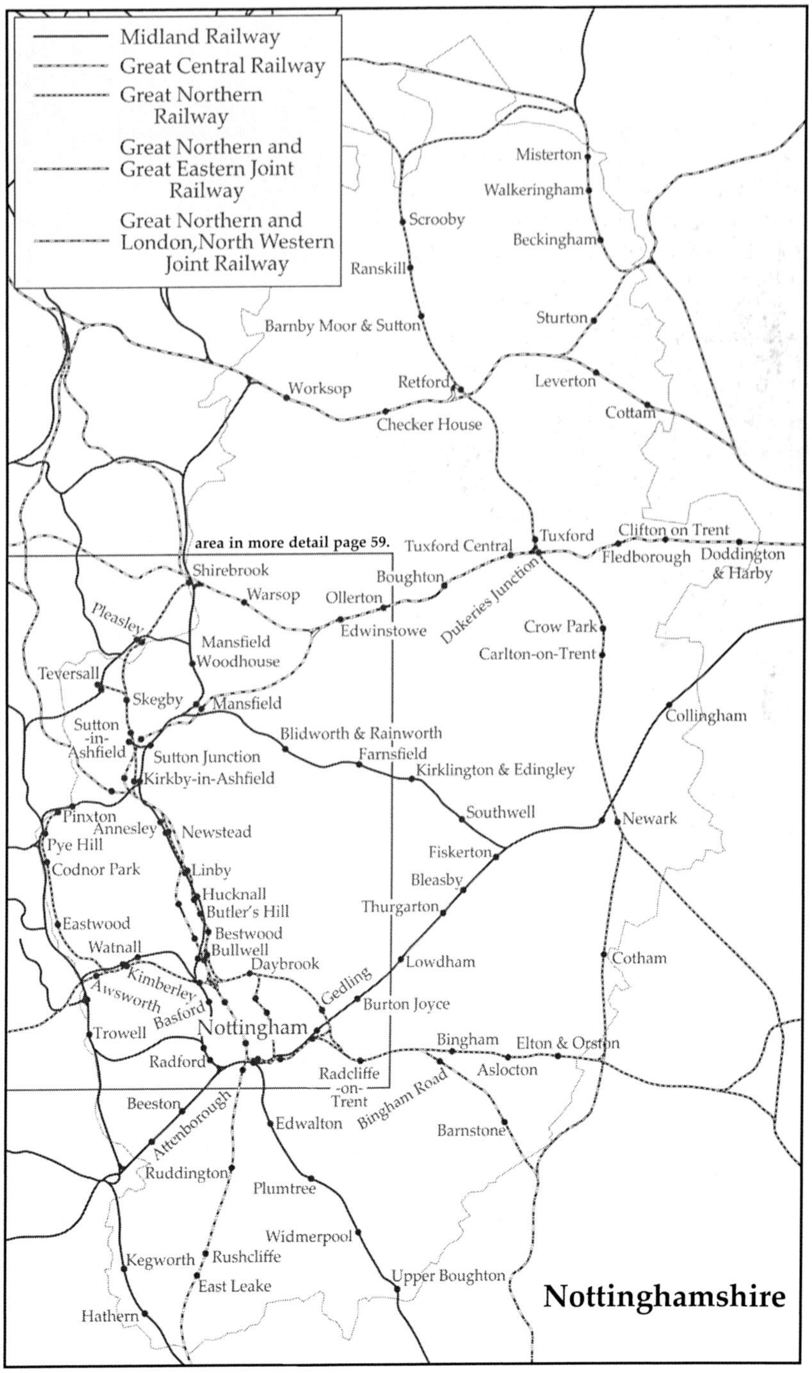

European loading gauge to connect with a channel tunnel – a century before that dream became reality – and offering a service built on all the accumulated wisdom of sixty years of railway development; and yet it was also a meteoric one. The comparison with the Midland – over whose station it confidently strode – is striking; the Midland line was authorised in 1836, arrived in Nottingham in June 1839 and is still there, 170 years later; the Great Central came and went within just seventy years.

Nottinghamshire's branch lines tended to owe their origins to coal, even if, like the line through Southwell to Rolleston Junction on the Midland's Lincoln route, they ran through agricultural countryside rather than the coalfield itself. It was certainly coal which kept them going, sometimes long after their owners had despaired of passengers and bowed to the competitive pressure of the electric street tramway, the motor bus and later the private car. But coal was not for ever, even if there are still large reserves under the ground waiting to be extracted. The run-down of the mining industry in Nottinghamshire spelt the end for the lines which it had sustained, though a number still keep going to transport coal to power stations – though this particular coal tends to come from Poland and eastern Europe, shipped in through the port of Immingham.

One of the coal-hauling lines, or more correctly a route made out of several originally separate ones, has provided Nottinghamshire with an example of railway renaissance. The lines through the Leen valley to the west of Nottingham have seen a revival as the 'Robin Hood Line' – what else? – during the 1990s when it eventually began to dawn on national and local governments that the 1960s solution to urban transport – the car – was actually no solution at all, but a dead-end. Nottingham, which has a growing problem of traffic congestion around its centre, also became one of the pioneers of the reintroduction of another long-abandoned aspect of urban transport, the electric tram. The routes which run through the city centre, and which connect with the Robin Hood line along the way, make use of the abandoned Great Central line bridges and viaducts to reach the southern extent of their present network, an interesting example of the principle of recycling.

Another renaissance has been a further part of the Great Central's London Extension. Although the section from Loughborough southwards to Quorn & Woodhouse had reopened in 1974, followed by the extension to Rothley two years later and then on to Belgrave & Birstall – now renamed Leicester North – in 1991, the removal of the bridge carrying the line over the Midland route to Leicester seemed to mean that there would be no expansion northwards. Yet the line as far as Ruddington had remained *in situ* to serve the Gypsum works at East Leake and a Ministry of Defence depot. This was transformed into the Great Central Railway (Nottingham) and the Nottingham Transport Heritage Centre during the 1990s and now there is every possibility that the sections of the line north and south of Loughborough will be reunited in the future.

Even so, there remains much of Nottinghamshire's railway network which is unlikely ever to see a train again. As in other counties, lines have closed and all but disappeared into their surroundings. Though there are traces, the Nottingham Suburban Railway and other Great Northern routes around the city have largely vanished, their cuttings and tunnels filled in, their embankments and bridges bulldozed and their station sites submerged under new building. There is, in one way, a certain symmetry to all this; the railways were part of a major social upheaval which transformed all of British society during the nineteenth century and the disappearance of so many lines has been part of a further and in many ways equally far-reaching transformation in our own time. It is sobering to think that just as many people mourn the passing of lines today, so several generations ago there were plenty of our ancestors who deplored their coming. Even so, it is sad to glimpse the remains of Victoria Station in Nottingham and think on the splendour – albeit a rather smoky splendour – of the past; or wonder what the Leen Valley might have looked like in the early years of the twentieth century with three routes running alongside each other through Basford, Bulwell and Hucknall; or to think of travelling on the 'Southwell Paddy' along the valley of the Trent from Rolleston or on the 'Penny Emma' to Sutton-in-Ashfield. Though these sights and sounds are long gone, hopefully these pages will evoke their memory once again.

**Rail tour at Wellbeck Colliery Platform, July 1960.**

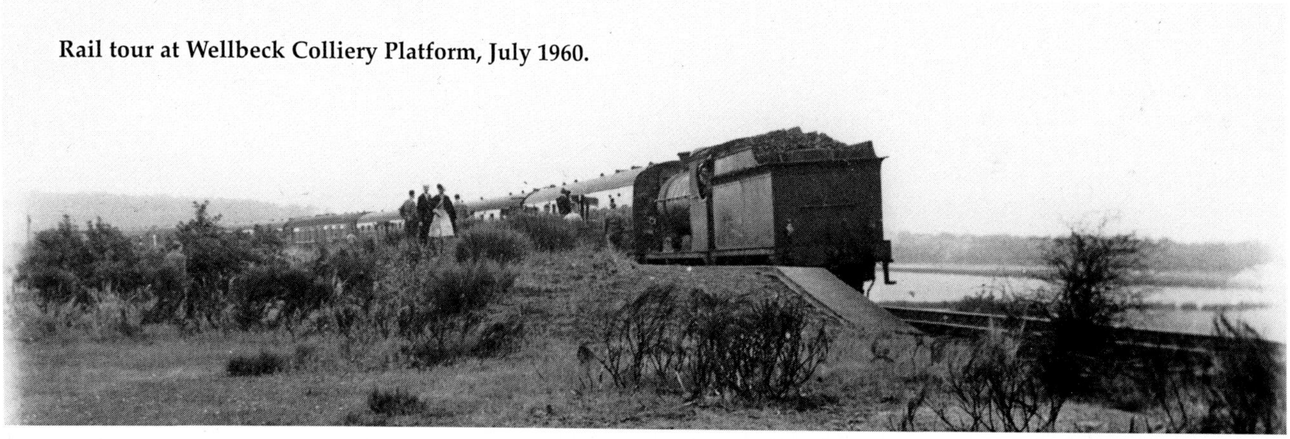

* Note: closed lines are listed alphabetically, followed by sections on lines in the Leen Valley, the Great Northern and London & North Western joint lines and closed stations on lines that remain open to passenger services.

# Alfreton – Mansfield *

| | |
|---|---|
| *Passenger services withdrawn* | 27 July 1930 |
| *Length* | $11\frac{1}{2}$ miles |
| *Original owning company* | Midland Railway |

| | |
|---|---|
| *Stations closed* | *Date of closure* |
| Whiteborough ** | 4 October 1926 |
| Teversall | 27 July 1930 |
| Pleasley | 27 July 1930 |
| Mansfield Woodhouse | 12 October 1964 |

* The closed station on this line that was in Derbyshire was Tibshelf & Newton.
** Originally named Woodend until 1 October 1908, then Woodened for Hucknall Huwthwaite until 20 January 1893, then Whiteborough for Hucknall Huwthwaite until 1 January 1908. The town is half in Derbyshire and half in Nottinghamshire.

This was a line built to open up the coalfield which survived far longer as a mineral carrier than as a passenger route. Originally authorised in 1861, it was opened in 1866 to link the Erewash Valley line at Tibshelf South Junction to Mansfield, the route joining the Leen Valley line north of Mansfield Woodhouse at Pleasley Junction. The line crossed the Great Northern Leen Valley Extension in two places, near Teversall and again near Pleasley, and threw off a number of colliery branches along the way. Passenger services were sparse, four trains in each direction between Mansfield and Pye Bridge in 1910, reduced to three twelve years later. The Depression saw the passenger service end completely in 1930, though coal traffic continued into the 1980s.

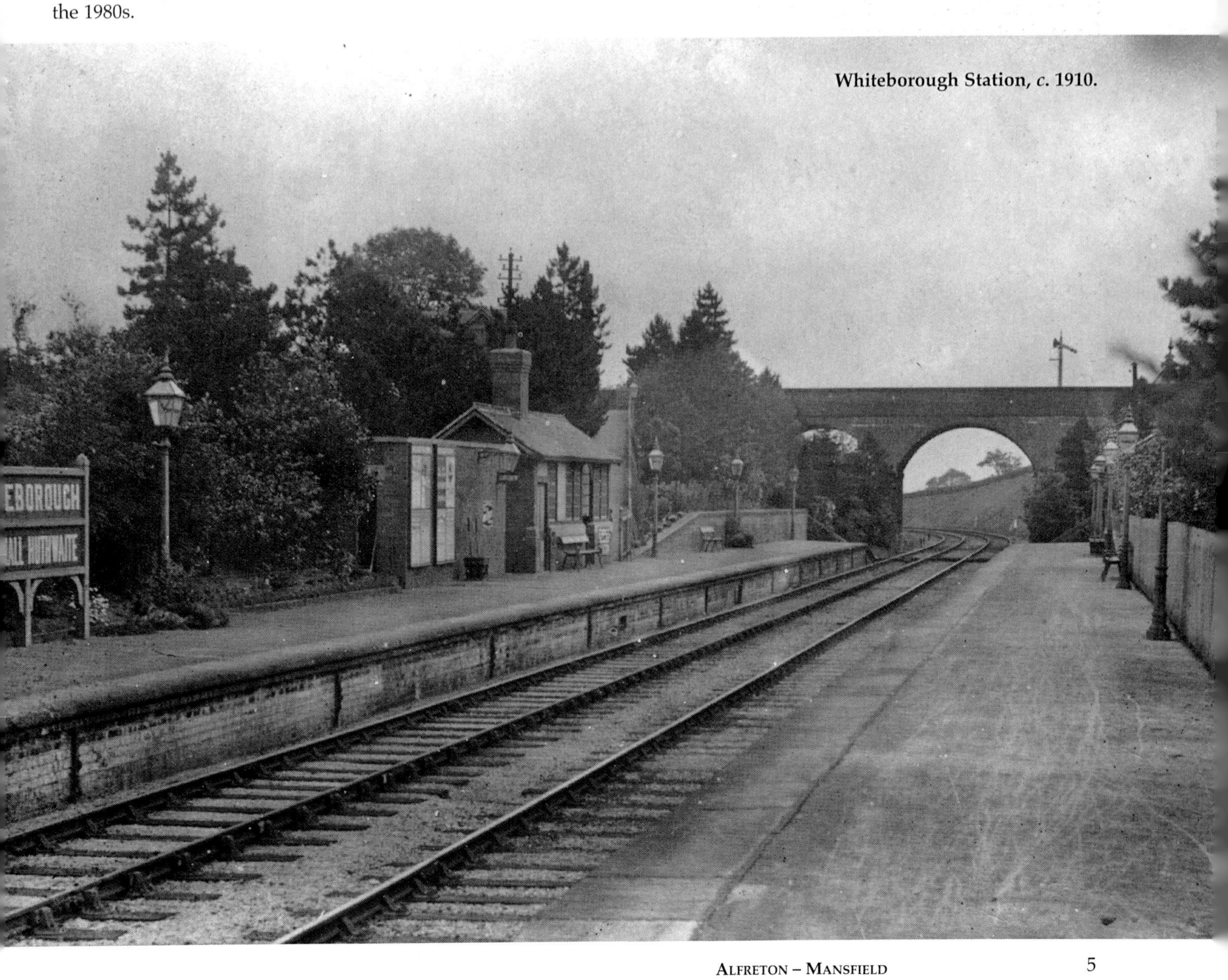


**Whiteborough Station, *c.* 1910.**

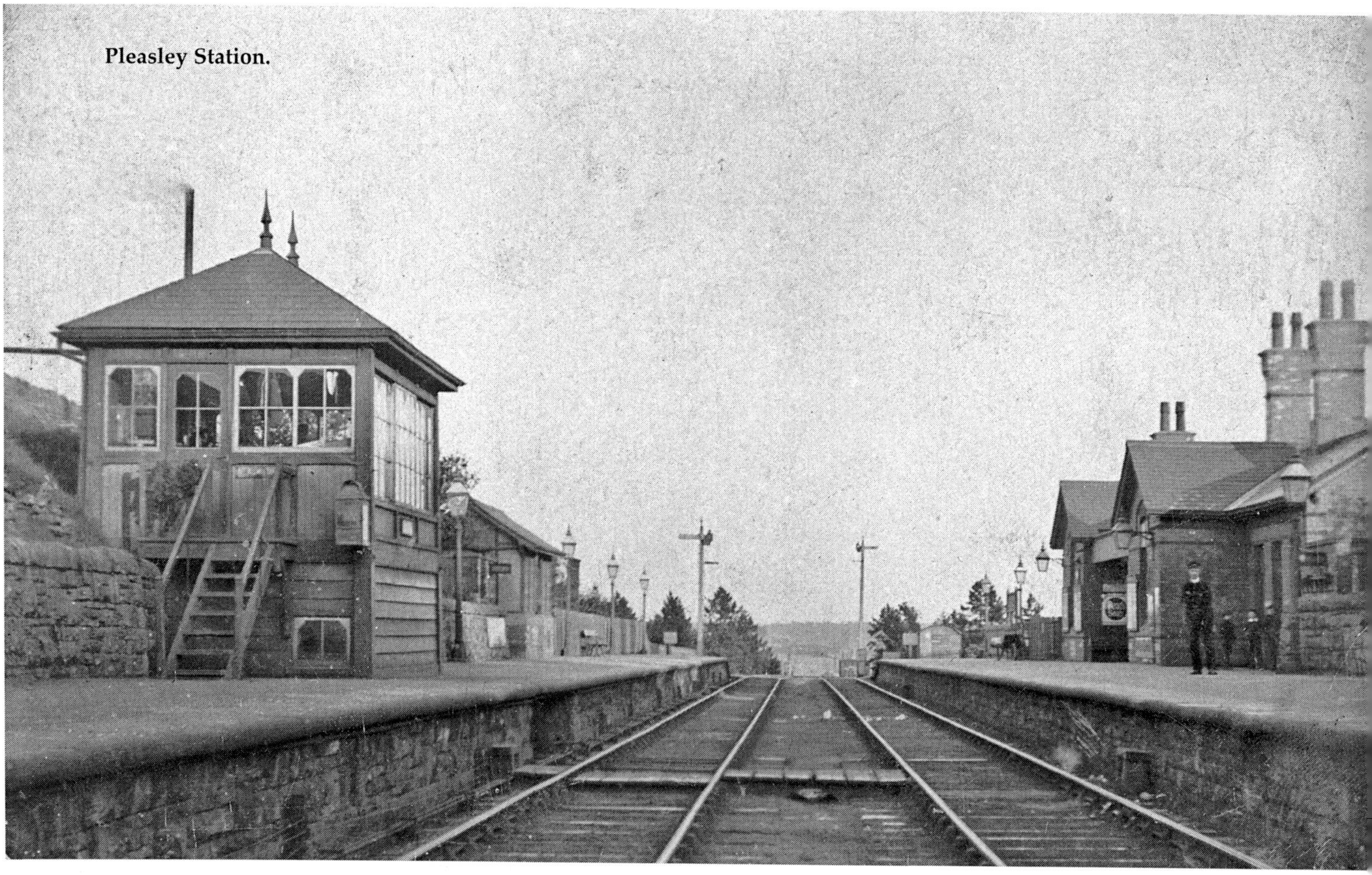

Pleasley Station.

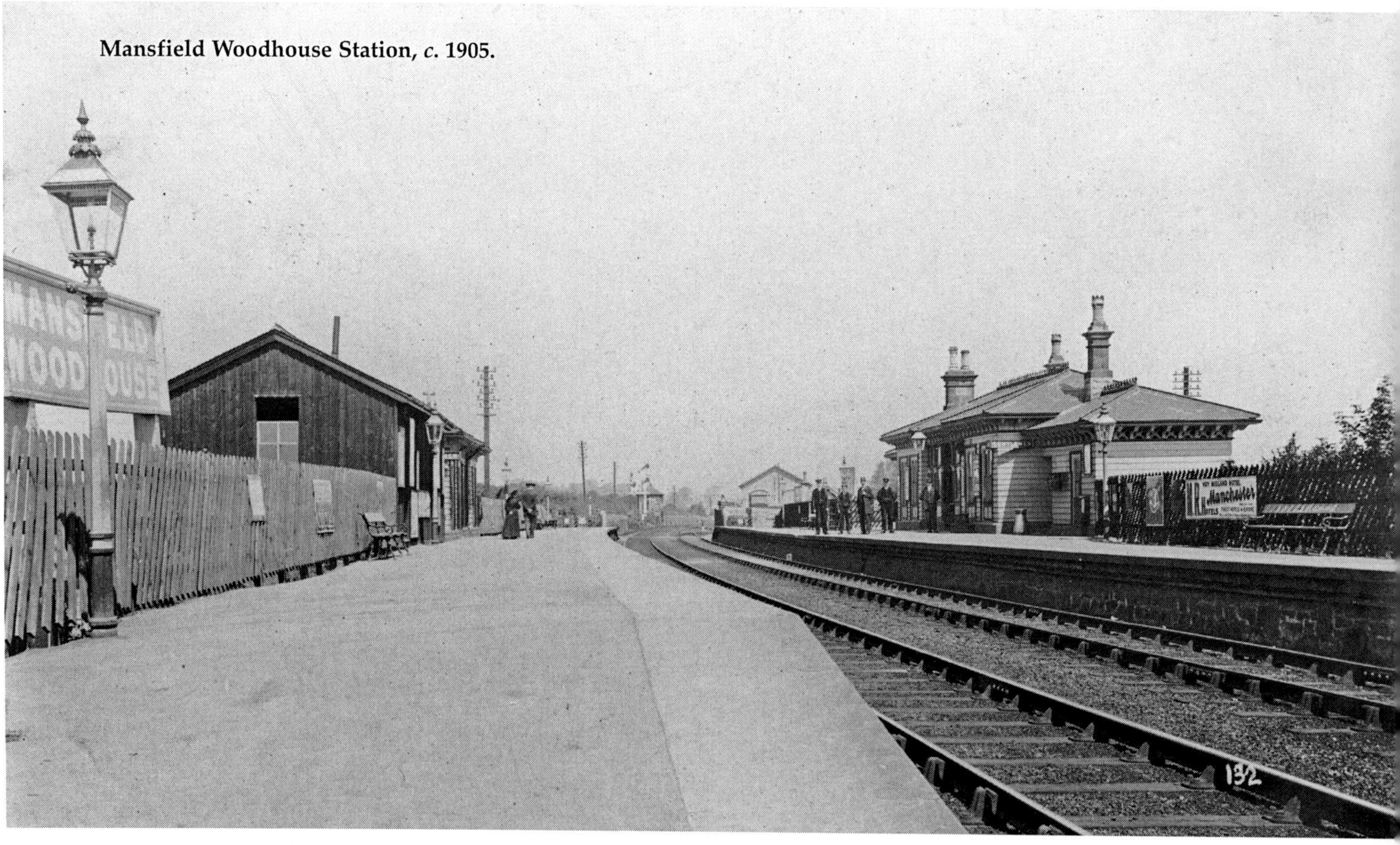


Mansfield Woodhouse Station, *c.* 1905.

# Bennerley Junction – Bulwell

| | |
|---|---|
| *Passenger services withdrawn* | 1 January 1917 |
| *Length* | 4 miles (approx.) |
| *Original owning company* | Midland Railway |

| *Stations closed* | *Date of closure* |
|---|---|
| Kimberley | 1 January 1917 |
| Watnall | 1 January 1917 |

The incursions of the Great Northern into what the Midland had seen as its own undisputed territory caused some alarm in the boardroom and probably helped the company galvanise itself to expand its operations further. In *Derbyshire's Lost Railways* it was related how the Midland had closed the branch between Ilkeston Junction on the Erewash Valley line and Ilkeston Town between 1870 and 1879, the reopening being a reaction to the Great Northern's ambitions. At the same time as the Ilkeston branch trains reappeared, the Midland opened a connecting line between Bullwell Line Junction, a point just south of Bulwell on the Leen Valley line, and Bennerley Junction on Erewash Valley line, between Ilkeston Junction and Shipley Gate. There were two intermediate stations, at Kimberley and Watnall, but the main interest in constructing the line seems to have been the opportunity to serve Watnall Colliery and also Bennerley Ironworks. Passenger trains ran from Nottingham to Ilkeston Town via Kimberley and in 1910 there were seven return journeys a day Mondays to Saturdays and no Sunday service. However, Kimberley was better served by the Great Northern's line from Nottingham to Derby and in 1917 passenger services were withdrawn as a war economy and never reinstated. There is an account suggesting that the track was removed between Kimberley and Bennerley Junction and sent to France for use on the railways serving the Western Front, though it was lost on the way when the ship carrying it was torpedoed. However, a similar story is told of track removed from other lines, so it may be apocryphal. The remainder of the line continued to be used for goods and mineral traffic, including a sub-branch to Digby Colliery, until 1954, when it closed completely.

The fate of the line's passenger service illustrates how the railways recognised that they had entered a new era after the end of the Great War. During the Victorian age they were often vigorously competitive, and the story of the lines in the Leen Valley (qv) illustrates how the hope of cornering a traffic as lucrative as coal could encourage a level of duplication – or triplication – of facilities in even quite small communities. By the 1920s, the railways – which had been reorganised into the four large groups in 1923 – were not only facing a harsher economic climate generally, but were having to compete with road transport for passengers and some categories of goods. The Midland's willingness to forego passenger traffic to Kimberley in favour of the Great Northern is a small part of that overall change of outlook.

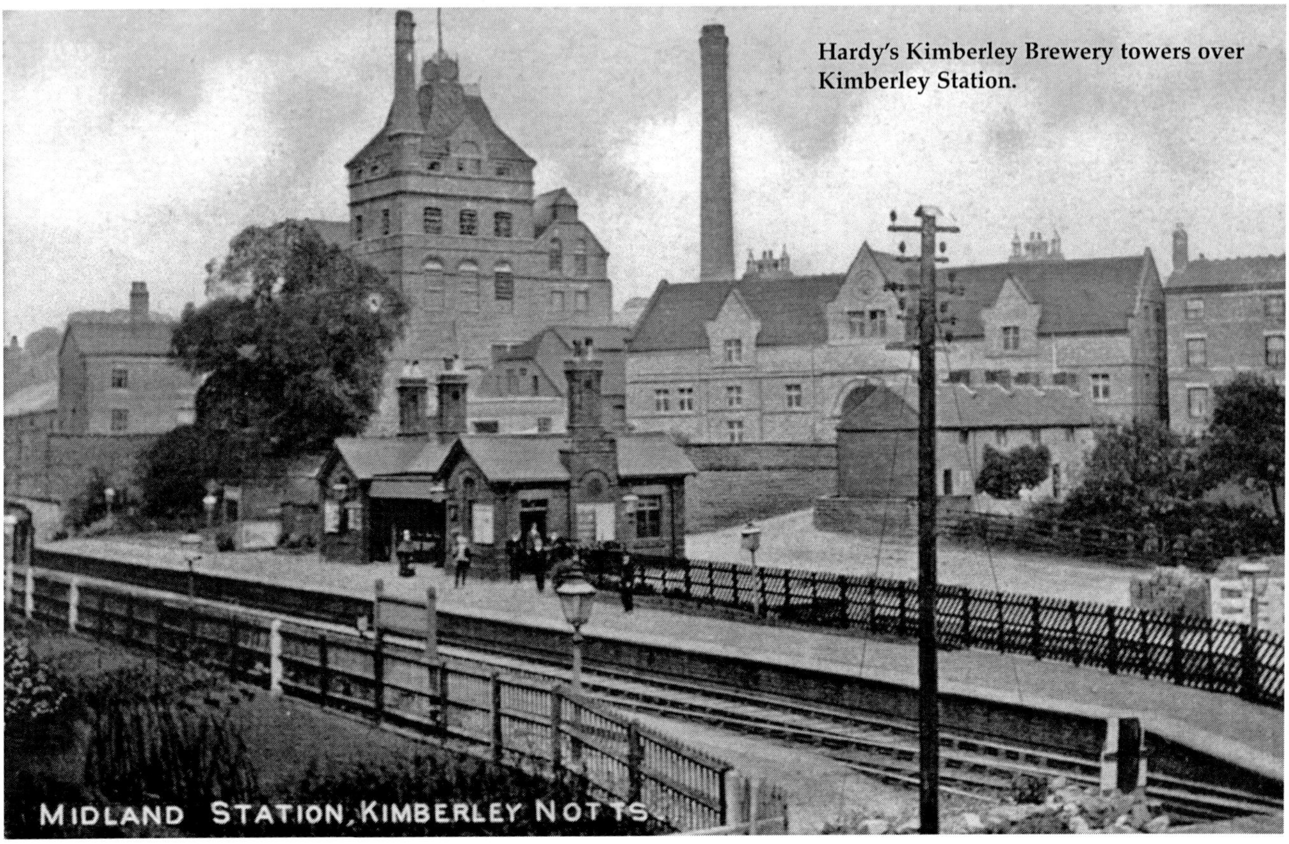


Hardy's Kimberley Brewery towers over Kimberley Station.

# Chesterfield – Lincoln *

| | |
|---|---|
| *Passenger services withdrawn* | 19 September 1955 |
| *Length* | $37\frac{1}{2}$ miles |
| *Original owning company* | Lancashire, Derbyshire & East Coast Railway (Great Central from 1907) |

| *Stations closed* | *Date of closure* |
|---|---|
| Warsop | 19 September 1955 |
| Edwinstowe | 2 January 1956 |
| Ollerton | 19 September 1955 |
| Boughton | 19 September 1955 |
| Tuxford Central | 19 September 1955 |
| Dukeries Junction | 6 March 1950 |
| Fledborough | 19 September 1955 |
| Clifton-on-Trent | 19 September 1955 |
| Doddington & Harby | 19 September 1955 |

* Closed stations on this line that were in Derbyshire were Chesterfield Market Place, Arkwright Town, Bolsover, Scarcliffe and Shirebrook North. The closed station in Lincolnshire was Slellingthorpe.

The story of the Lancashire, Derbyshire & East Coast Railway, a company which reached neither end of its expected route and which served most of its existence as a route across the Nottinghamshire and Derbyshire coalfield to Lincoln, has been recounted in both *Lincolnshire's Lost Railways* and *Derbyshire's Lost Railways*. The grandiose plans for a line from Wigan through the Peak District to Chesterfield came to nothing and the intention to press on east of Lincoln to a new deep-water port at Sutton-on-Sea were at first postponed because the line's principal ally, the Great Eastern Railway, was primarily interested in seeing the Chesterfield – Lincoln section open in order to allow it access to the coalfield from Lincoln. Having obtained its objective, the Great Eastern lost interest in the extension to the Lincolnshire coast altogether. In the event, the line was opened in 1897 and acquired ten years later not by its ally, but one of its most trenchant opponents, the Great Central, which used it as a second route between the coalfield and Grimsby, dubbing it 'the Dukeries route'. The passenger service between Chesterfield and Shirebrook North was withdrawn in 1951 and the whole line closed to regular passenger trains four years later, though it was used for two decades more as a route for excursion traffic to the Lincolnshire coast. Goods ceased over the through route in 1980 after an accident at Clifton-on-Trent damaged the track beyond economic repair. The section through Ollerton to Fledborough remained open until the early years of this century to supply coal to High Marnham power station, hard by the Trent, but this ceased when the power station closed.

Sections of the line around Ollerton still see occasional trains of minerals and there are plenty of reminders of the route in the form of embankments, cuttings, bridges and occasional buildings. The greatest landmark is the huge viaduct across the Trent at Fledborough, which remains intact but with the trackbed on the approach viaducts badly overgrown. Even so, to stand by the river and look up one could imagine that at any time an O2 or O4 2-8-0 might come into view, straining every nerve to shift its train of coal towards the Pyewipe yard and the far-off east coast.

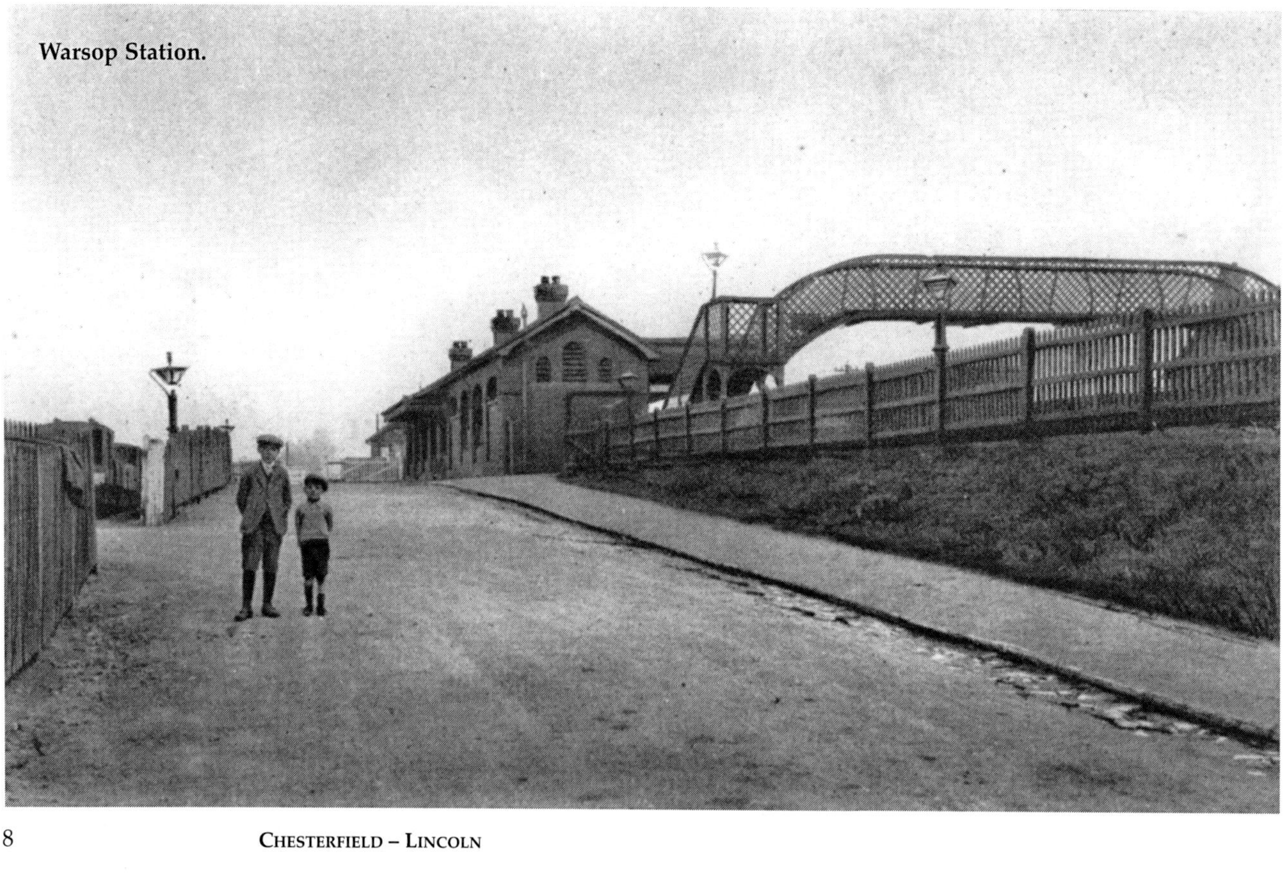
**Warsop Station.**

LNER tank engine No. 4528 with the 4.00 p.m. from Chesterfield to Lincoln, May 1946.

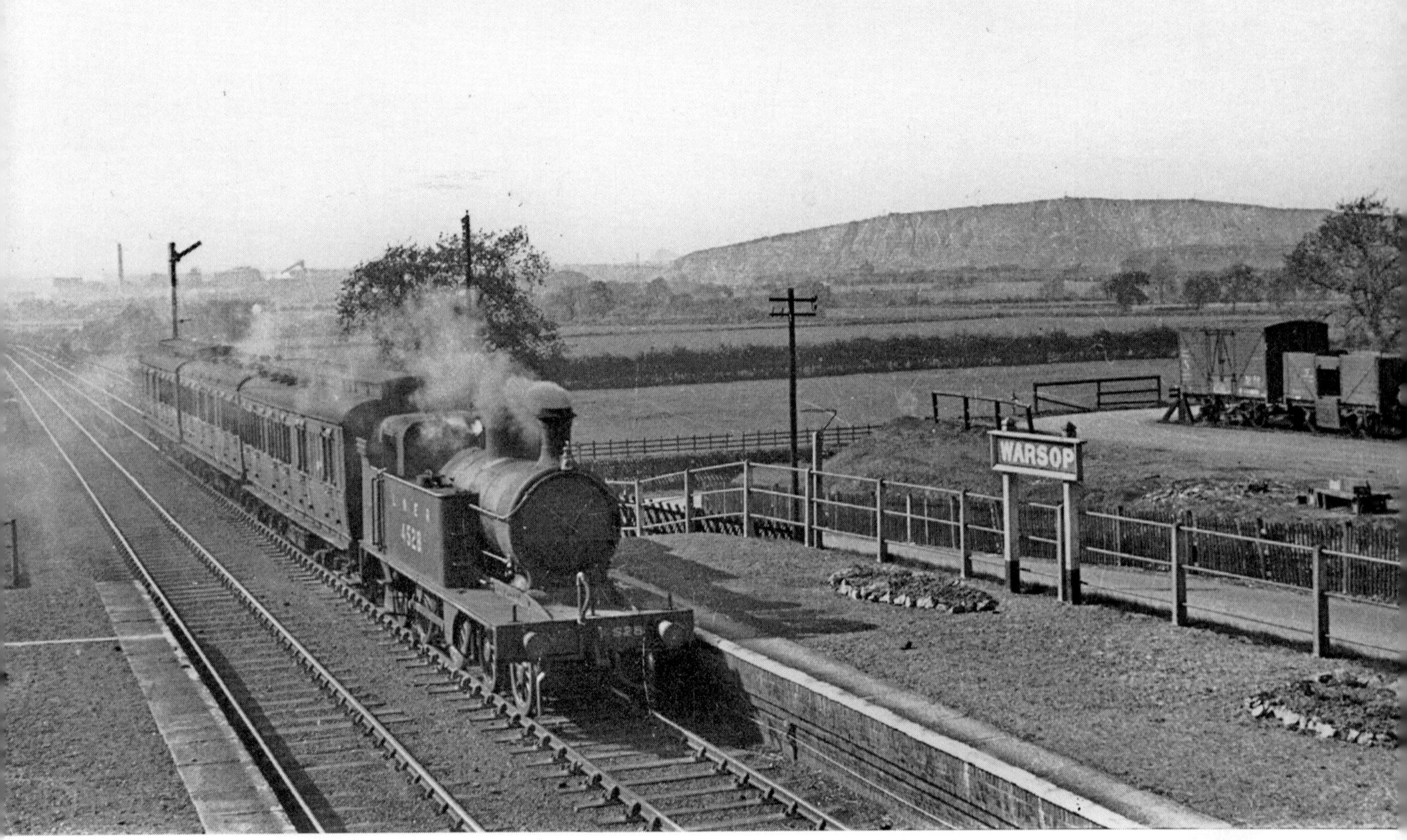


Warsop facing east, September 1955.

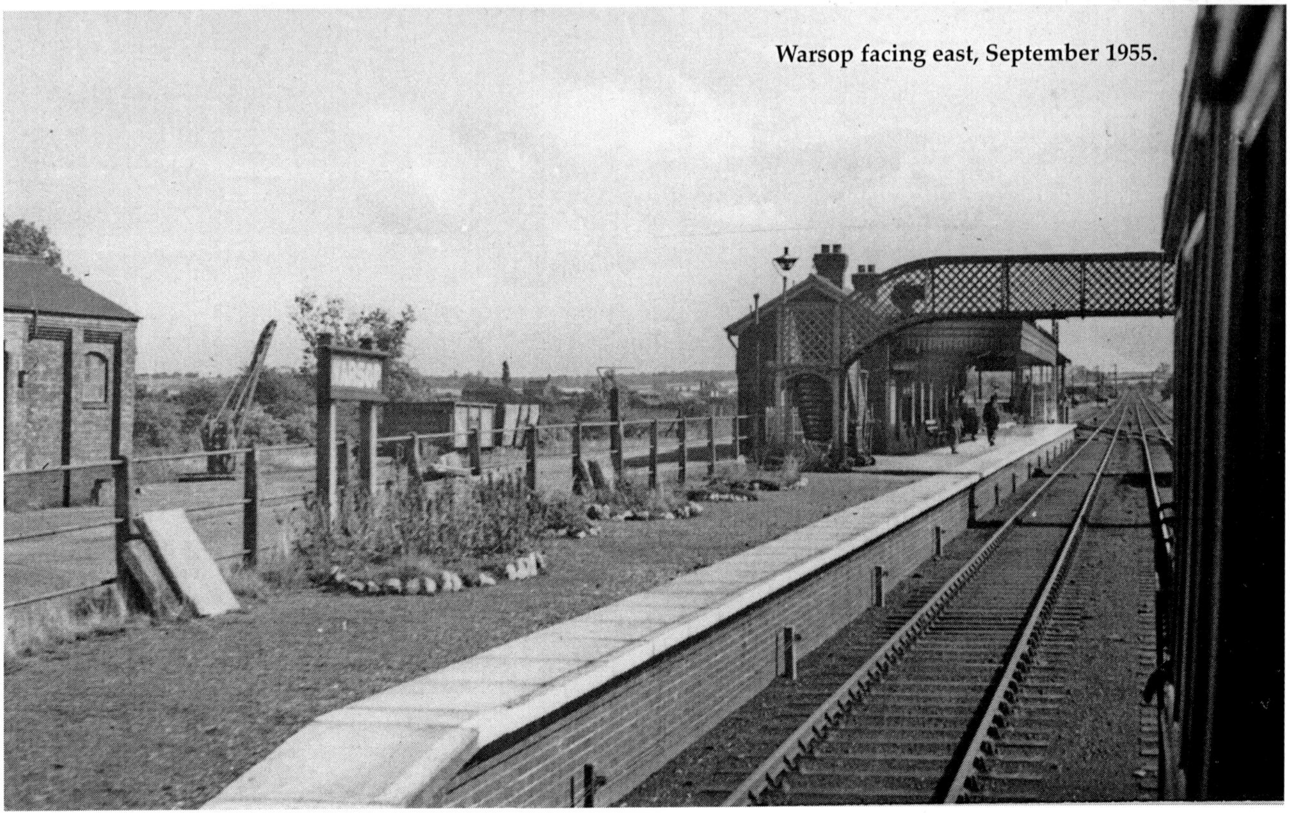

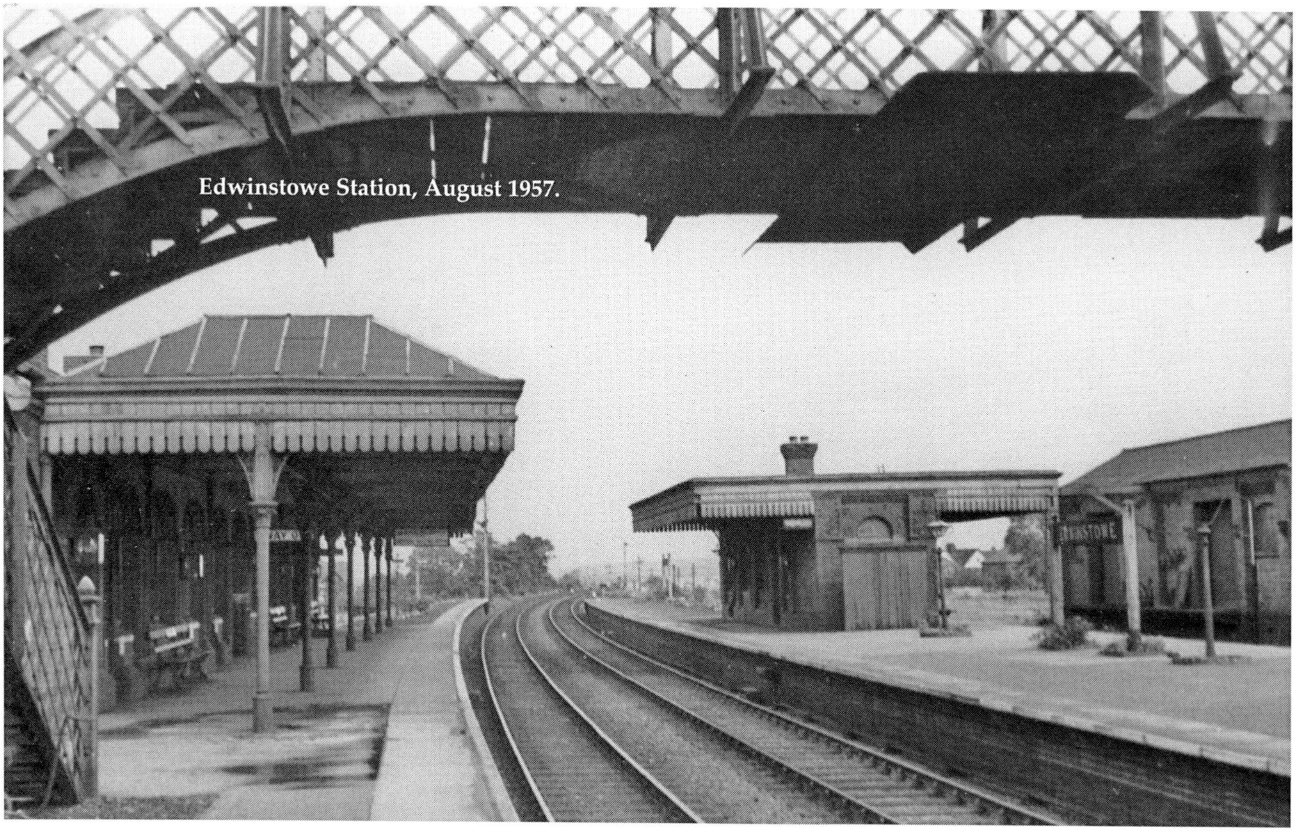

Edwinstowe Station, August 1957.

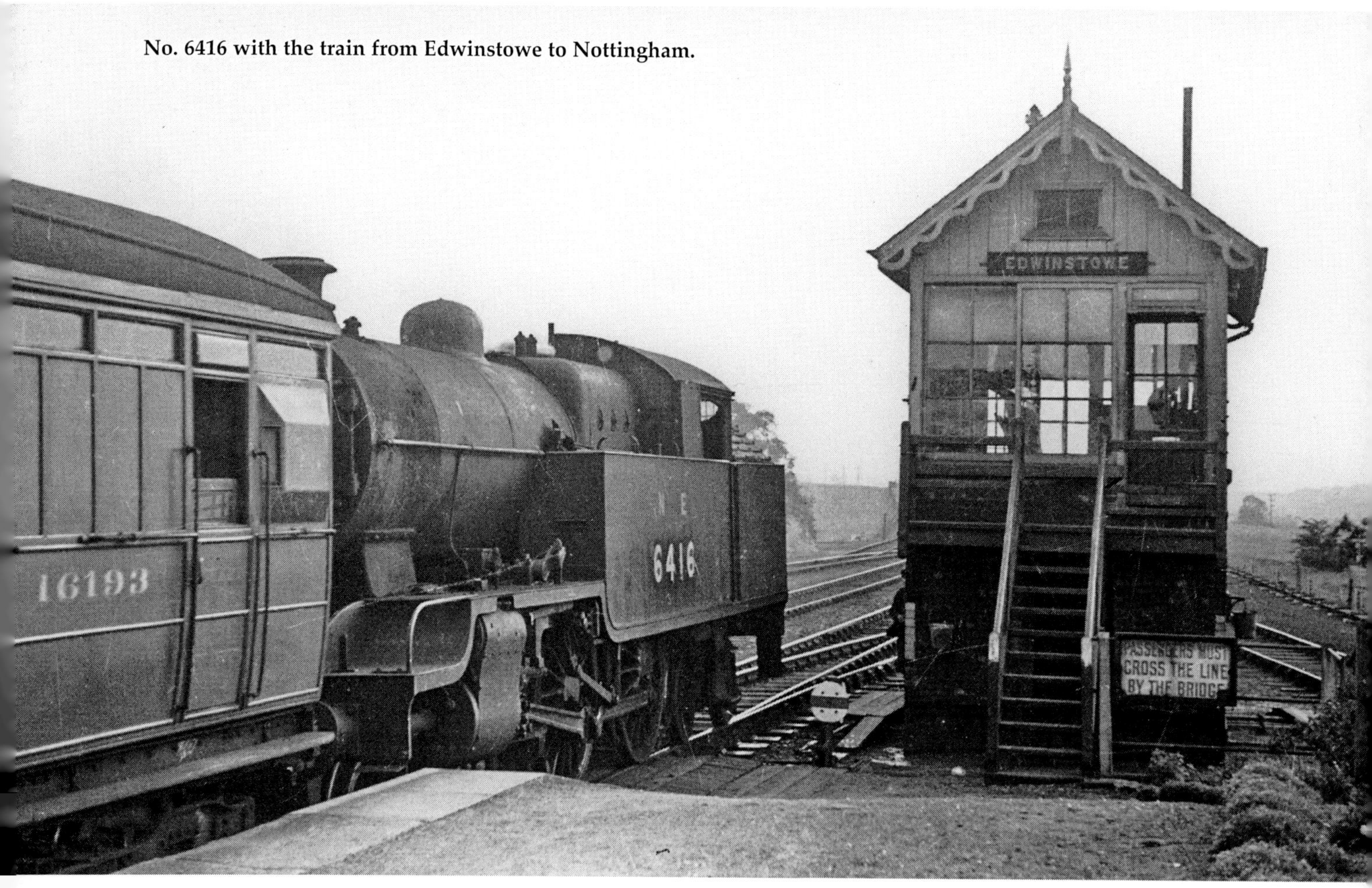


No. 6416 with the train from Edwinstowe to Nottingham.

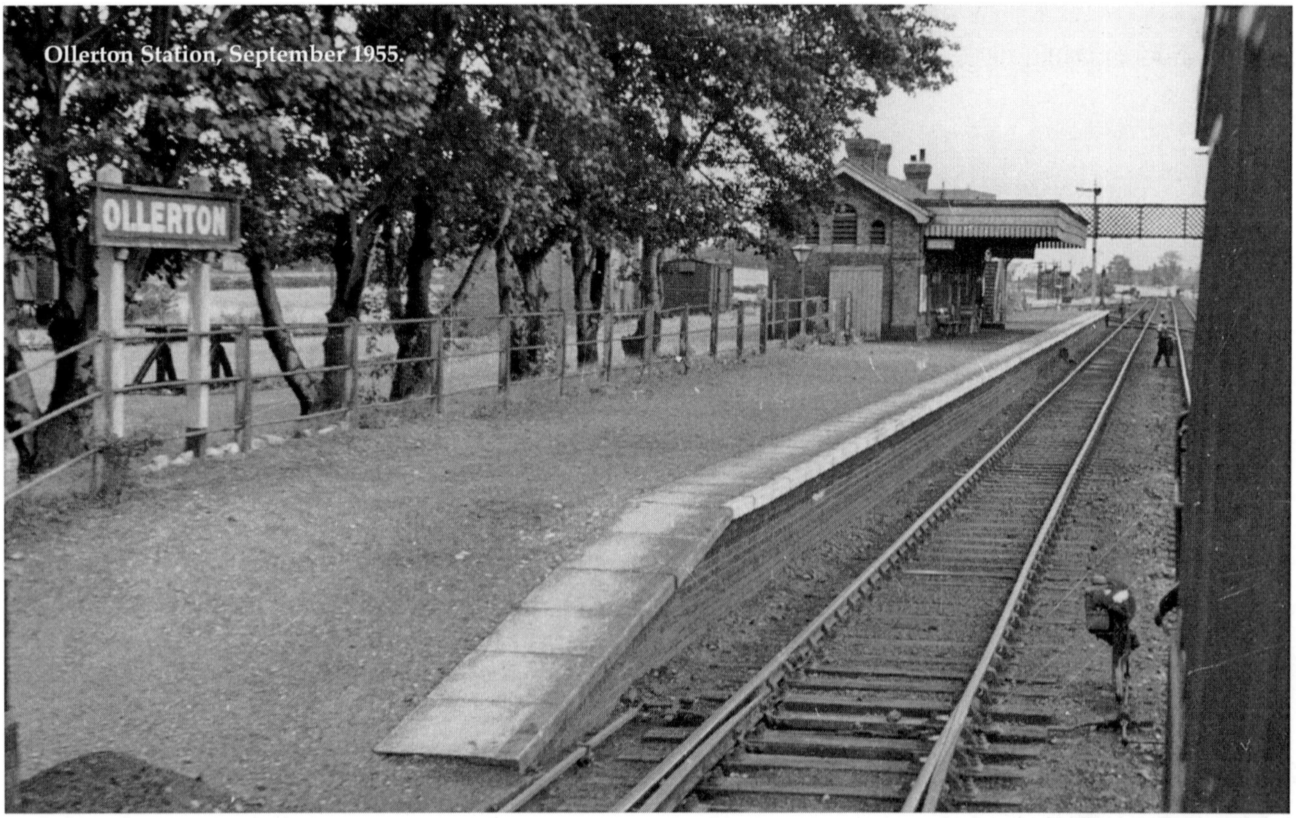


Ollerton Station, September 1955.

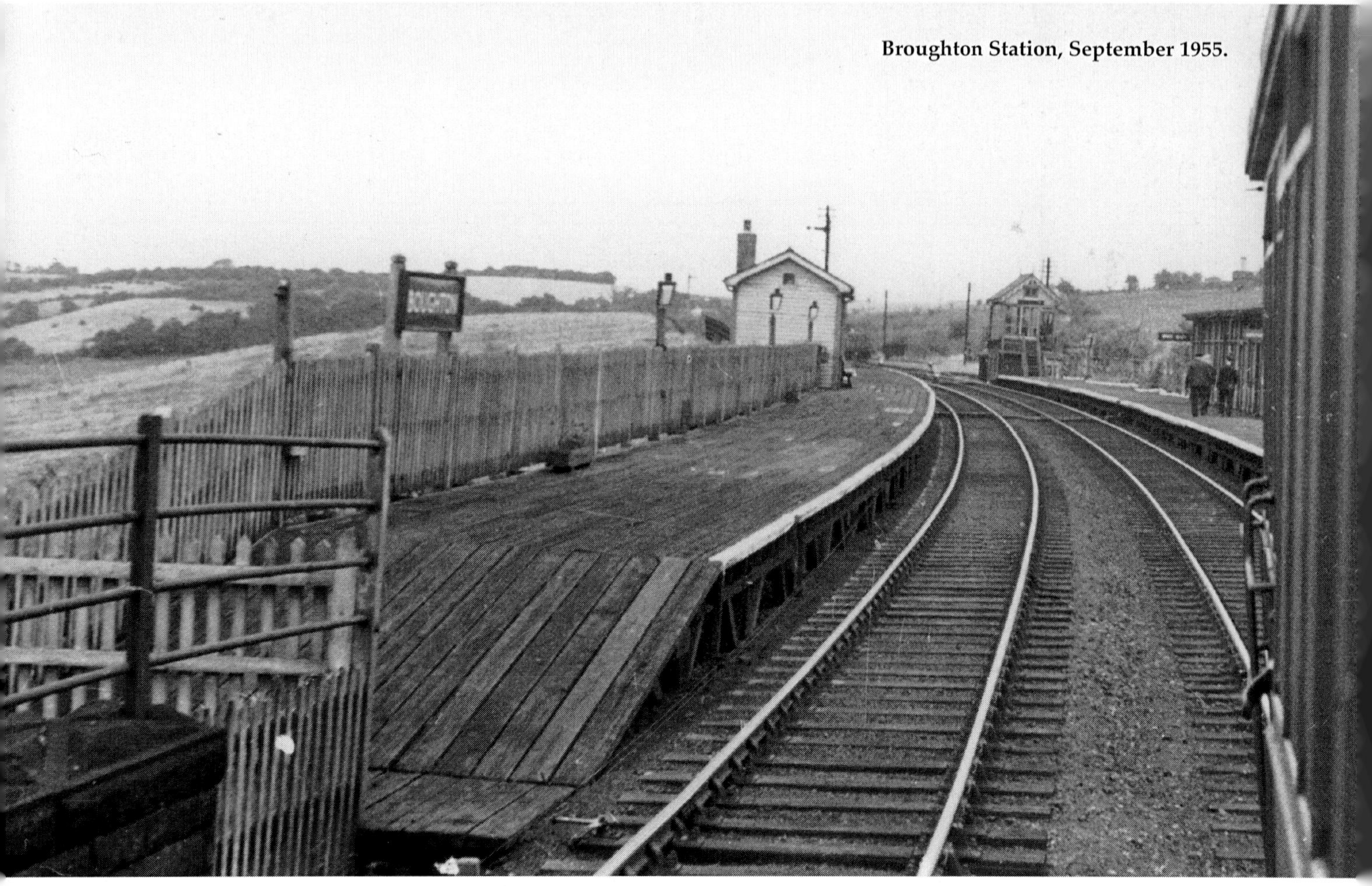

Broughton Station, September 1955.

Tuxford Central Station.

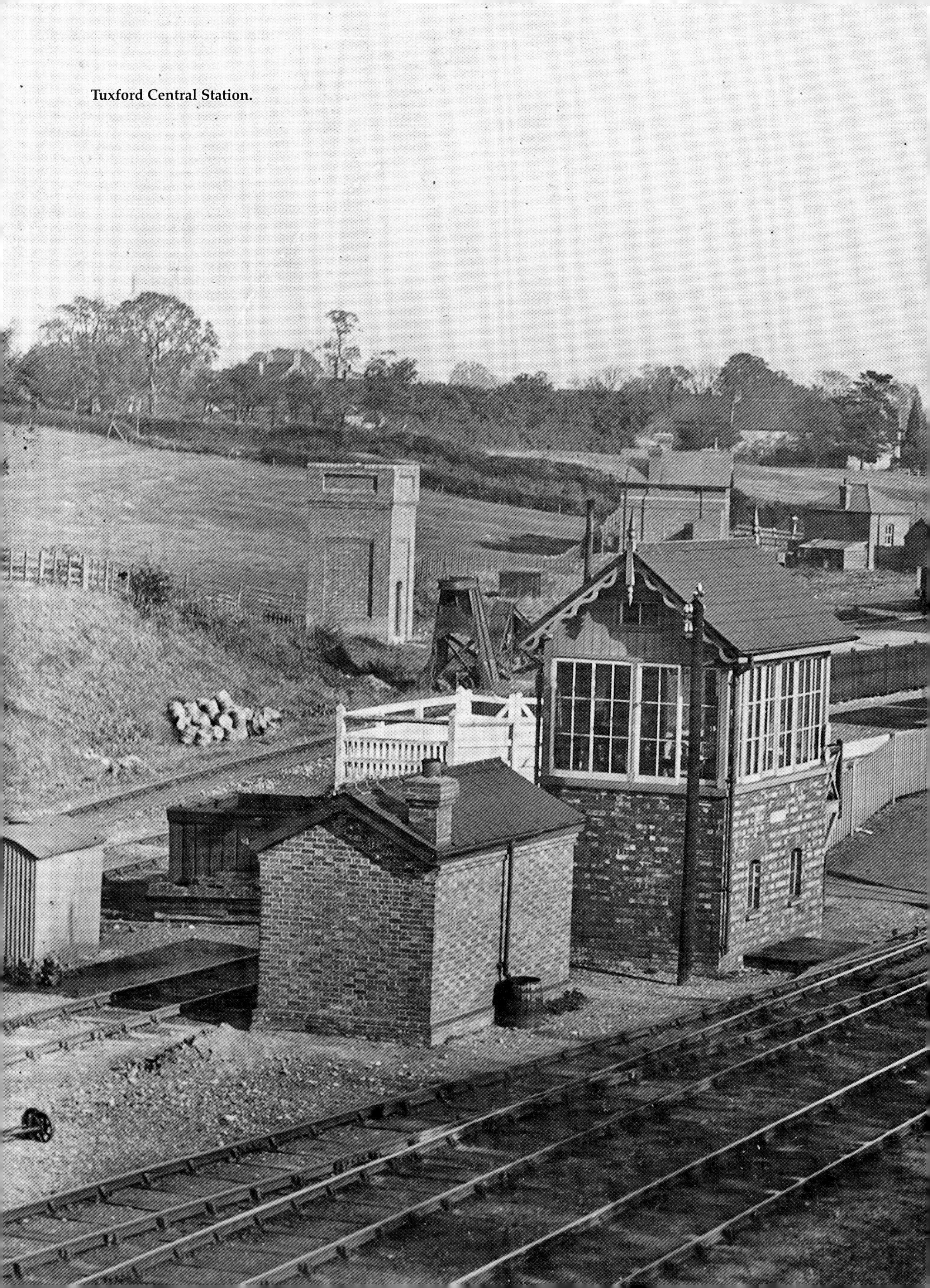

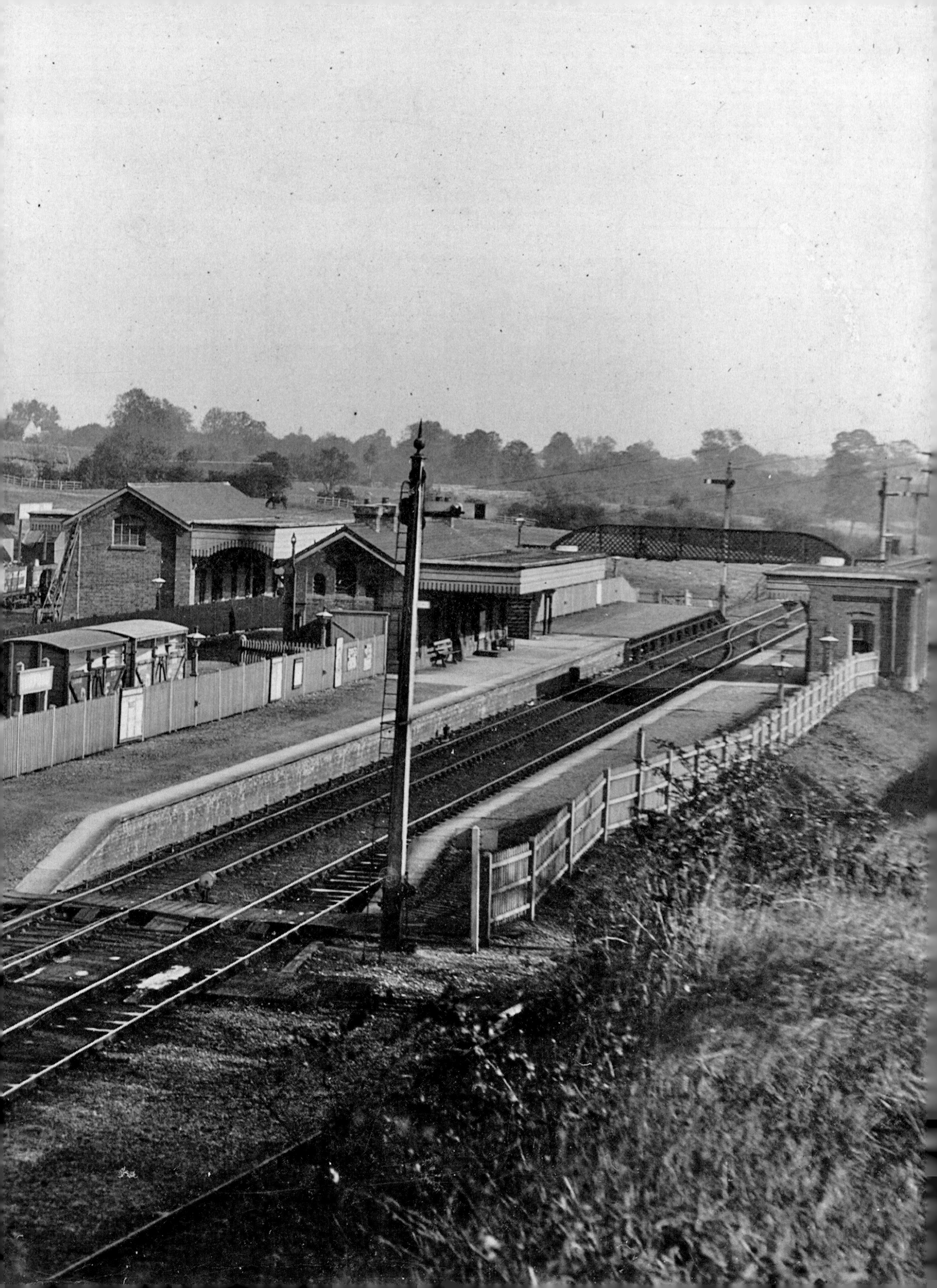

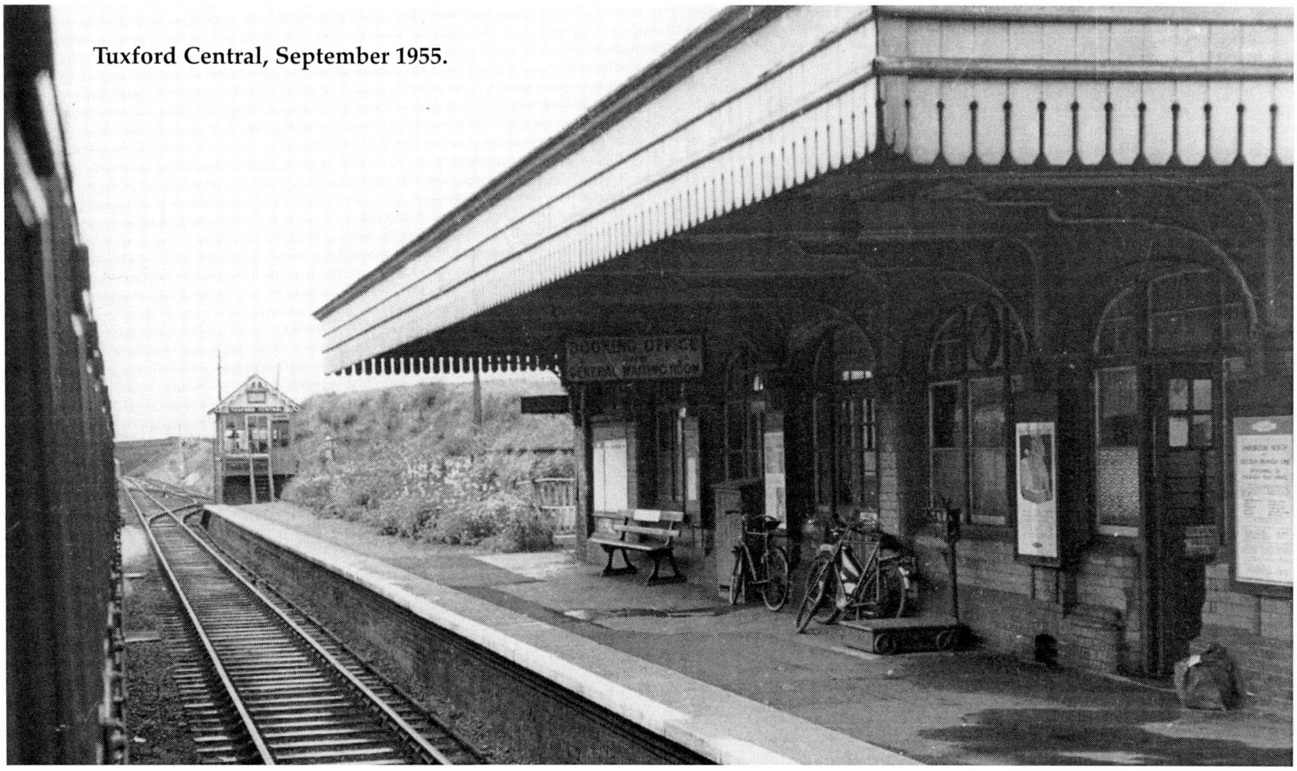

Tuxford Central, September 1955.

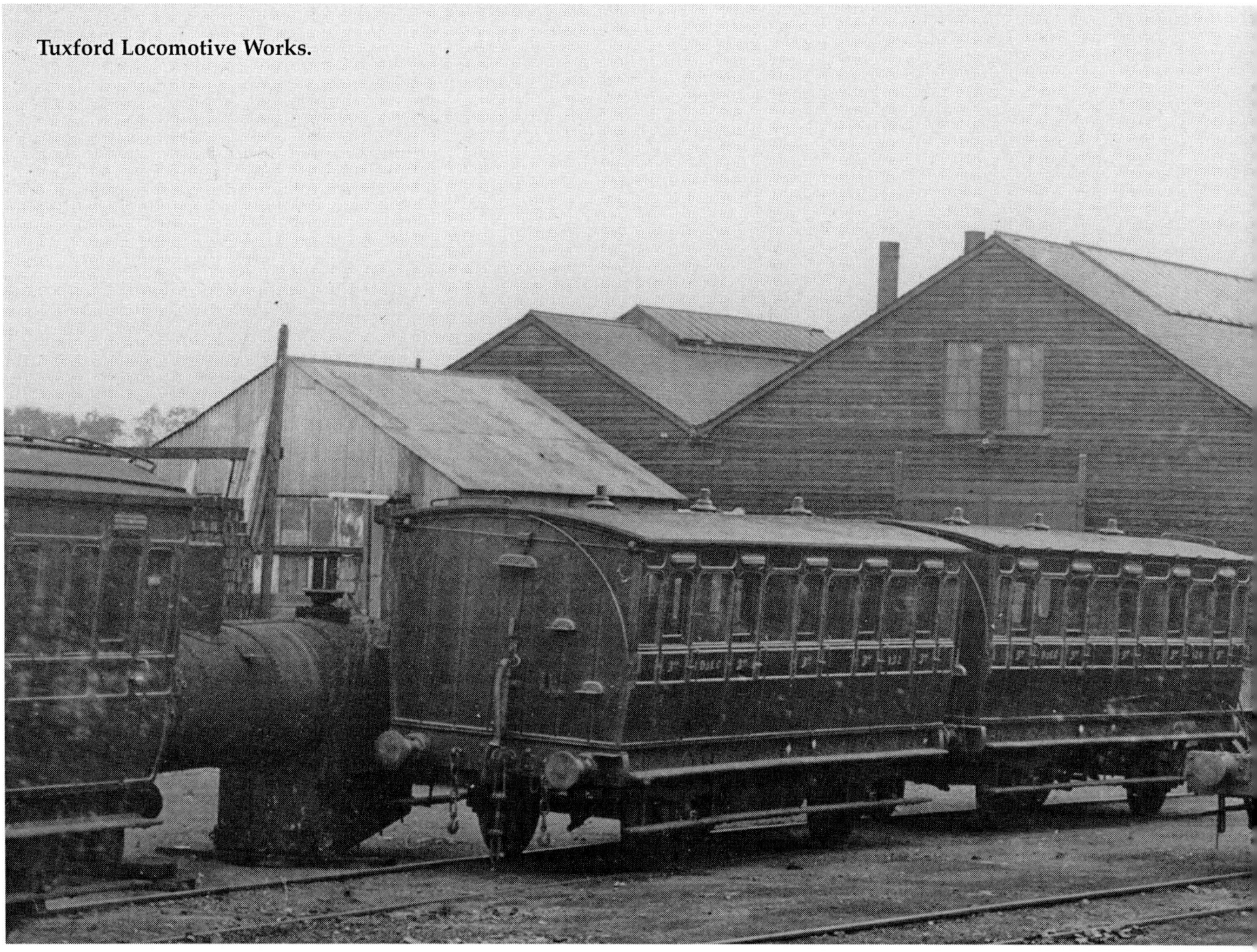

Tuxford Locomotive Works.

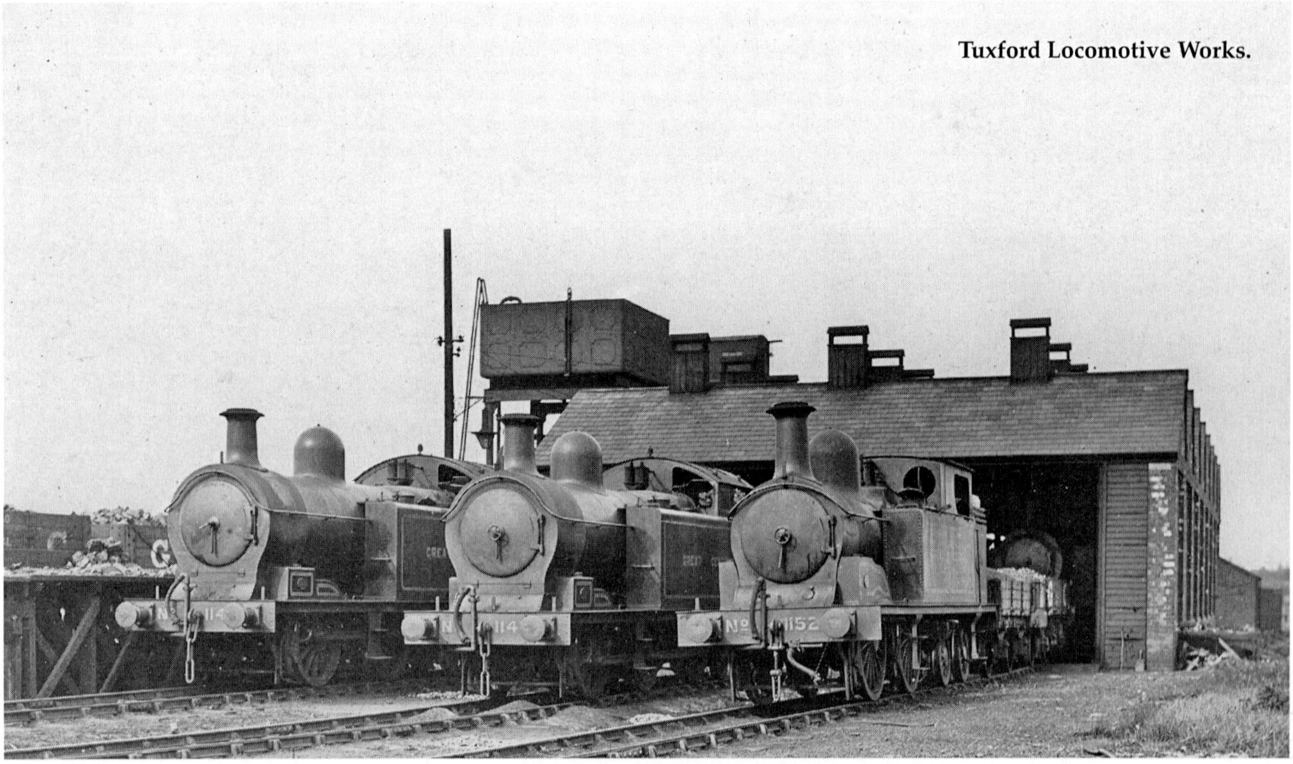

Tuxford Locomotive Works.

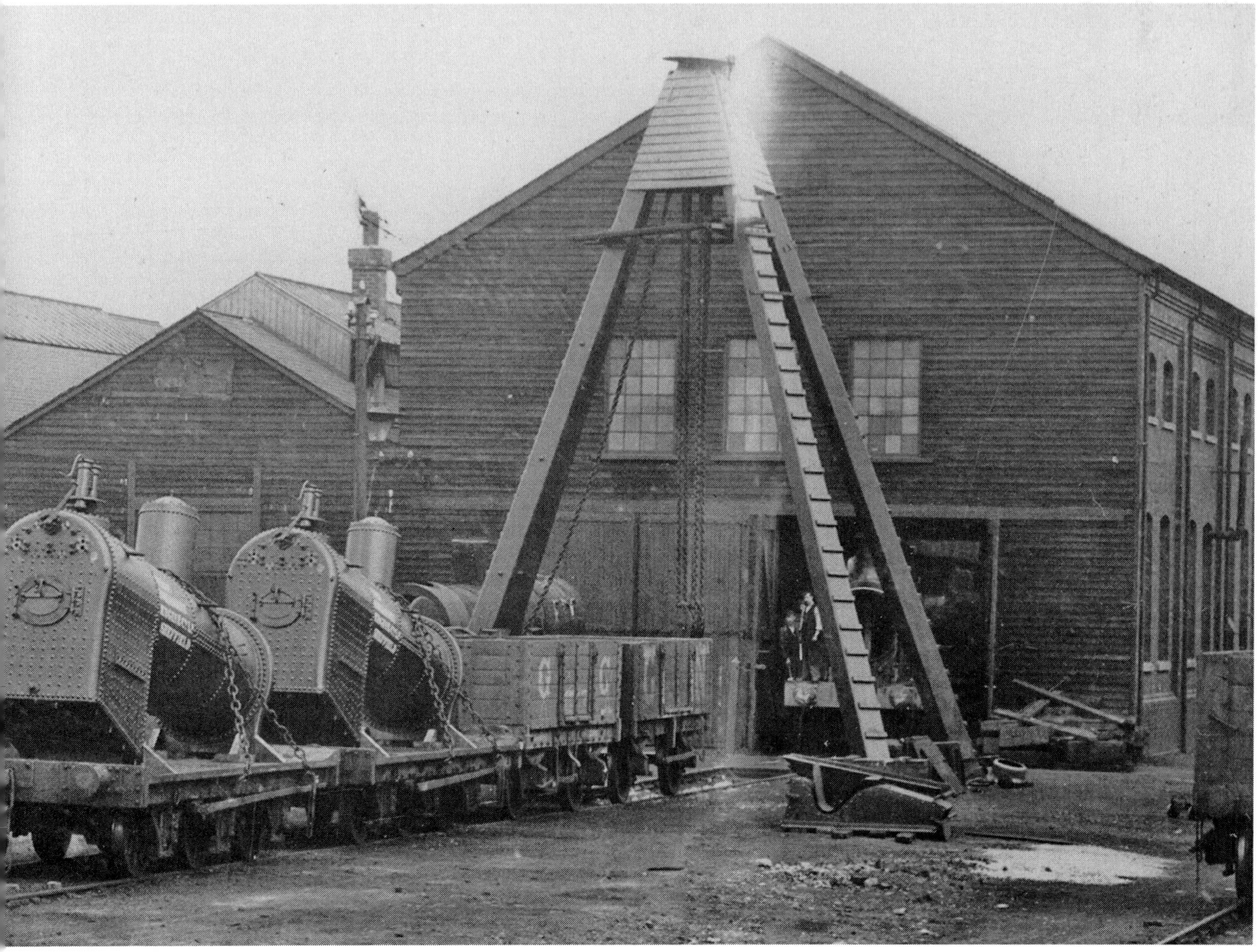

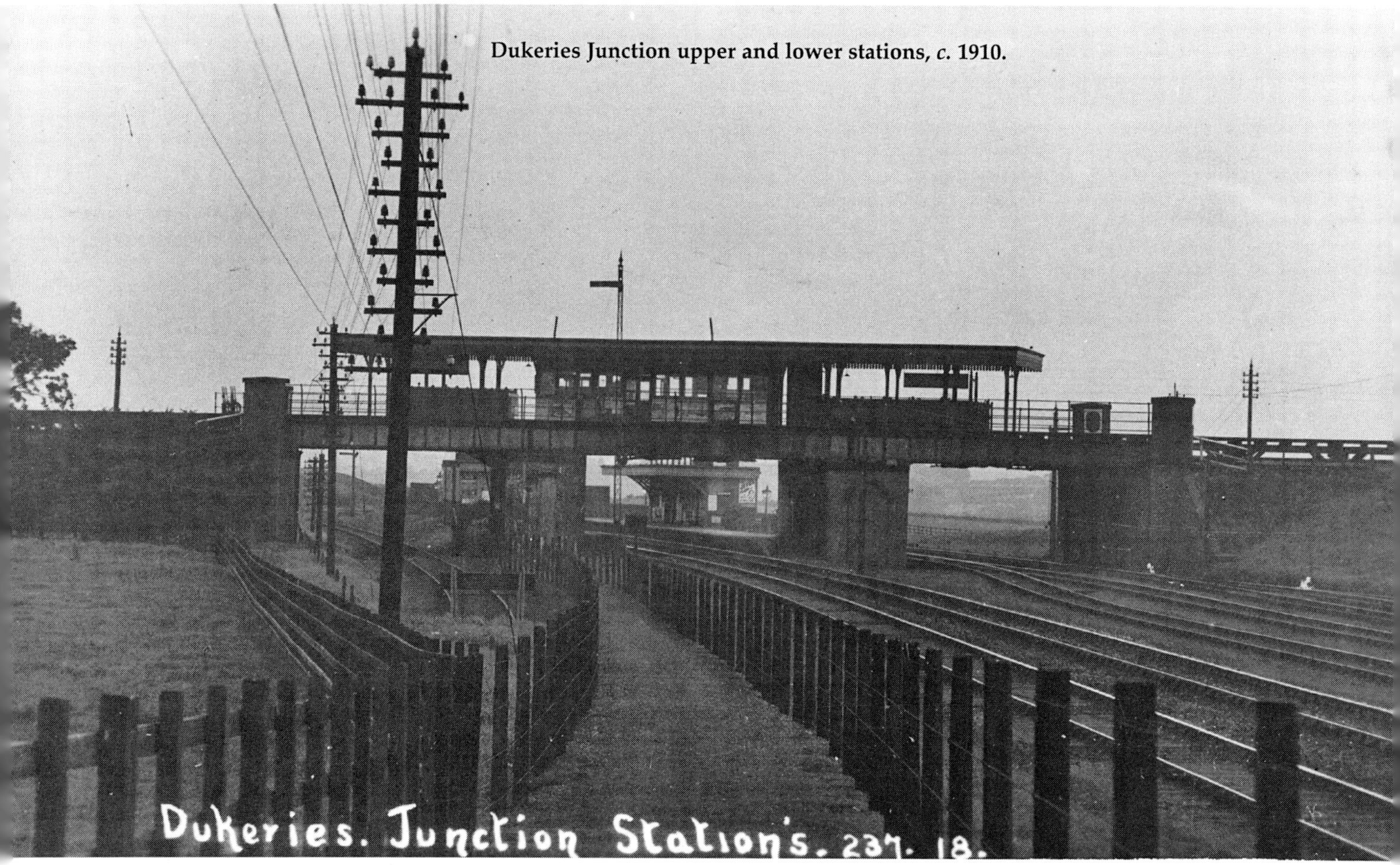


Dukeries Junction upper and lower stations, *c.* 1910.

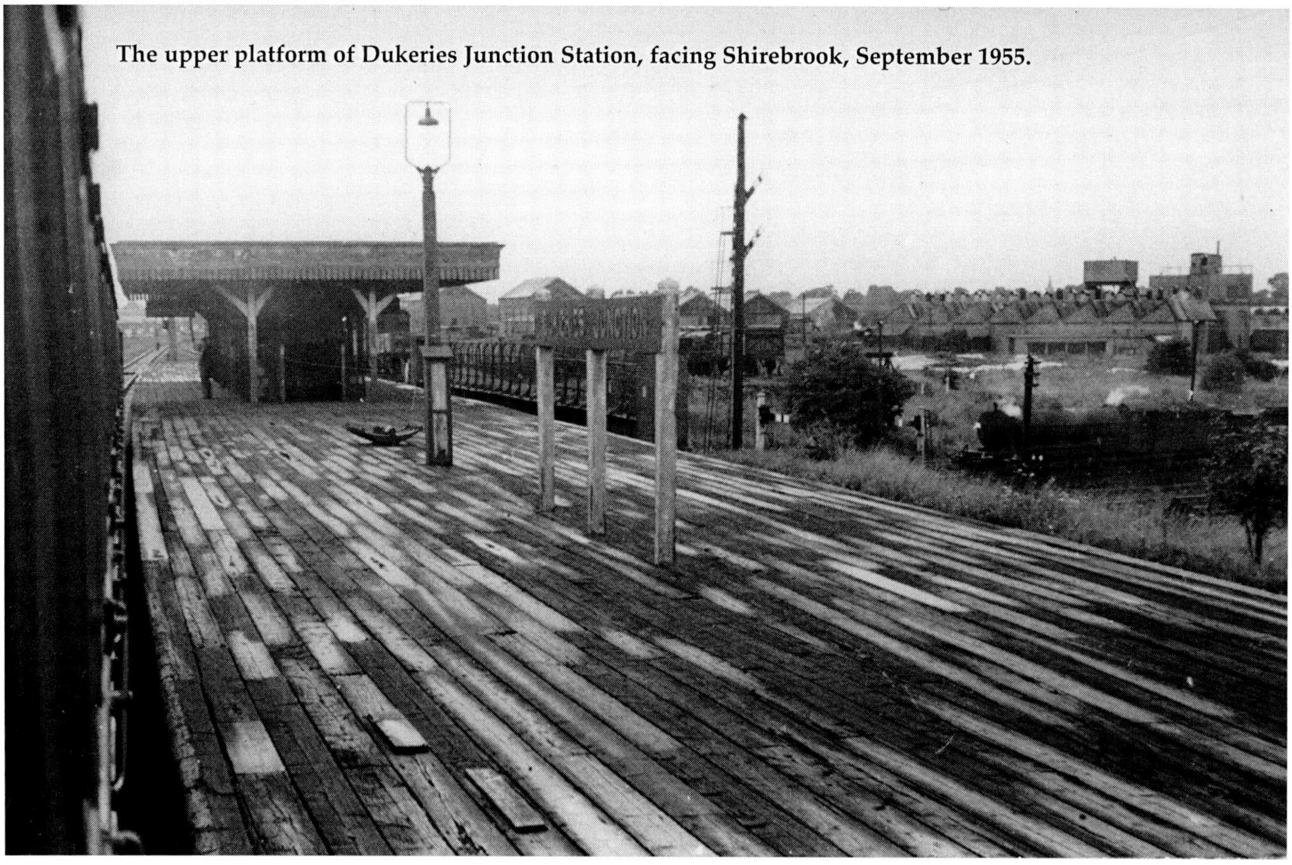

The upper platform of Dukeries Junction Station, facing Shirebrook, September 1955.

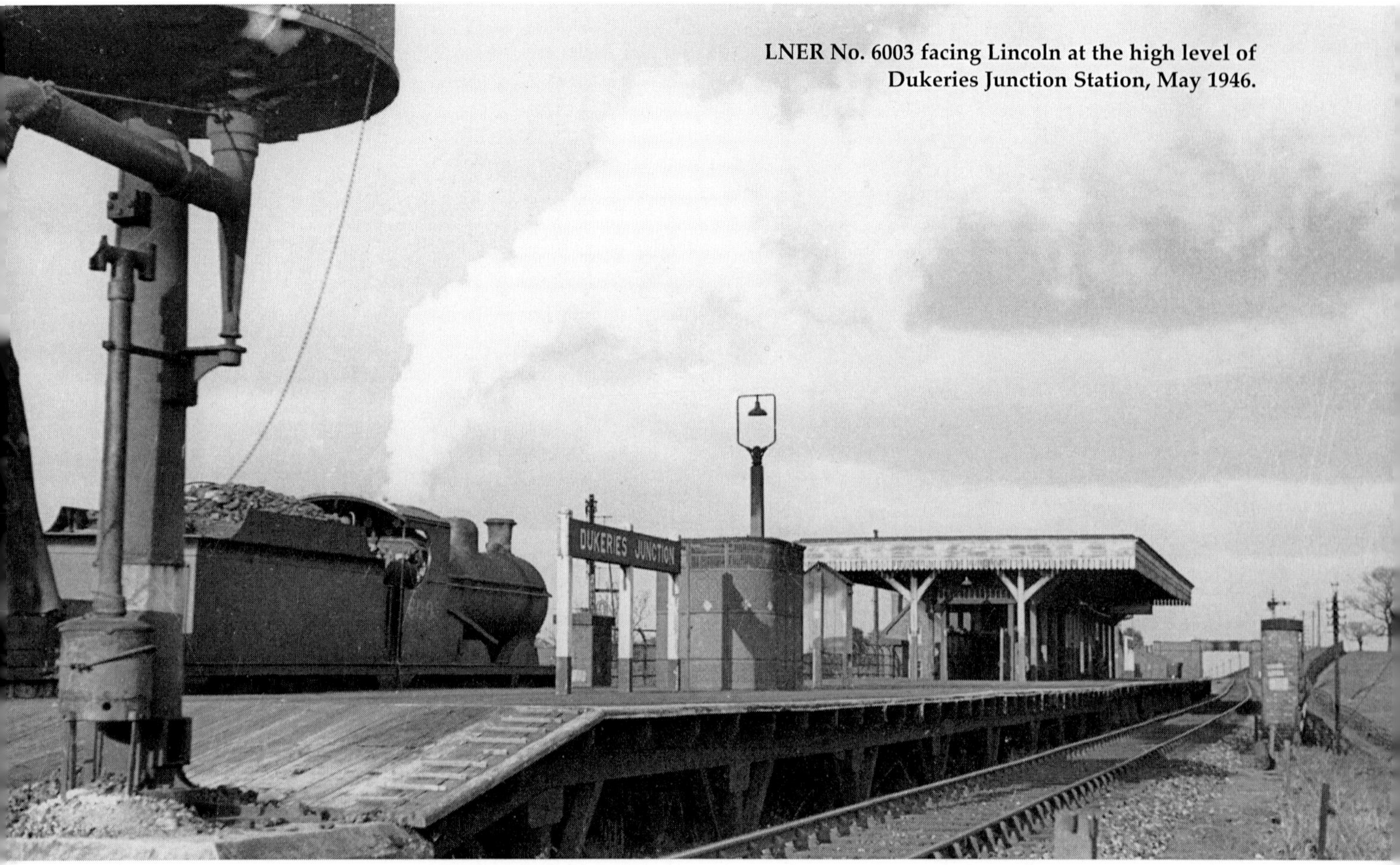


LNER No. 6003 facing Lincoln at the high level of Dukeries Junction Station, May 1946.

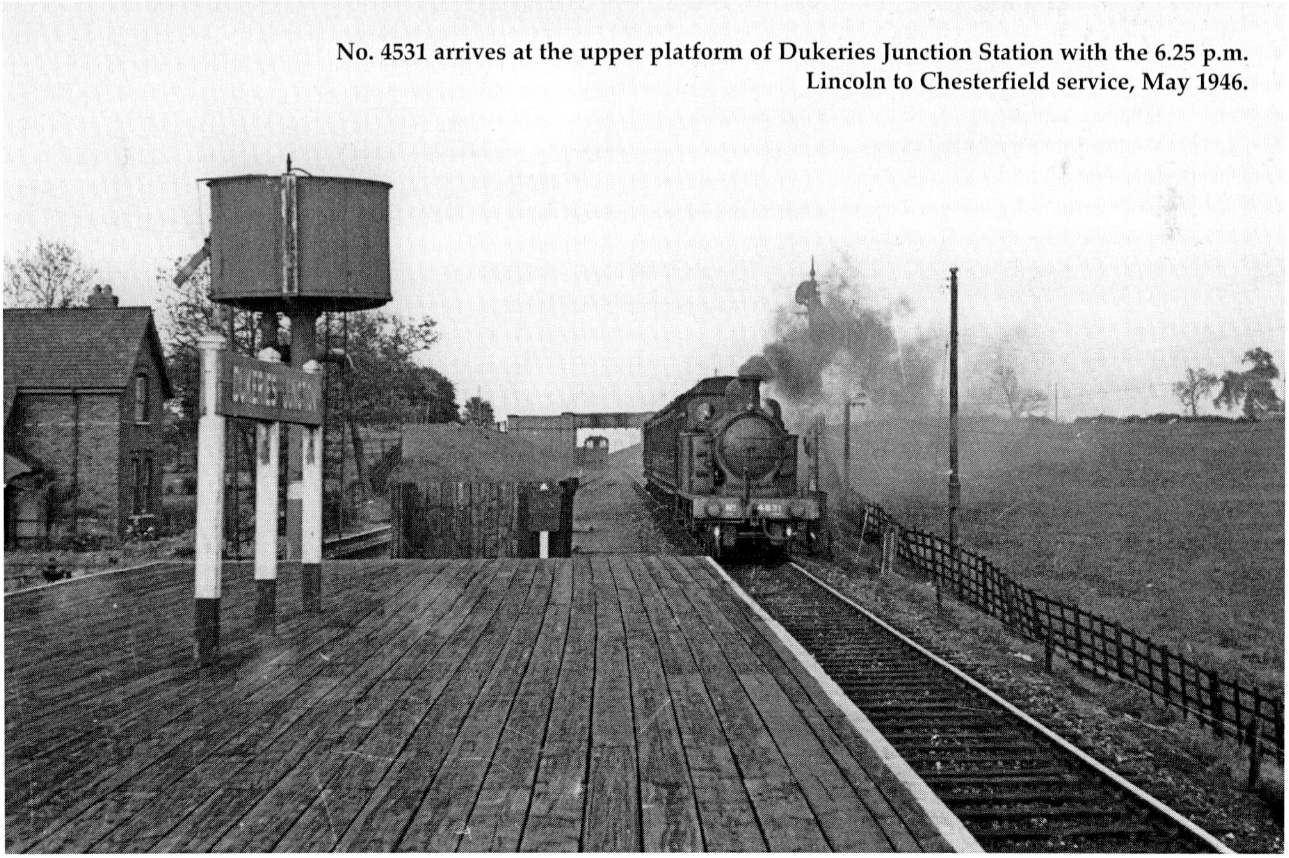

No. 4531 arrives at the upper platform of Dukeries Junction Station with the 6.25 p.m. Lincoln to Chesterfield service, May 1946.

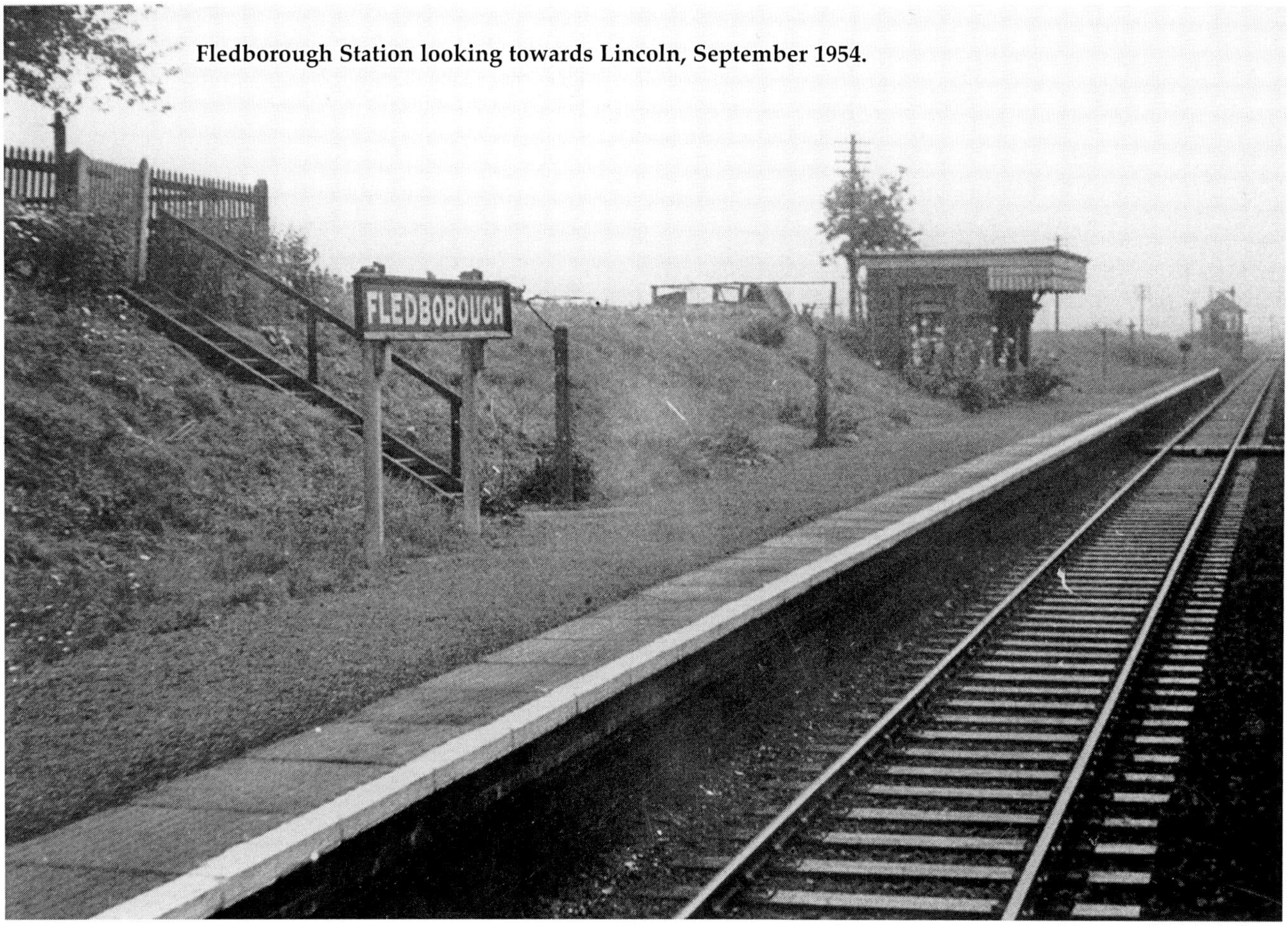

Fledborough Station looking towards Lincoln, September 1954.

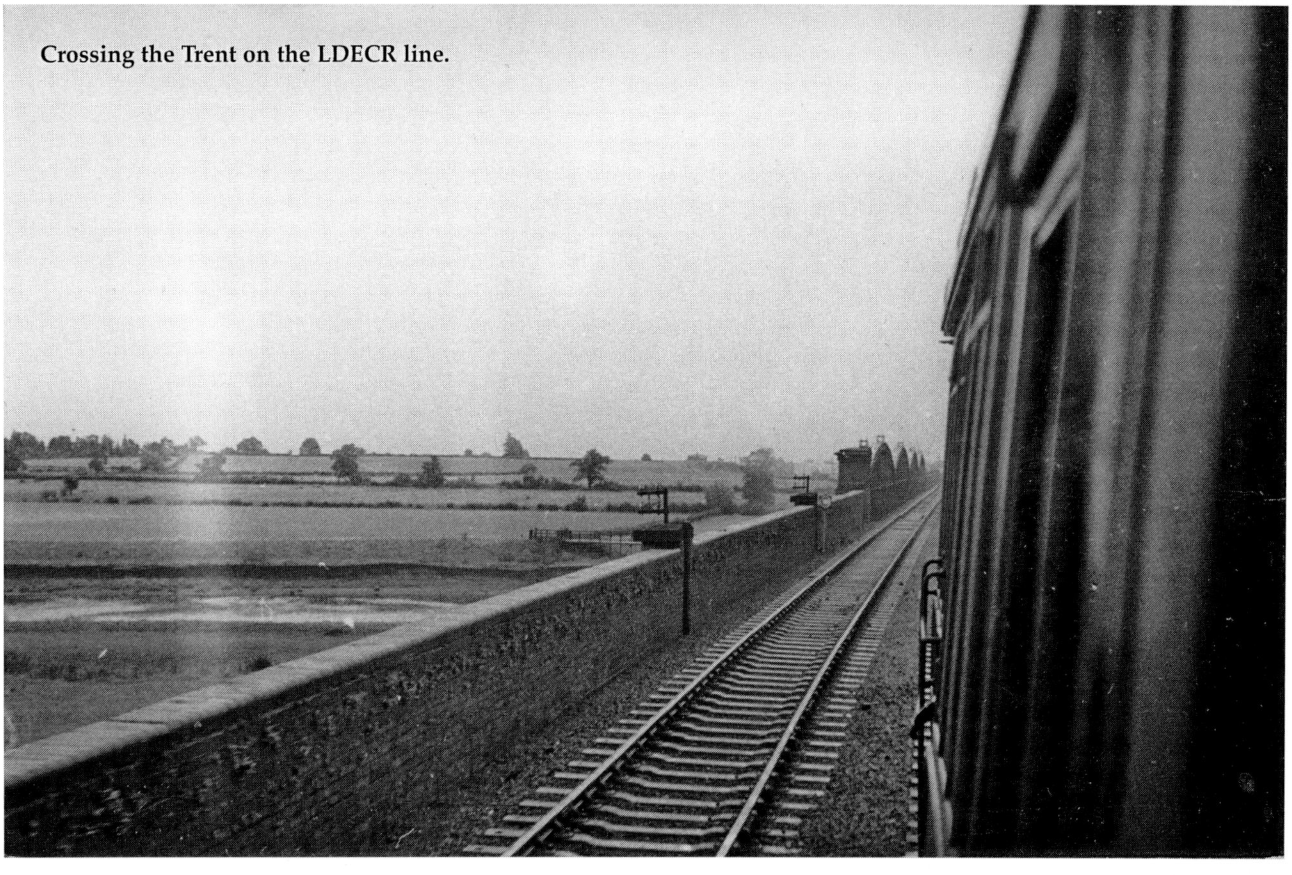
Crossing the Trent on the LDECR line.

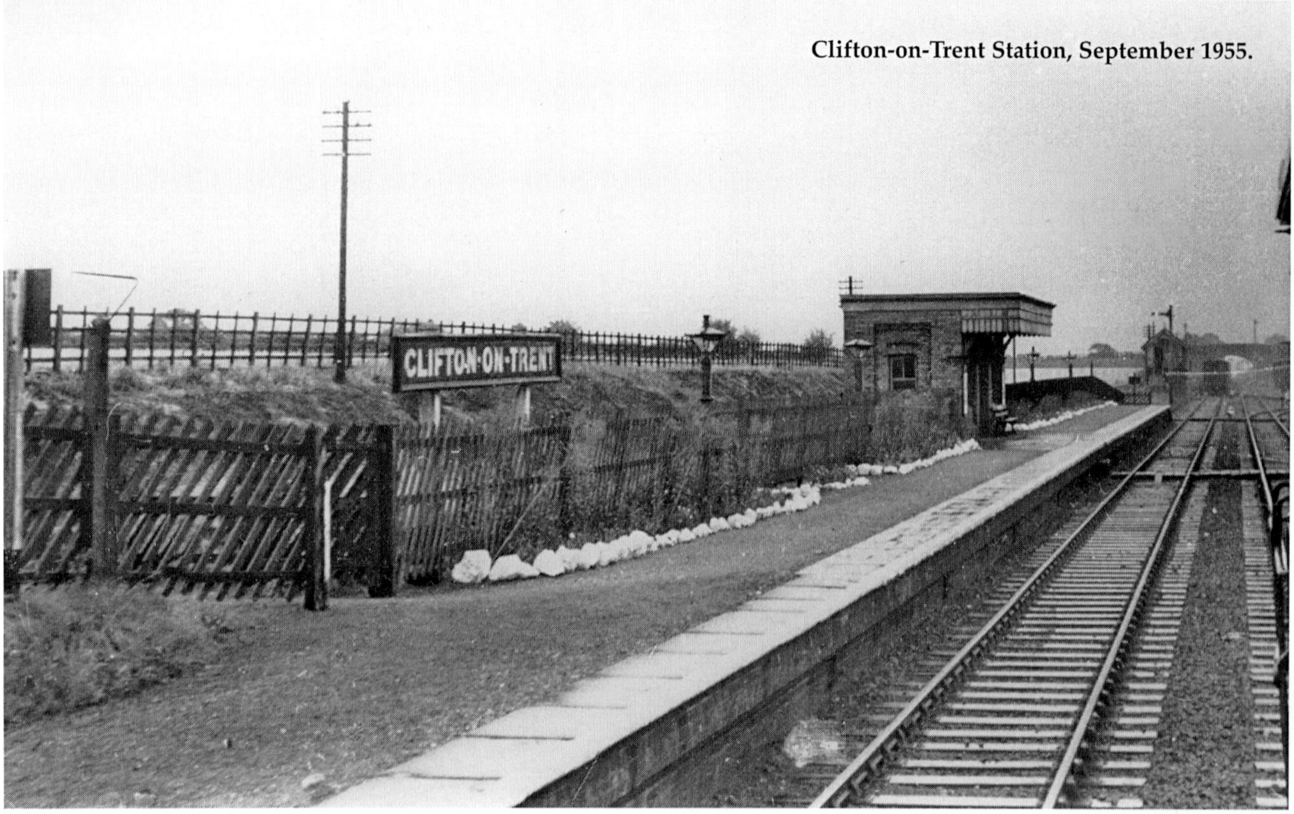

Clifton-on-Trent Station, September 1955.

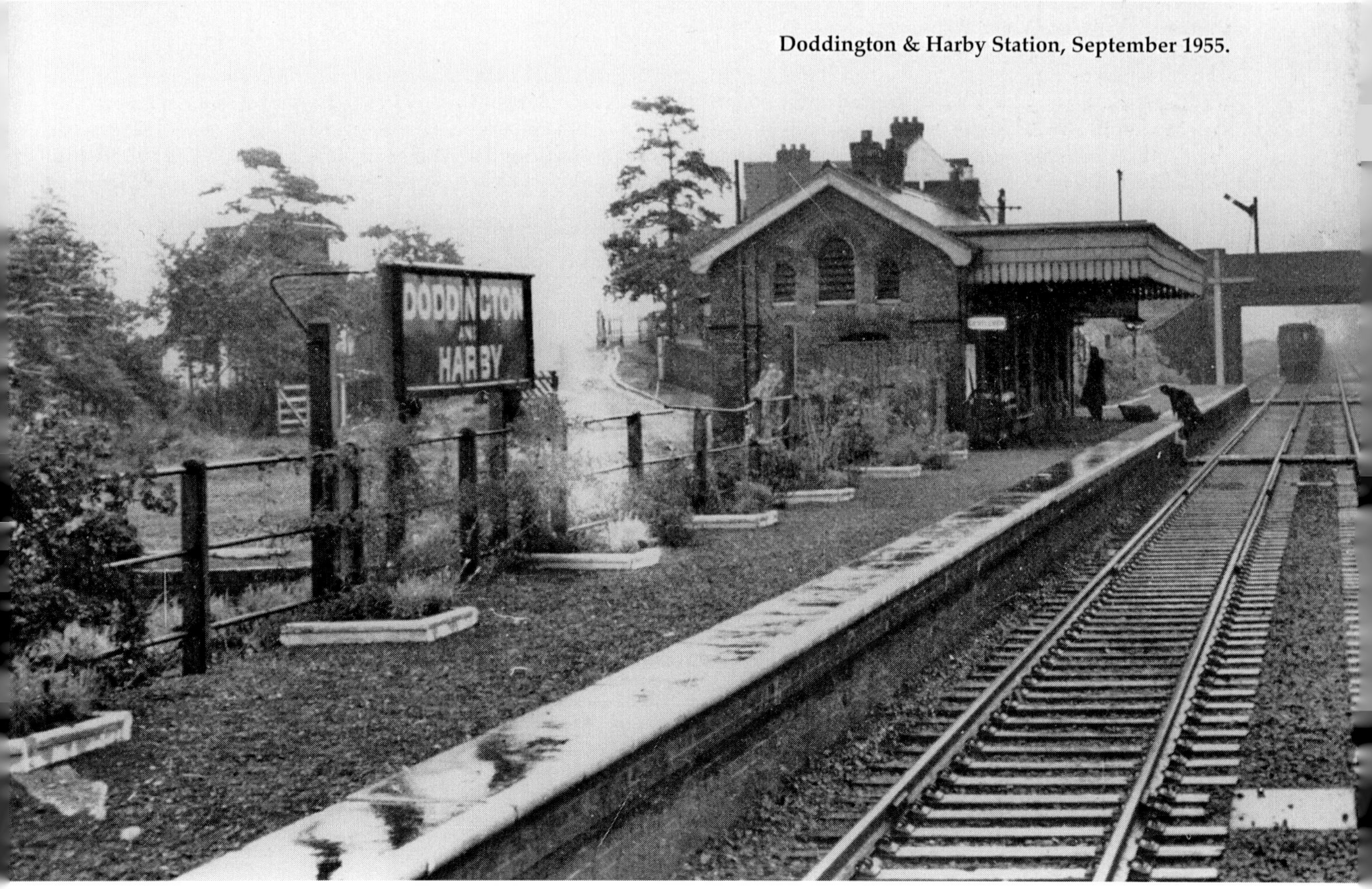

Doddington & Harby Station, September 1955.

# Chesterfield – Loughborough: The Great Central Main Line *

| | |
|---|---|
| *Passenger services withdrawn* | 4 September 1967 |
| *Length* | $36^1/_4$ miles (Chesterfield – Loughborough) |
| *Original owning company* | Manchester, Sheffield & Lincolnshire Railway (Great Central Railway from 1899) |

| *Stations closed* | *Date of closure* |
|---|---|
| Hucknall Central ** | 4 March 1963 |
| Bulwell Common | 4 March 1963 |
| New Basford | 7 September 1964 |
| Carrington | 24 September 1928 |
| Nottingham Victoria *** | 4 September 1967 |
| Nottingham Arkwright Street **** | 5 May 1969 |
| Ruddington | 4 March 1963 |
| Rushcliffe Halt | 4 March 1963 |
| East Leake | 5 May 1969 |

* Closed stations on this line that were in Derbyshire were Chesterfield Central, Grassmoor, Heath, Pilsley and Tibshelf Town. The closed station in Leicestershire was Loughborough Central.
** Originally named Hucknall Town until 1 July 1923.
*** Originally named Nottingham Joint by the Great Northern until 12 June 1900 (it was known as Nottingham Central by the Great Central).
**** Originally named Arkwright Street until 24 May 1900; closed between 4 March 1963 and 4 September 1967.

The Manchester, Sheffield & Lincolnshire Railway was, until the last decade of the nineteenth century, a provincial railway company concentrating its activities in the areas named in its title. During the 1890s it succeeded in transforming itself into a major trunk route from London to the north of England by the building of its London Extension, the last great main-line construction project before the Channel Tunnel rail link of recent years. Indeed, had the MS&LR's chairman, Sir Edward Watkin, had his way, it is he who would have built the Channel Tunnel, almost a century before the present one, and Nottingham would have had direct connection to Paris, Berlin and even St Petersburg.

The story of the upper end of the London Extension has been related in *Derbyshire's Lost Railways*. Suffice it to say that the initial project gave the MS&L access to Chesterfield by 1892 and in the following year it reached Annesley, gaining entry to Nottingham by running powers over the Great Northern. Over the next six years the company constructed its new line from Annesley, through Nottingham, Loughborough, Leicester and Rugby to Quainton Road Junction in Buckinghamshire, where it made an end-on connection with the Metropolitan Railway, another of Watkin's companies, to gain access to its new London terminus at Marylebone. The line was opened on 15 March 1899, by which time the Manchester, Sheffield & Lincolnshire had become the Great Central Railway.

The centrepiece of the line in Nottinghamshire was Nottingham Victoria Station, constructed in a huge cutting just south of the Mansfield Road tunnel, which pierced Sherwood Rise. The station was jointly owned with the Great Northern and was a vast cavernous structure with an overall glass roof, though this was less impressive than it might otherwise have been due to the depth of the cutting. After Victoria, the line plunged through Thurland Street tunnel before striding out across south Nottingham on a succession of viaducts, crossing both the Midland's rebuilt station and the River Trent, then making for Loughborough, Leicester and the capital.

The London Extension was a magnificent piece of engineering, but hardly a commercial success – it was wryly said that MS&L stood for 'Money Sunk & Lost', while GC stood for 'Gone Completely'! The line was run down during the late 1950s, lost many of its intermediate stations in 1963 and closed entirely in 1967, though a passenger service from Rugby continued for a further two years, stopping short of Victoria at Arkwright Street, close to the football grounds. Given that it had been constructed to European loading gauge and could, with the Channel Tunnel, have provided precisely the rapid access from France to northern England that Watkin envisaged, the closure must rate as one of the greatest single blunders in transport policy in the late twentieth century and a monument to short-term thinking.

Nottingham Victoria Station is no more, the site cleared for the construction of the Victoria shopping centre, though the station's brick-built clock tower remains amid the sea of glass and concrete. The viaducts and retaining walls to the south not only still exist, but some have been adapted to carry rail traffic again, in the shape of Nottingham's cross-city tram network. Further south, at Ruddington, a stub of the line remained in use to serve the British Gypsum works at East Leake and a Ministry of Defence depot. These have now become the basis of the northern end of the Great Central steam railway project and it is intended to link the section north of Loughborough to the established steam railway operating southwards to the former Belgrave & Birstall Station (now Leicester North), so that it will be possible to travel again by steam from the outer edges of Nottingham to the edges of Leicester by Great Central.

The Annesley Locomotive Sheds were opened by the Great Central Railway in 1898 on their main line north of Hucknall Central. Locomotives Nos. 5375 and 5385 sit at he head of a long line of LNER engines, June 1926.

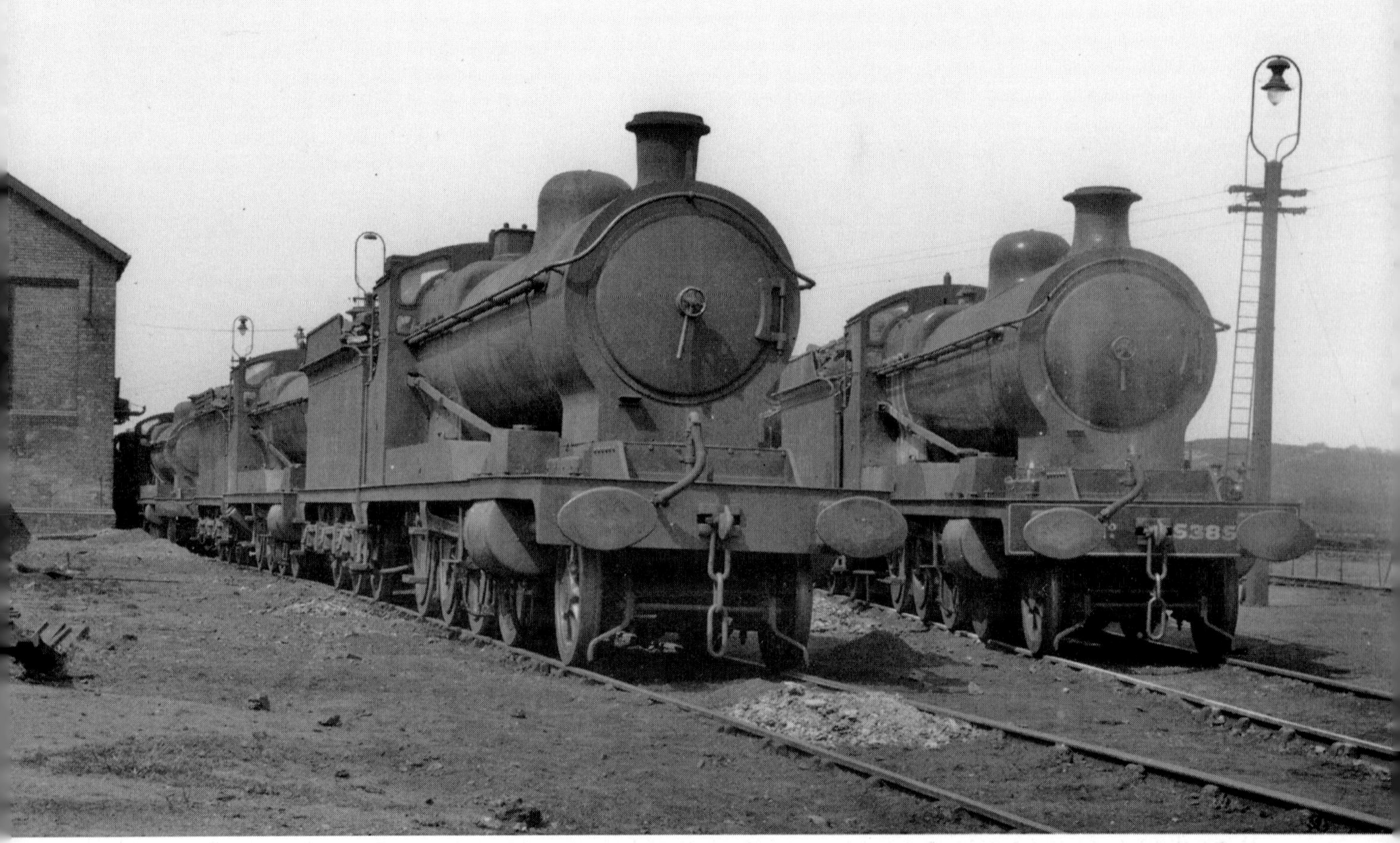


Locomotives Nos. 5770, 5767, 5290 and 5366 in storage at Annesley Locomotive Sheds, June 1926.

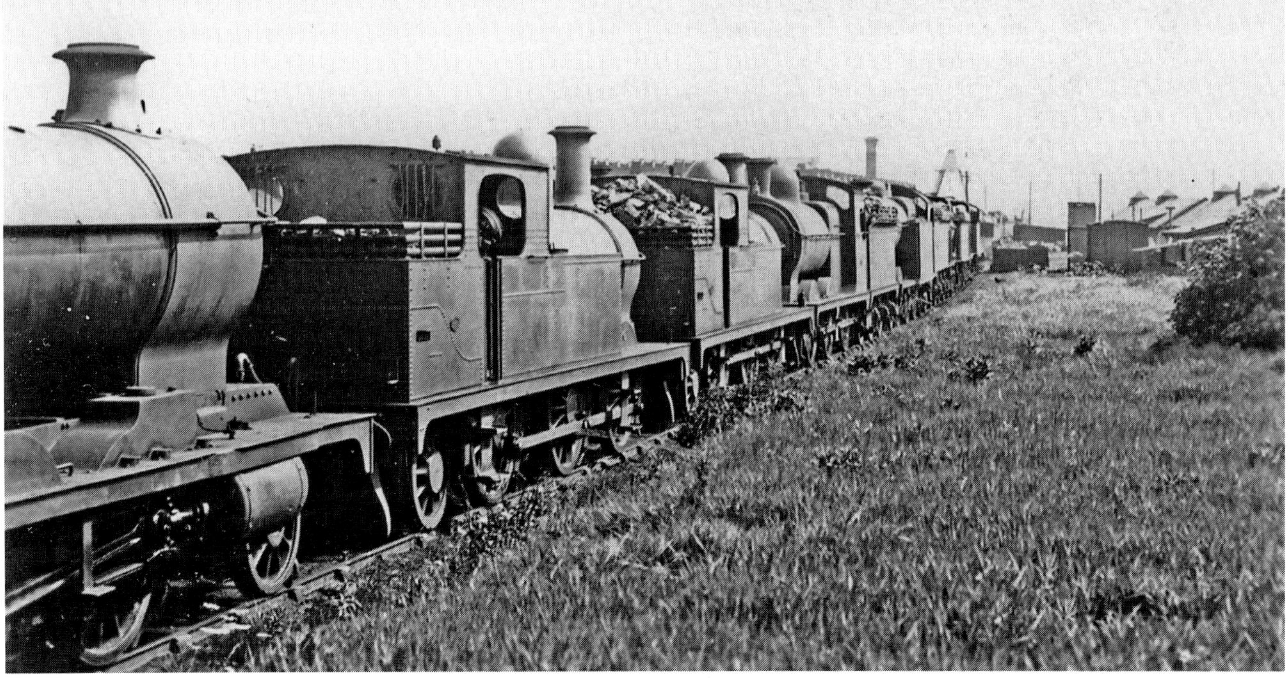

Annesley Locomotive Sheds, August 1954. Annesley Colliery's arial ropeway is in the background.

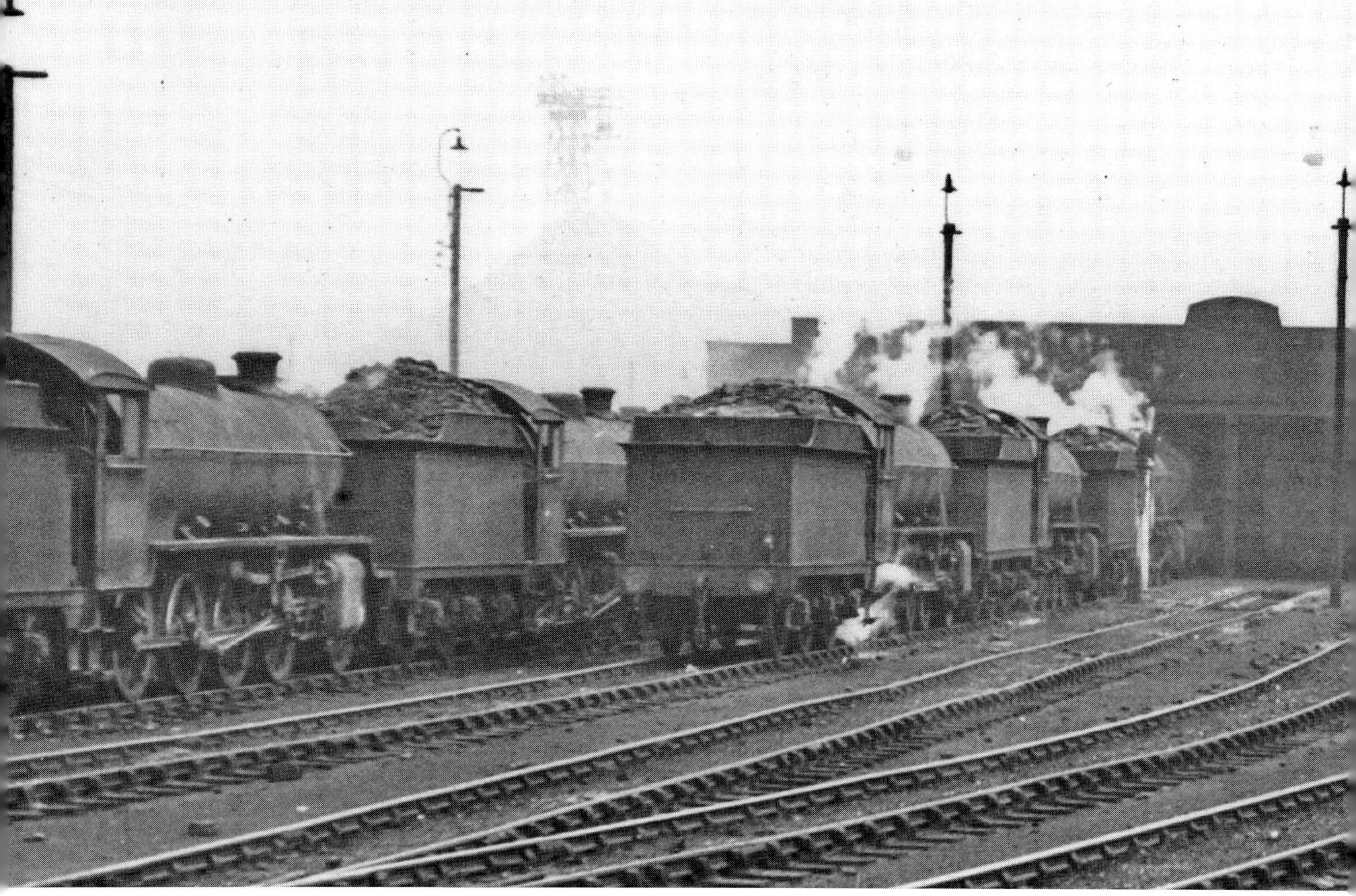

No. 6047 at Hucknall Central Station, May 1946.

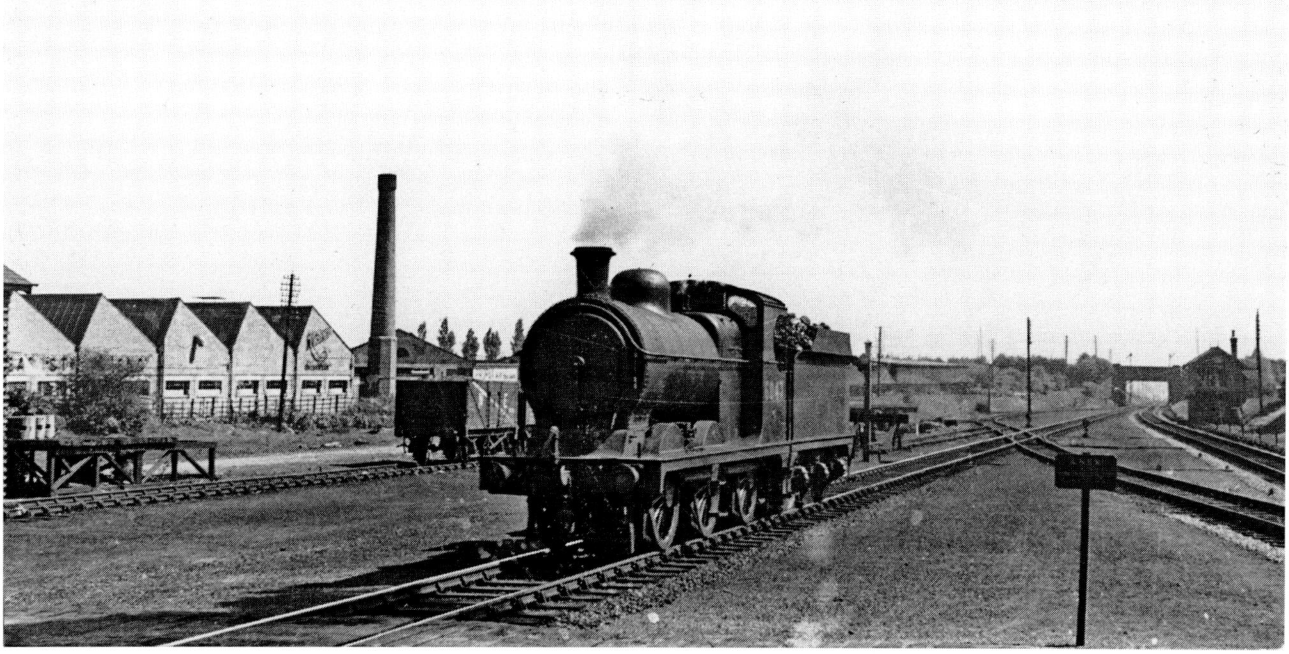

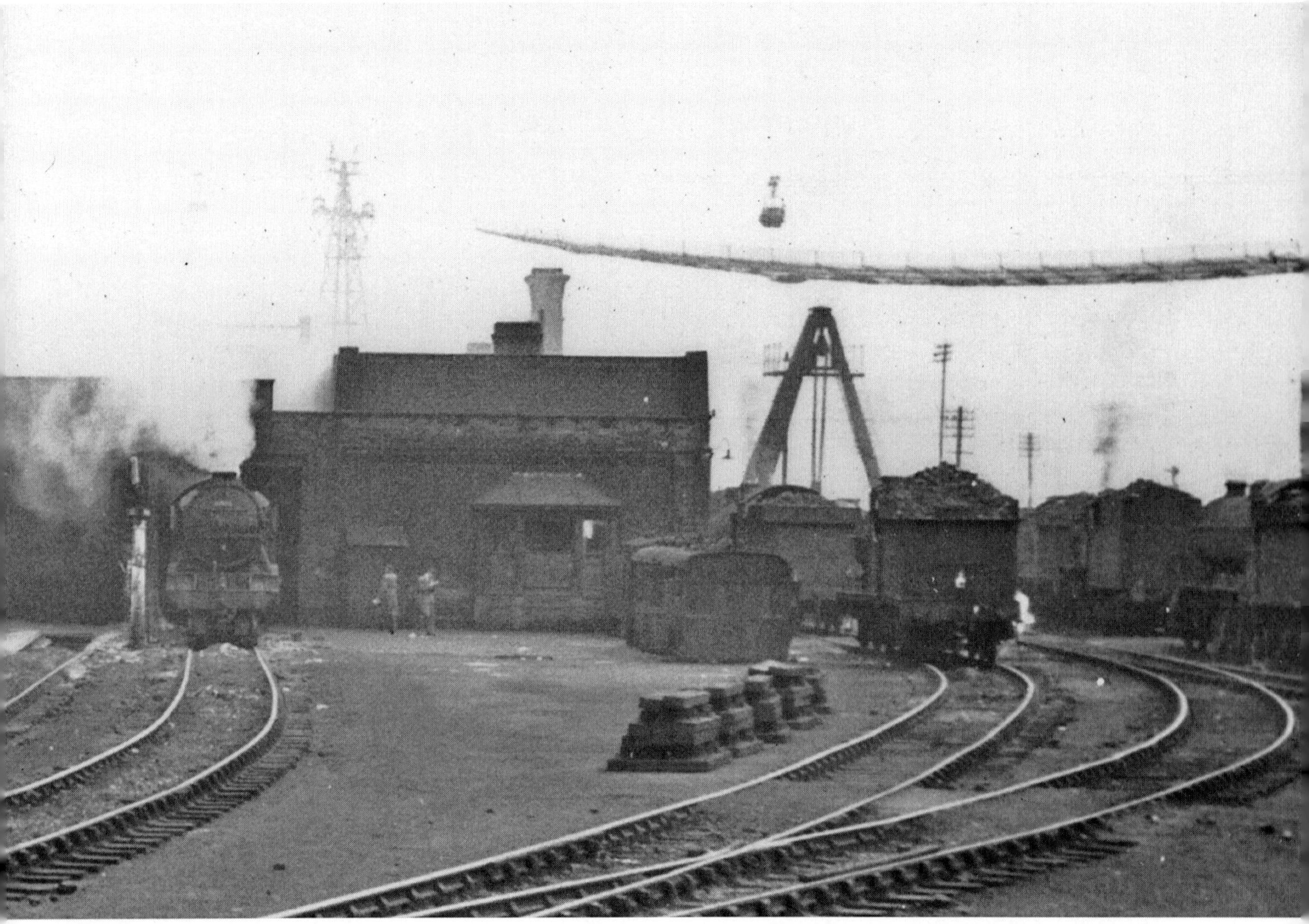

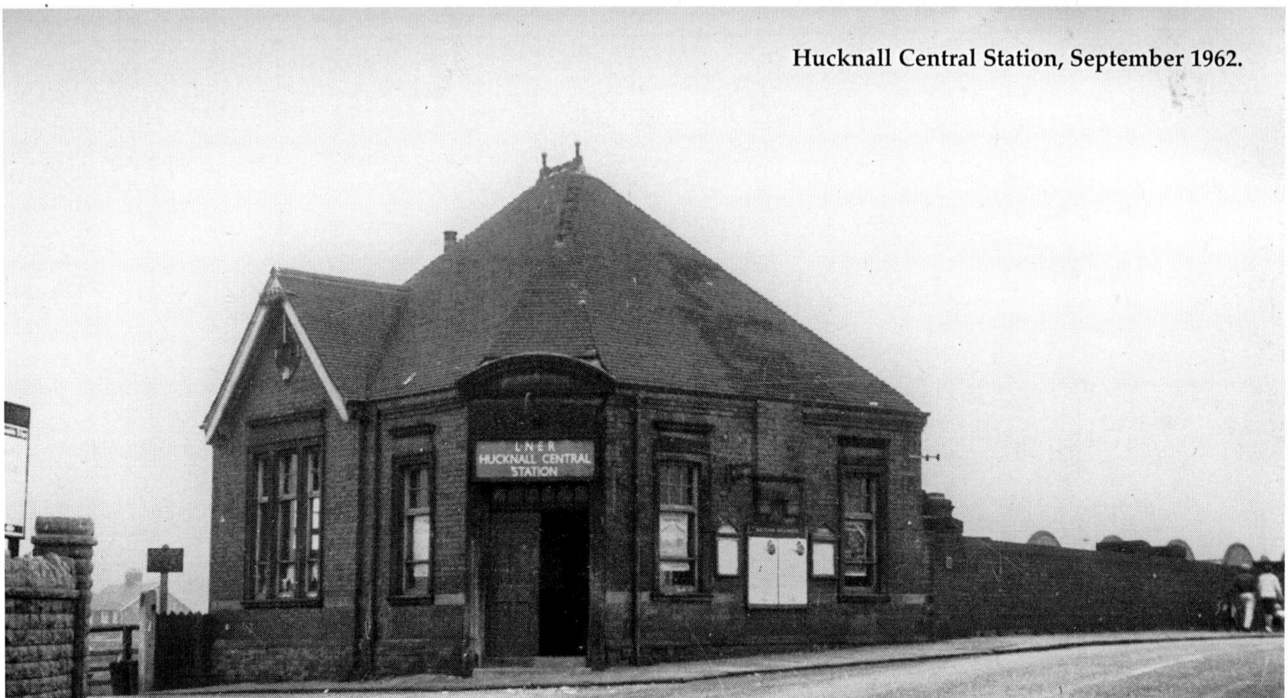


Hucknall Central Station, September 1962.

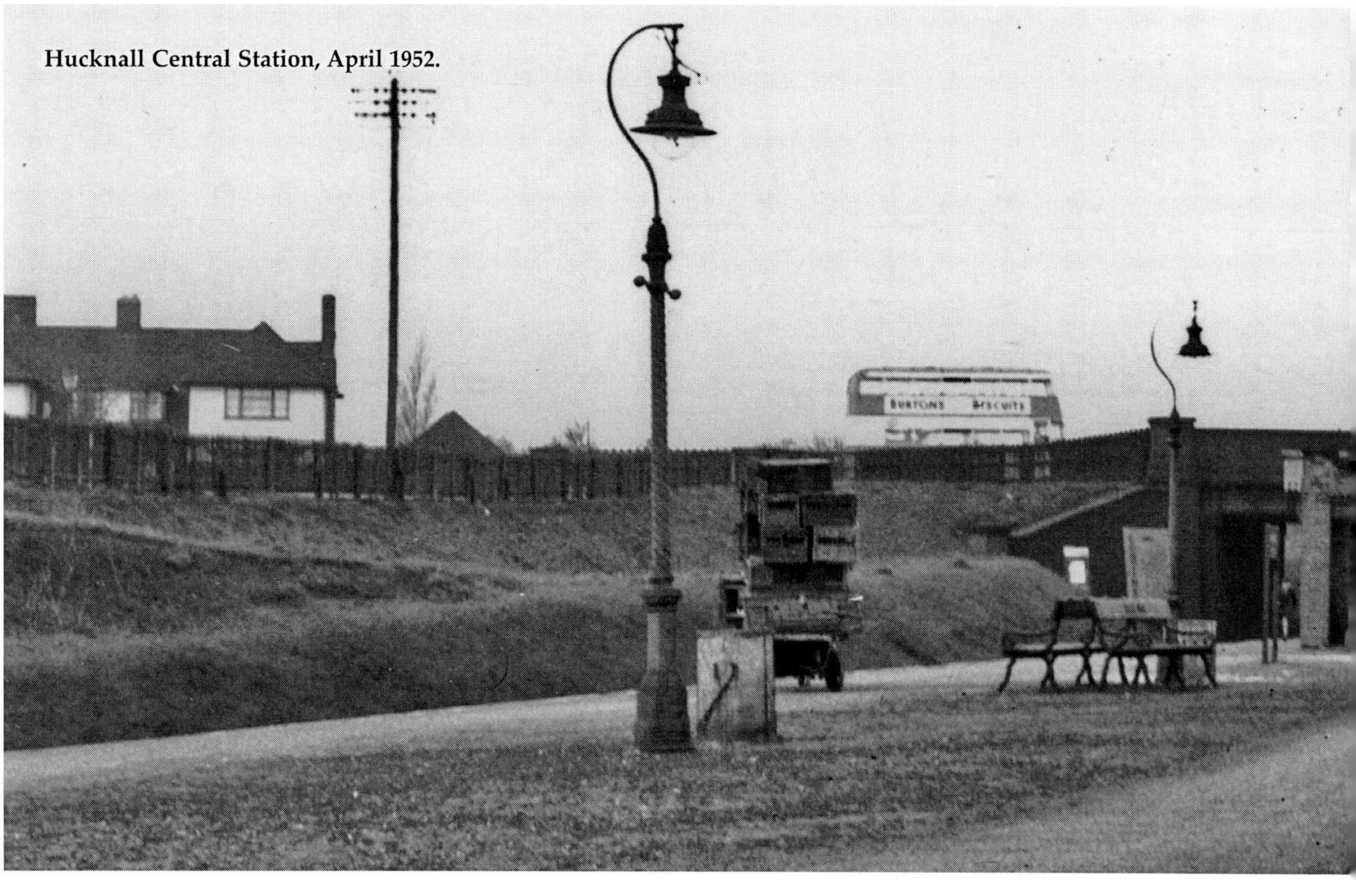
Hucknall Central Station, April 1952.

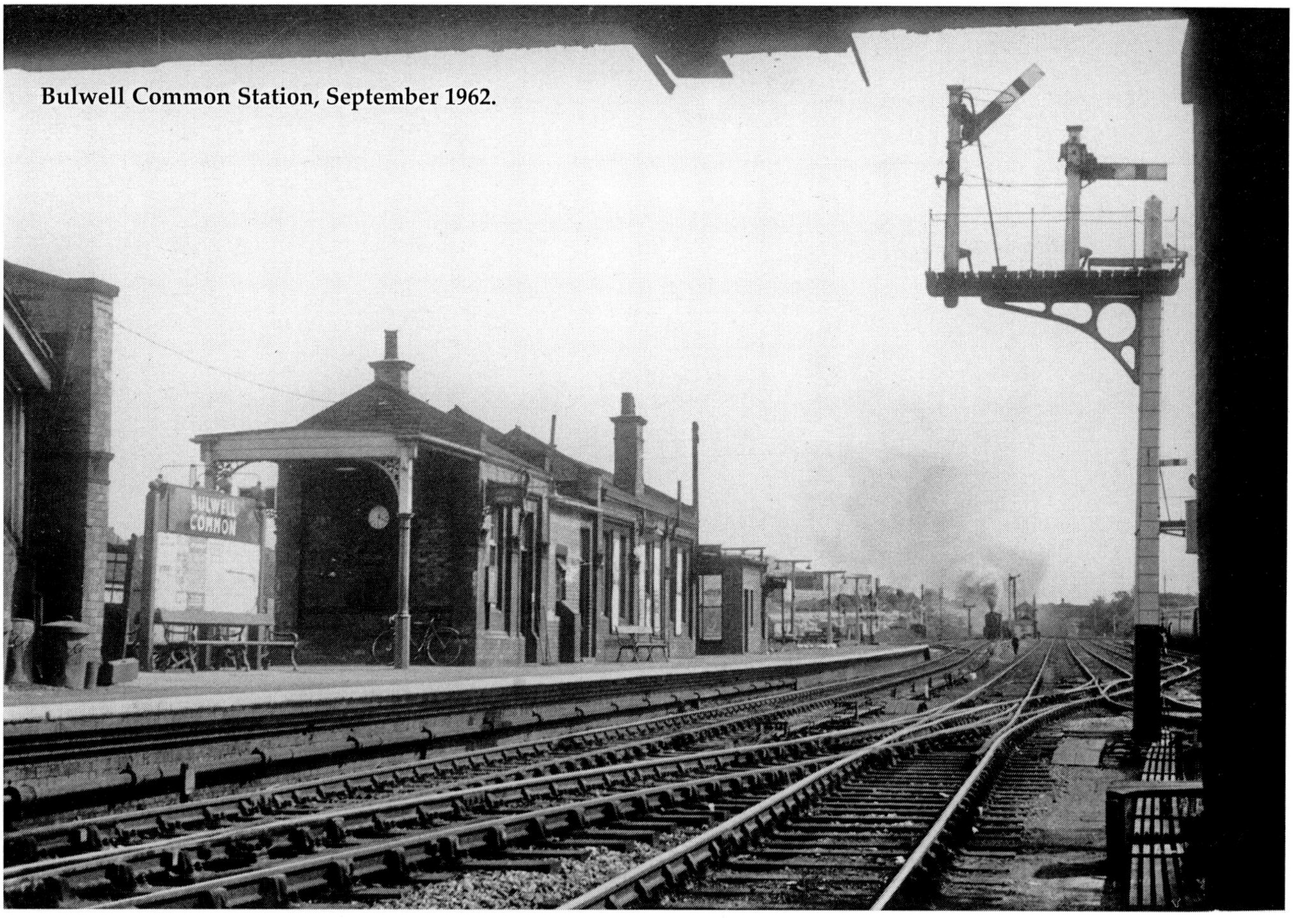

Bulwell Common Station, September 1962.

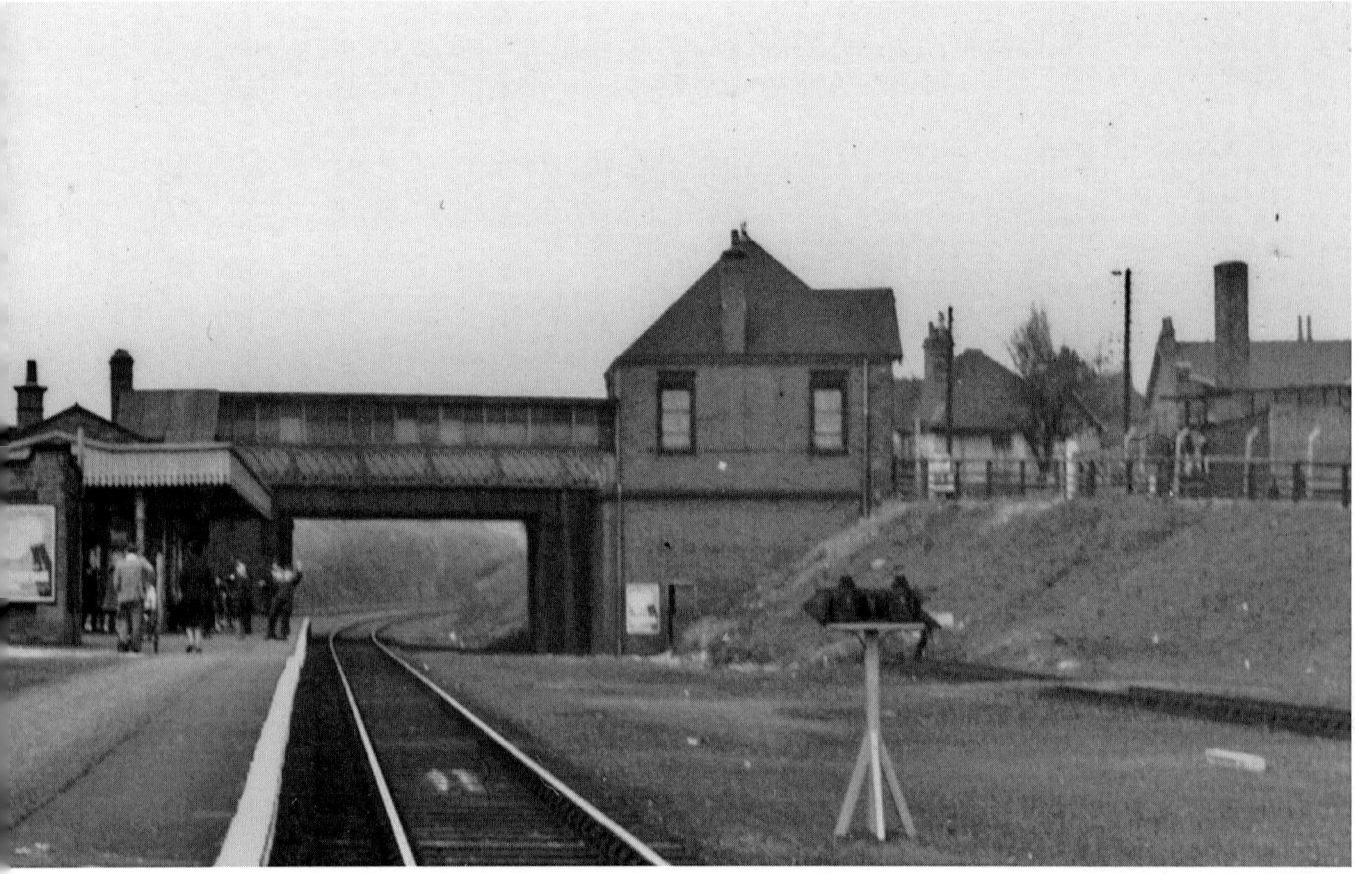

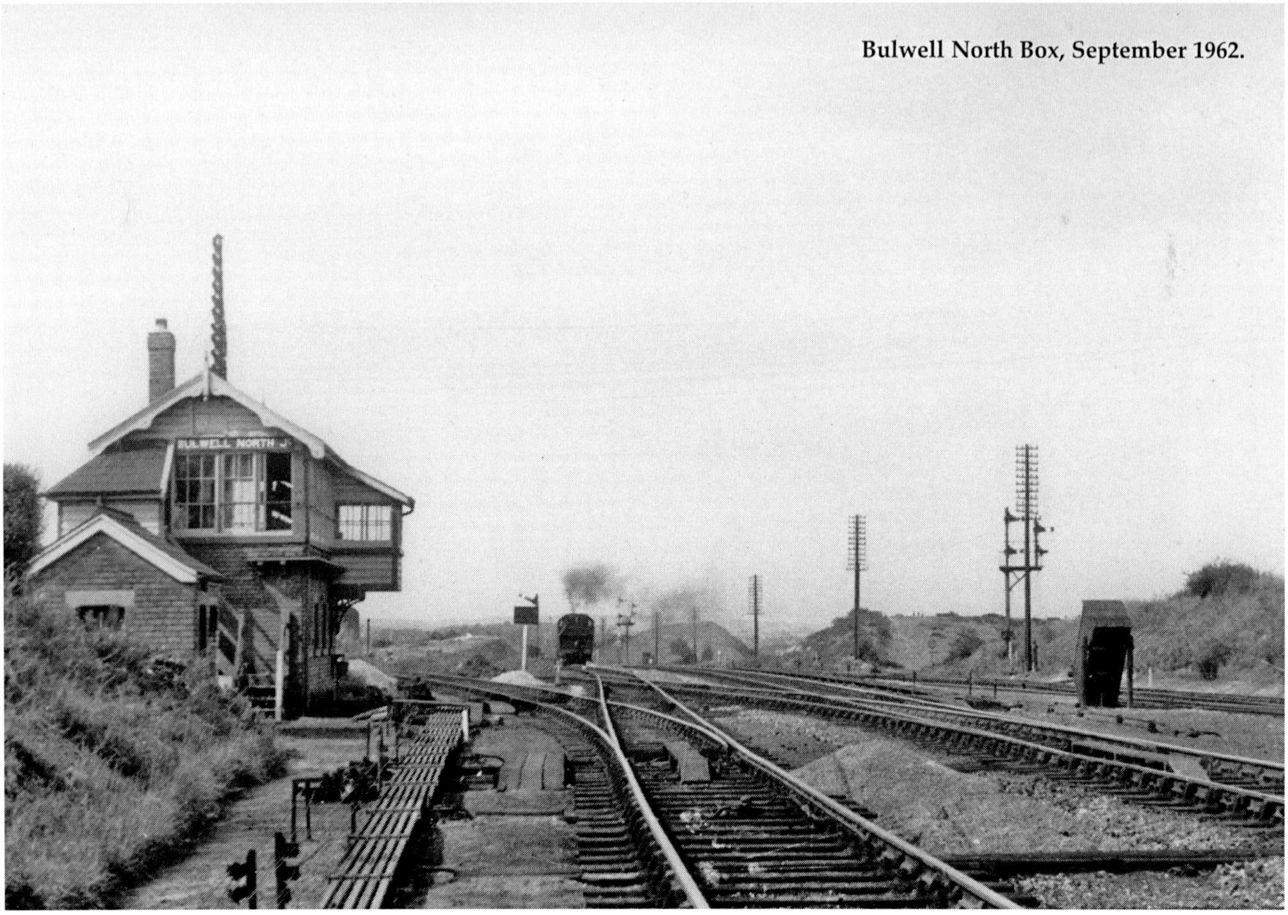

Bulwell North Box, September 1962.

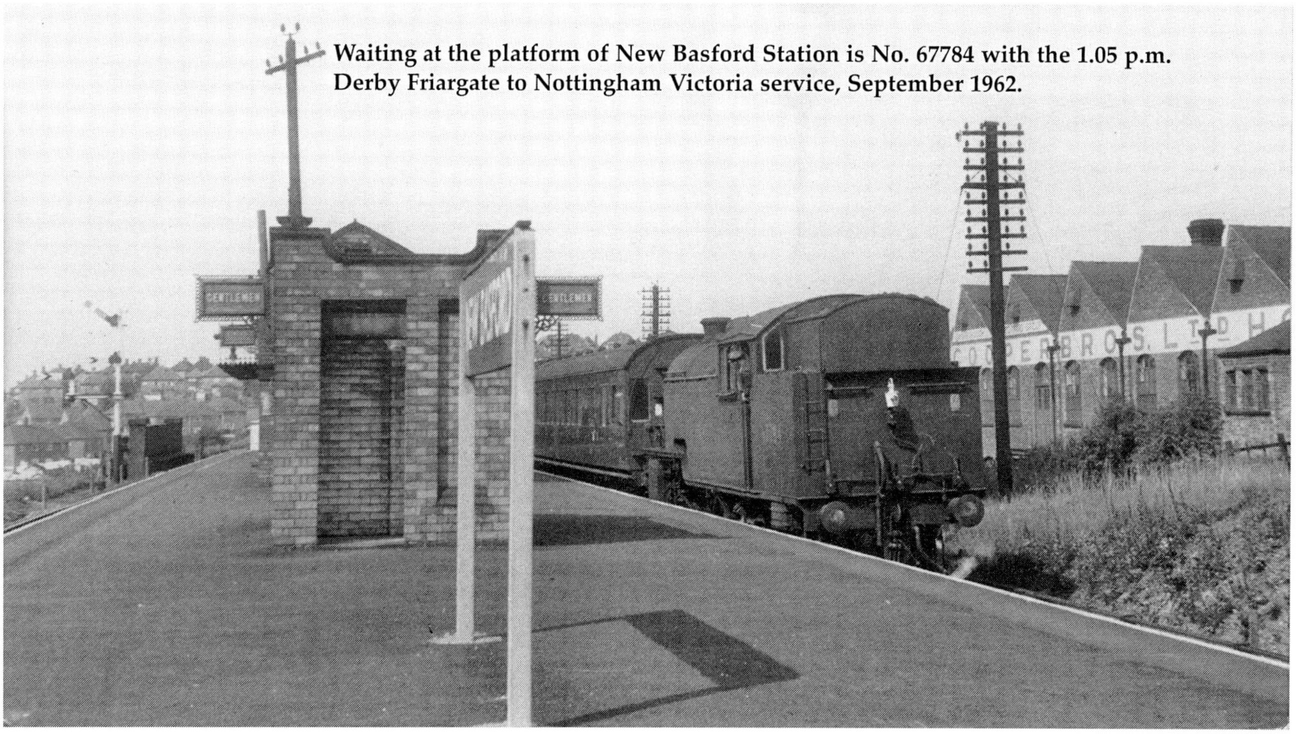


Waiting at the platform of New Basford Station is No. 67784 with the 1.05 p.m. Derby Friargate to Nottingham Victoria service, September 1962.

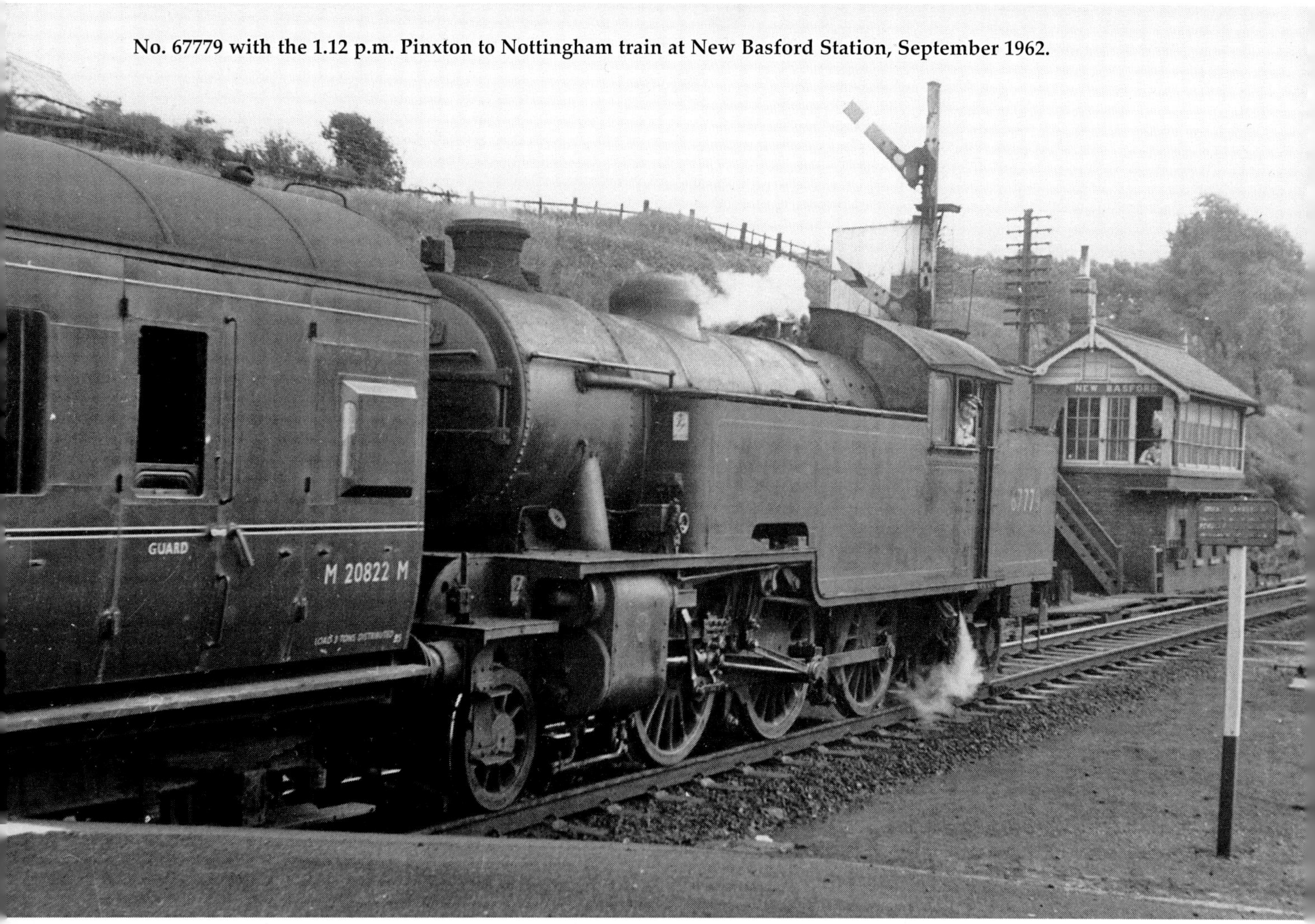


No. 67779 with the 1.12 p.m. Pinxton to Nottingham train at New Basford Station, September 1962.

The 6.55 p.m. Nottingham to Sheffield train pulled by No. 61877 at New Basford Station, July 1961.

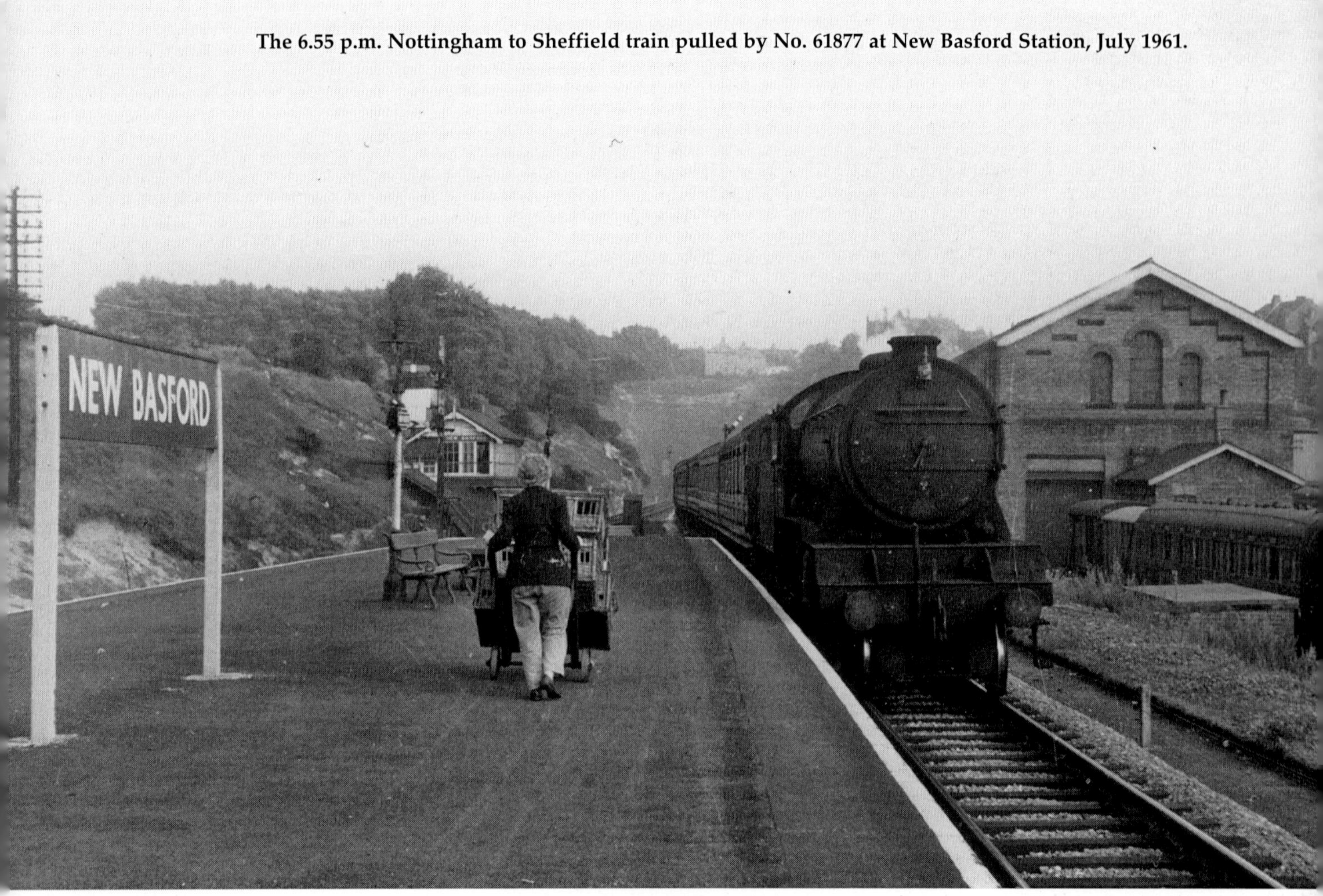


Nottingham Victoria Station.

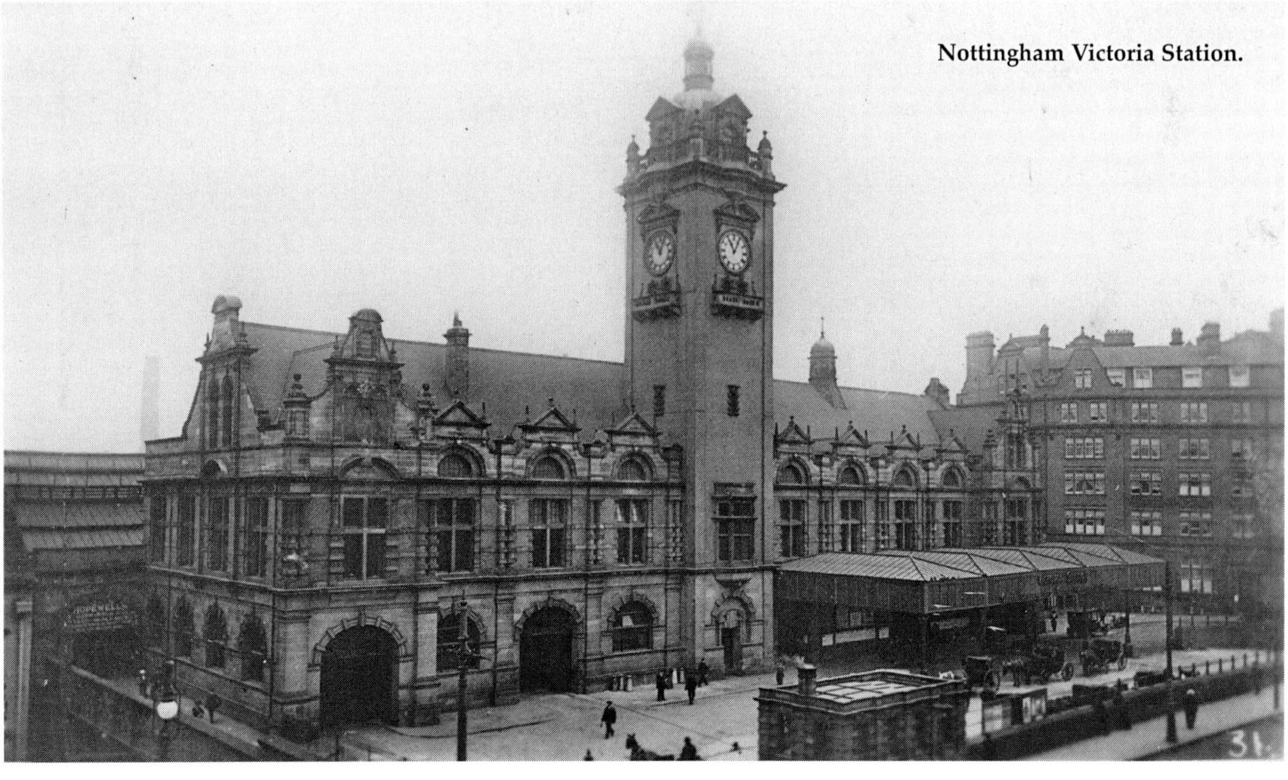

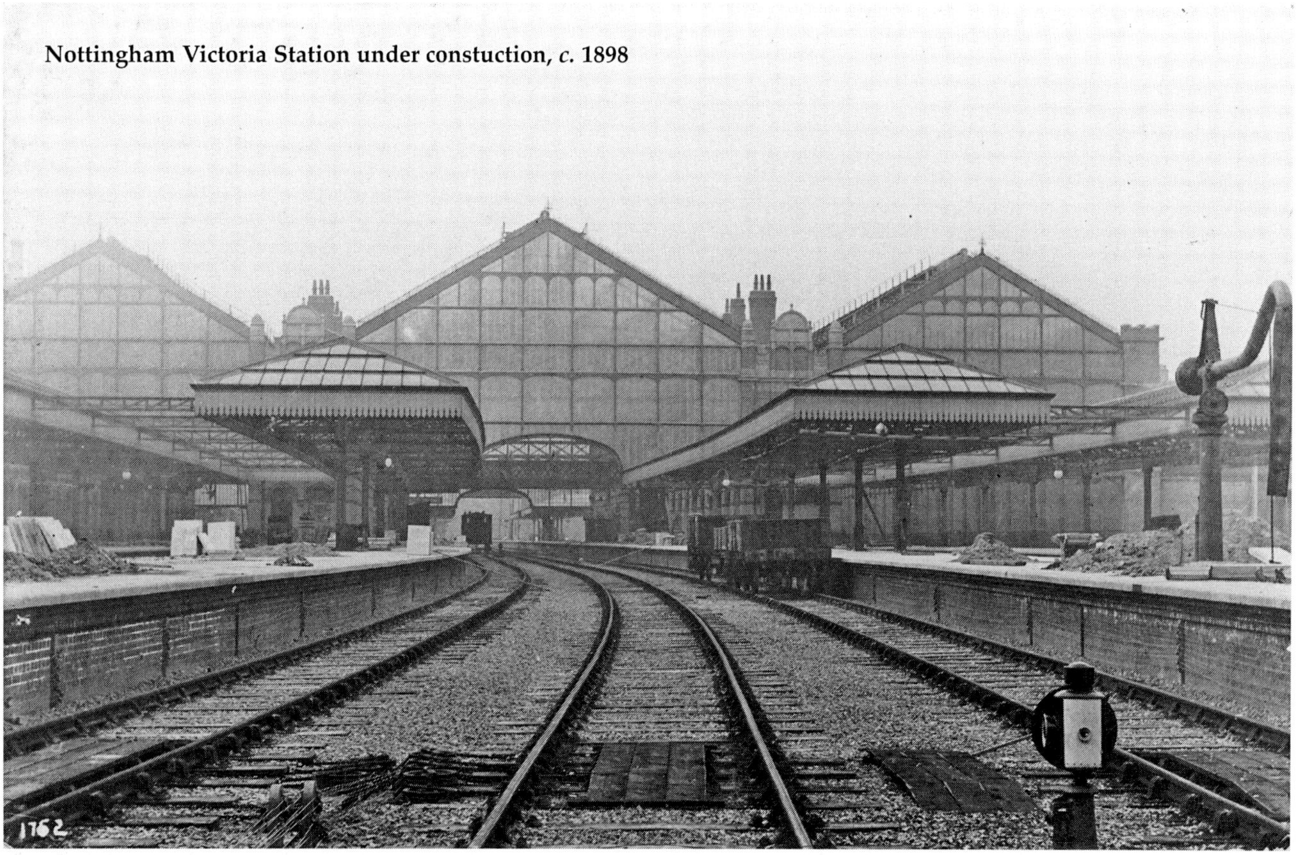


Nottingham Victoria Station under constuction, *c.* 1898

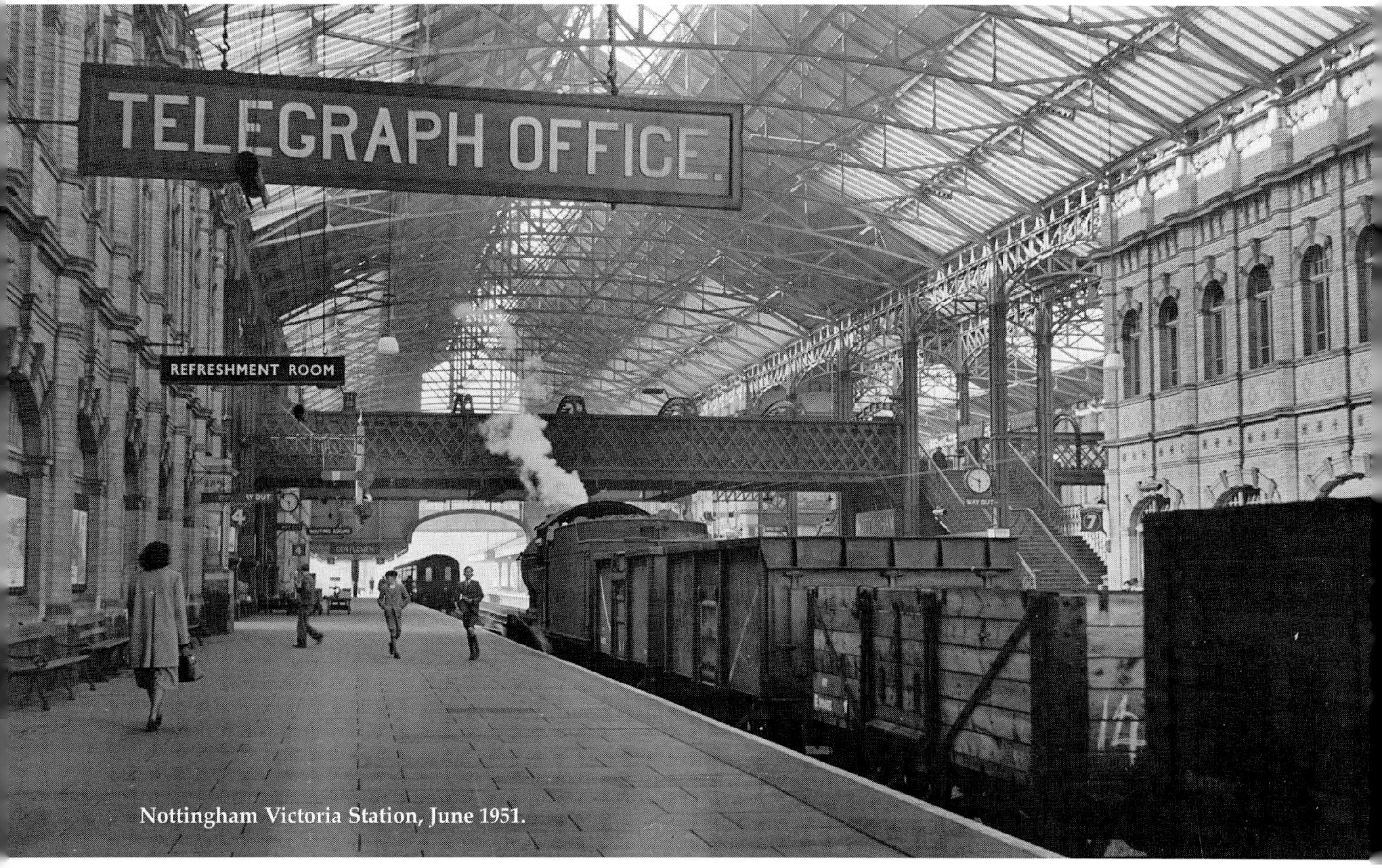


Nottingham Victoria Station, June 1951.

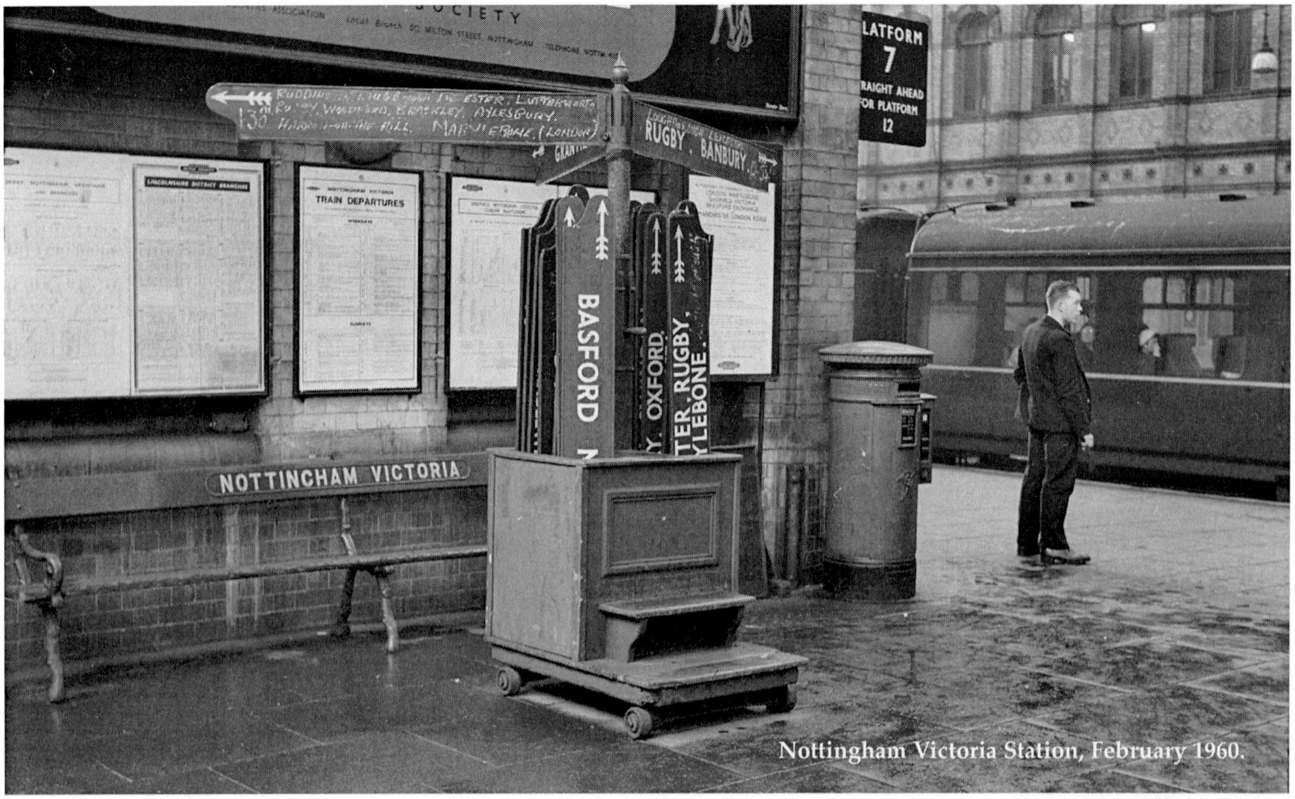


Nottingham Victoria Station, February 1960.

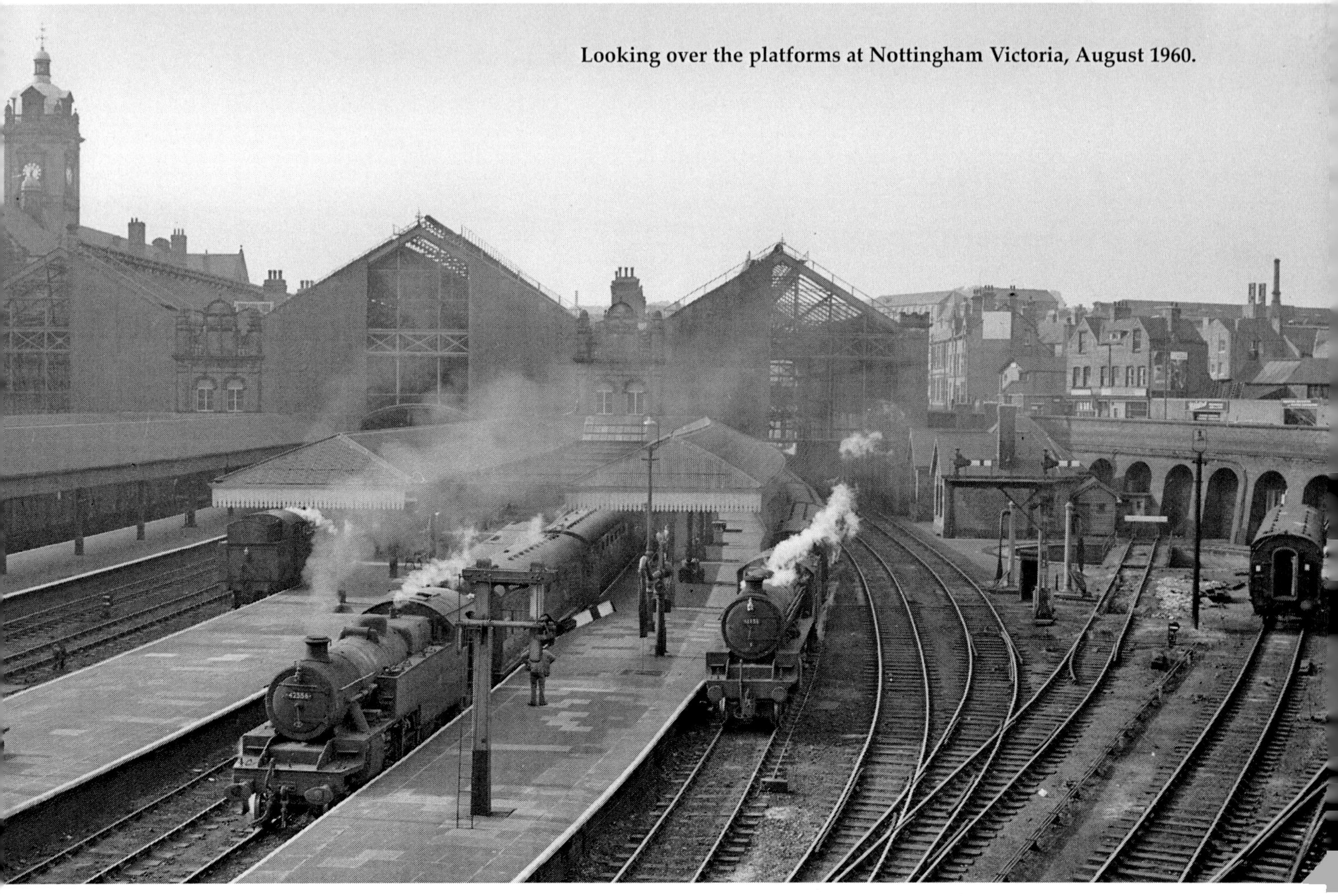

Looking over the platforms at Nottingham Victoria, August 1960.

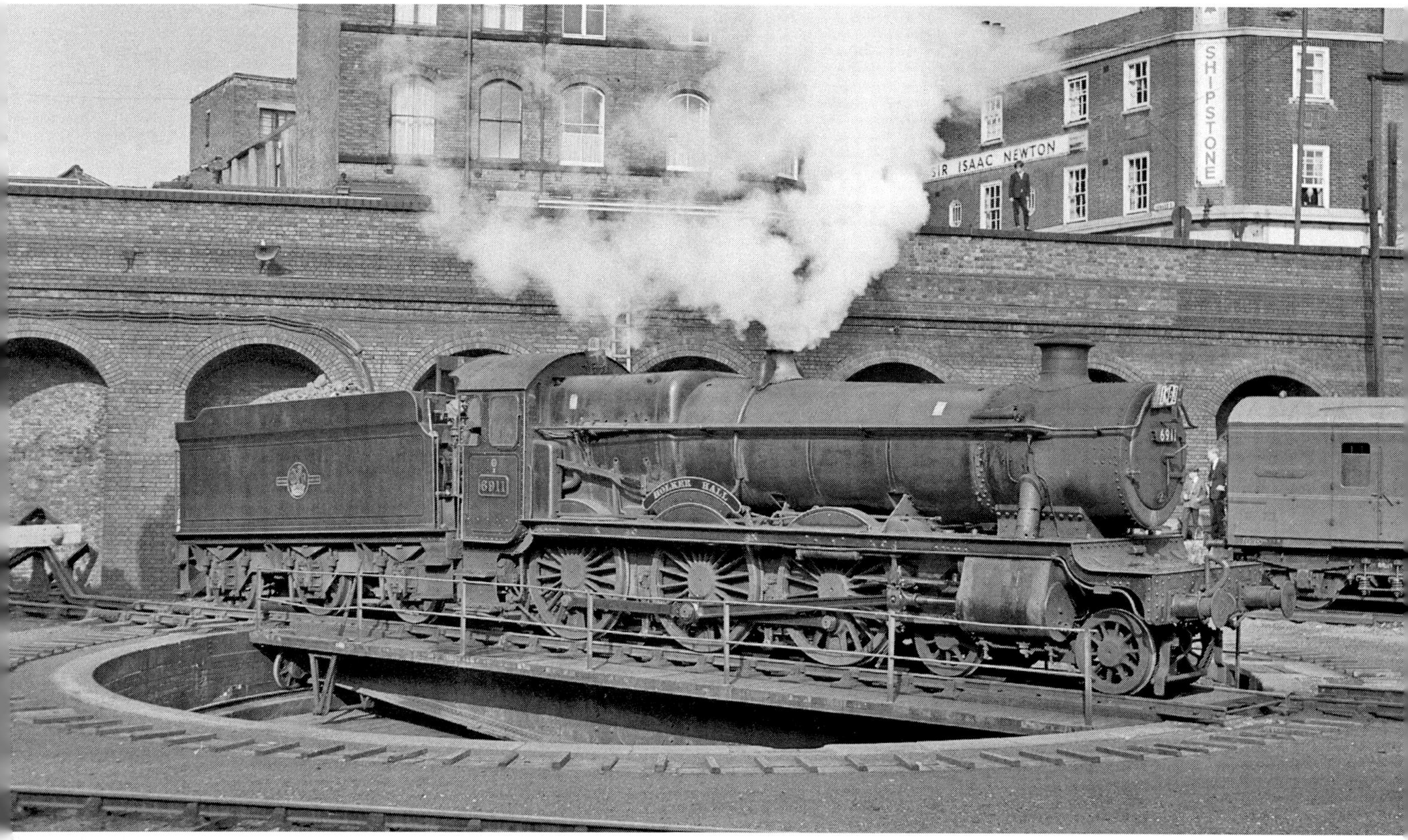


The south turntable of Nottingham Victoria Station, 8 August 1964. The crew were apparently unable to balance *Holker Hall* properly but they managed to get the turntable to move. Part way round it jammed, forcing the crew to re-adjust the balance. While trying to do so, they managed to get the rear wheels of the tender over the edge of the turntable.

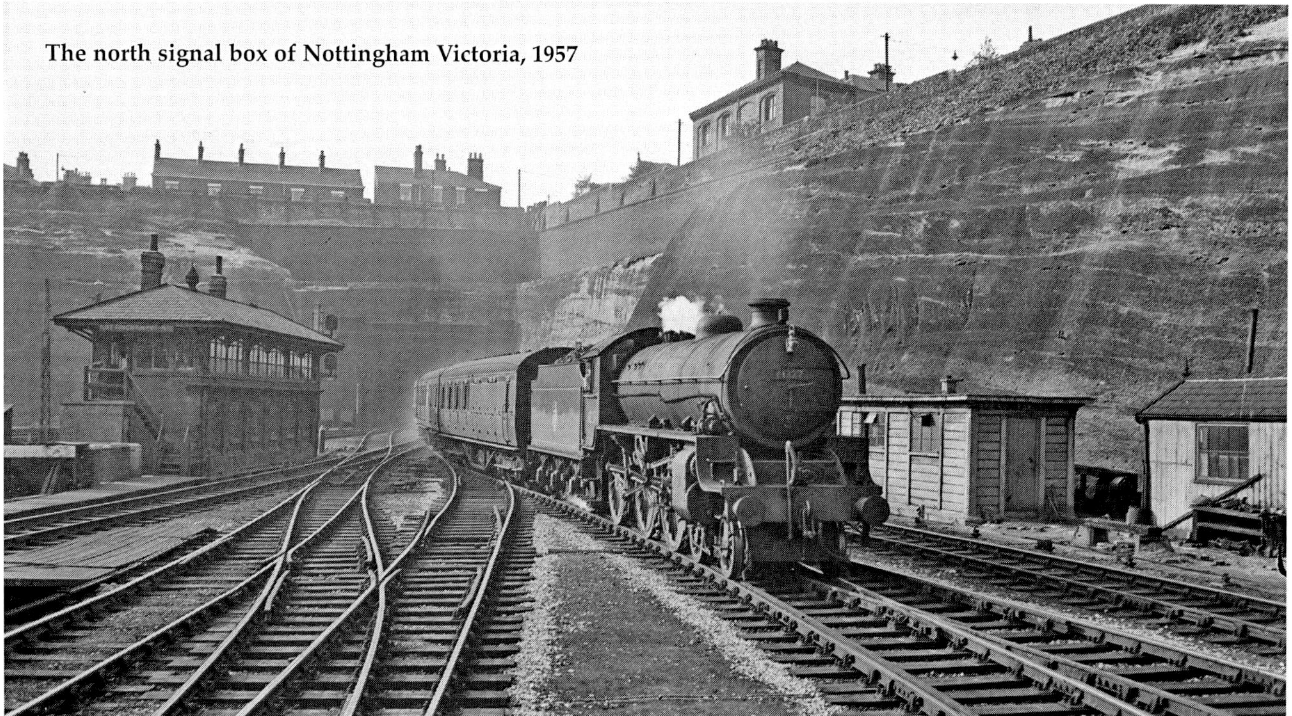

**The north signal box of Nottingham Victoria, 1957**

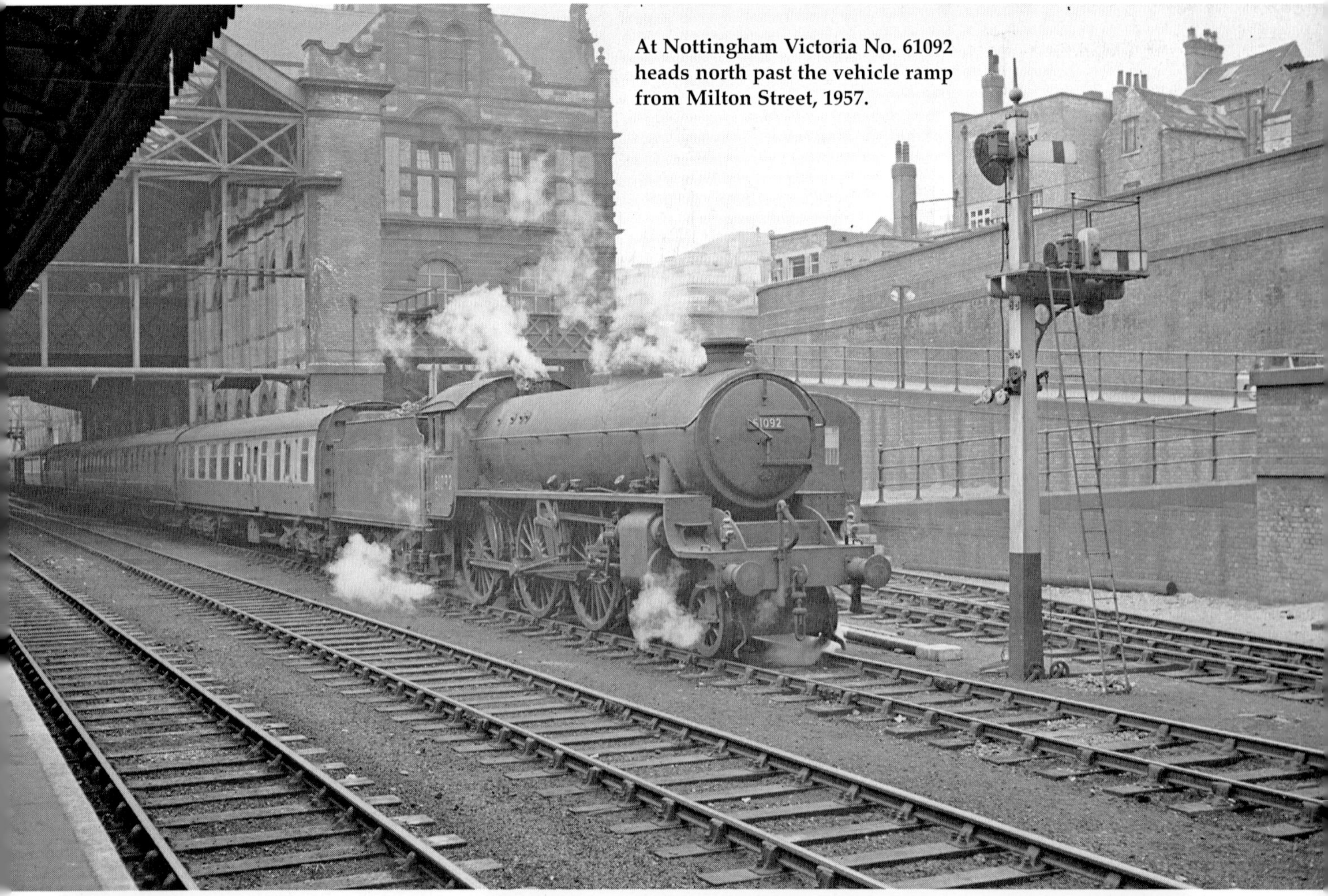


At Nottingham Victoria No. 61092 heads north past the vehicle ramp from Milton Street, 1957.

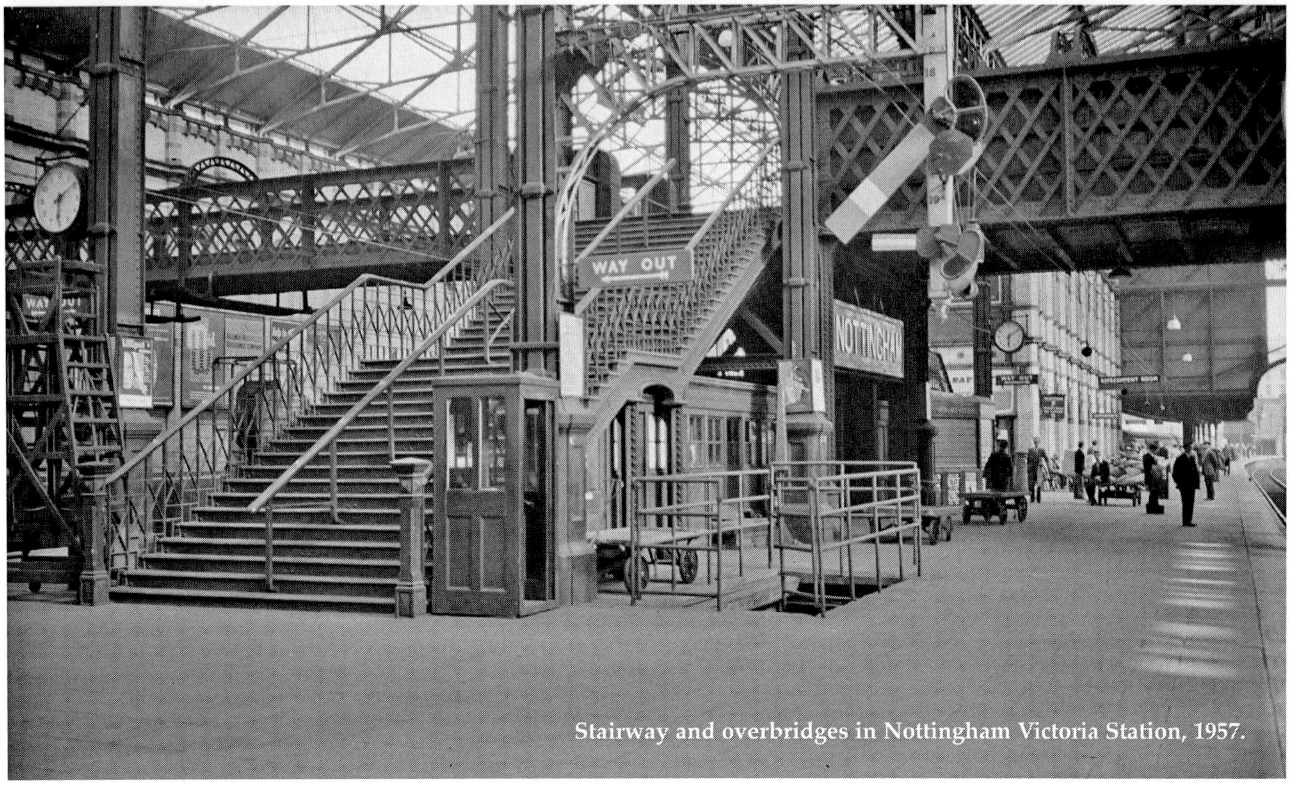


Stairway and overbridges in Nottingham Victoria Station, 1957.

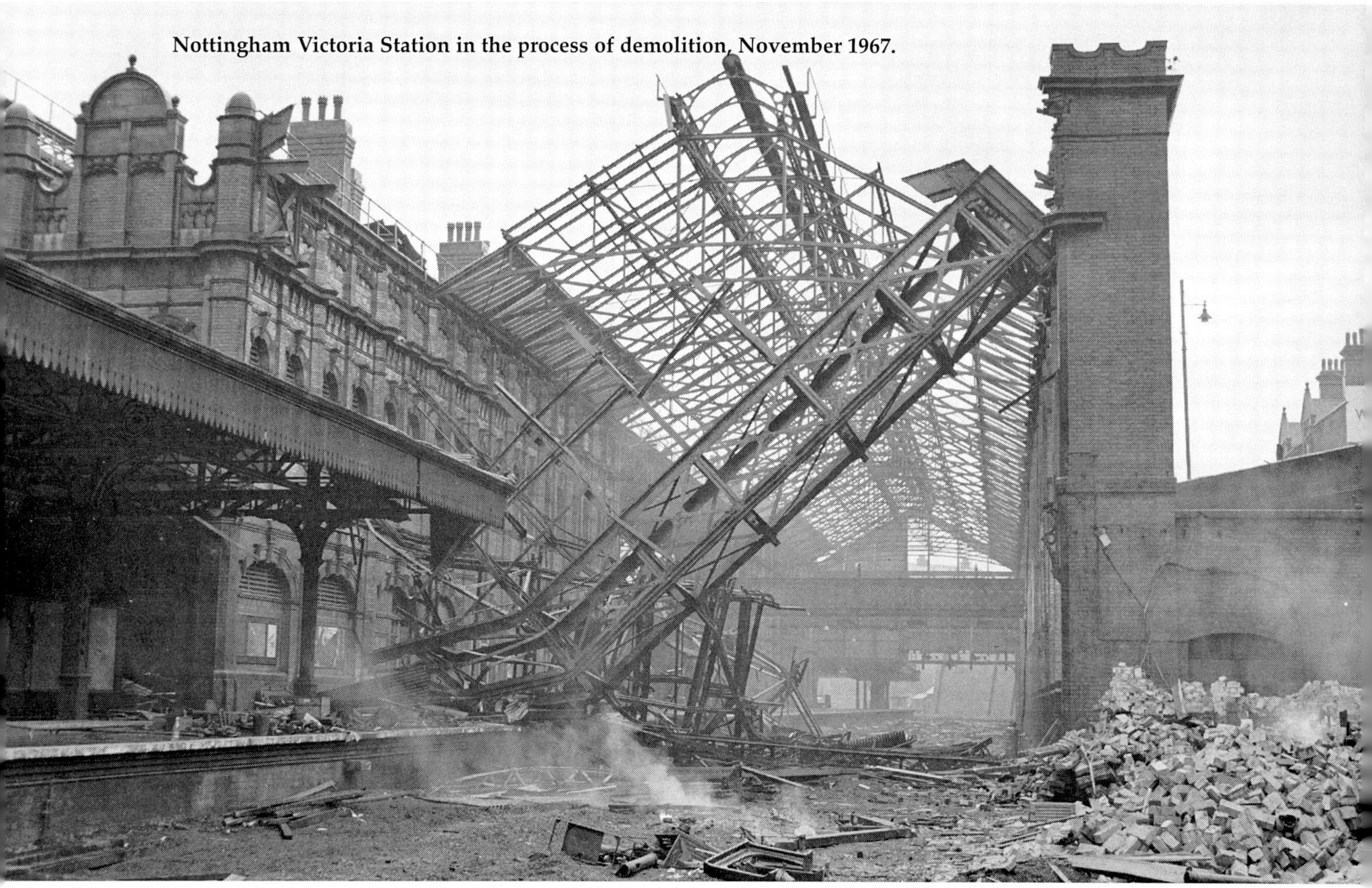

Nottingham Victoria Station in the process of demolition, November 1967.

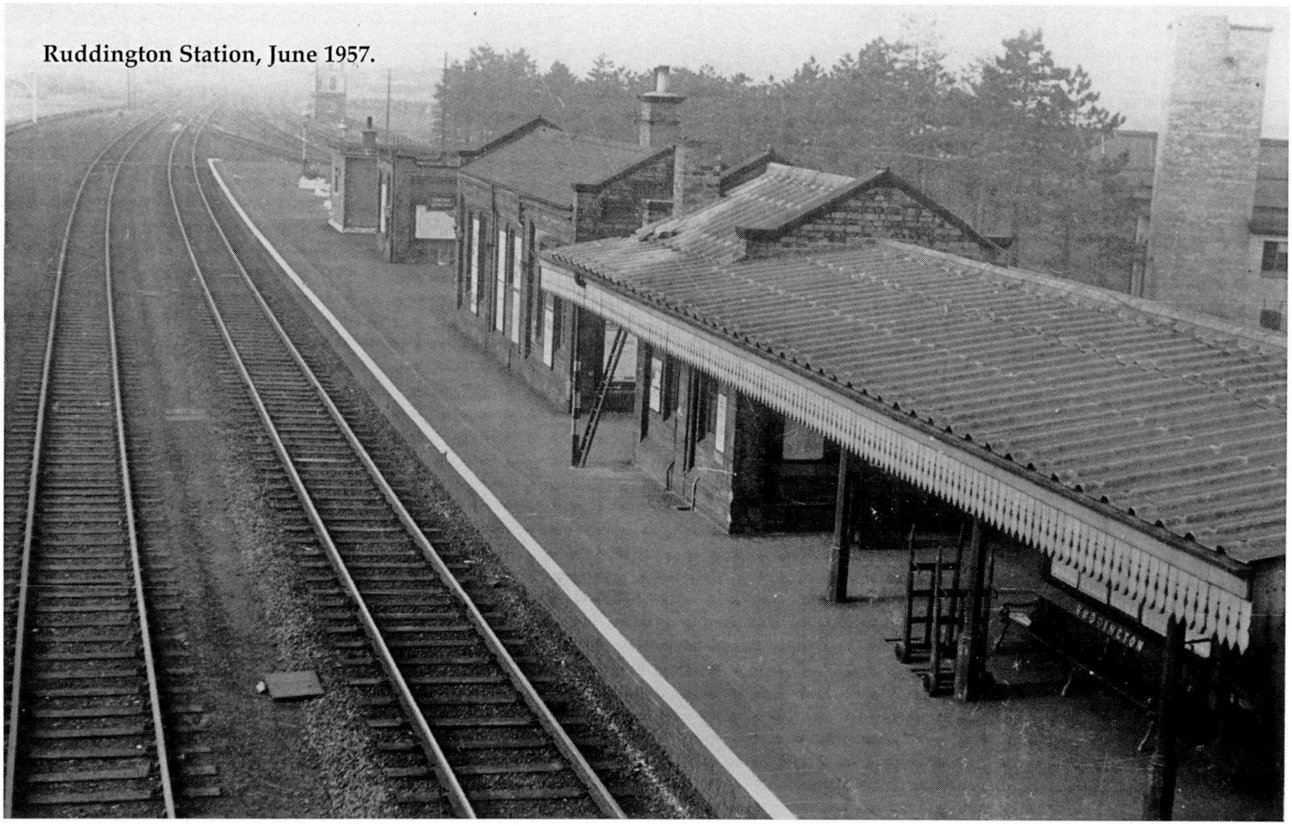

Ruddington Station, June 1957.

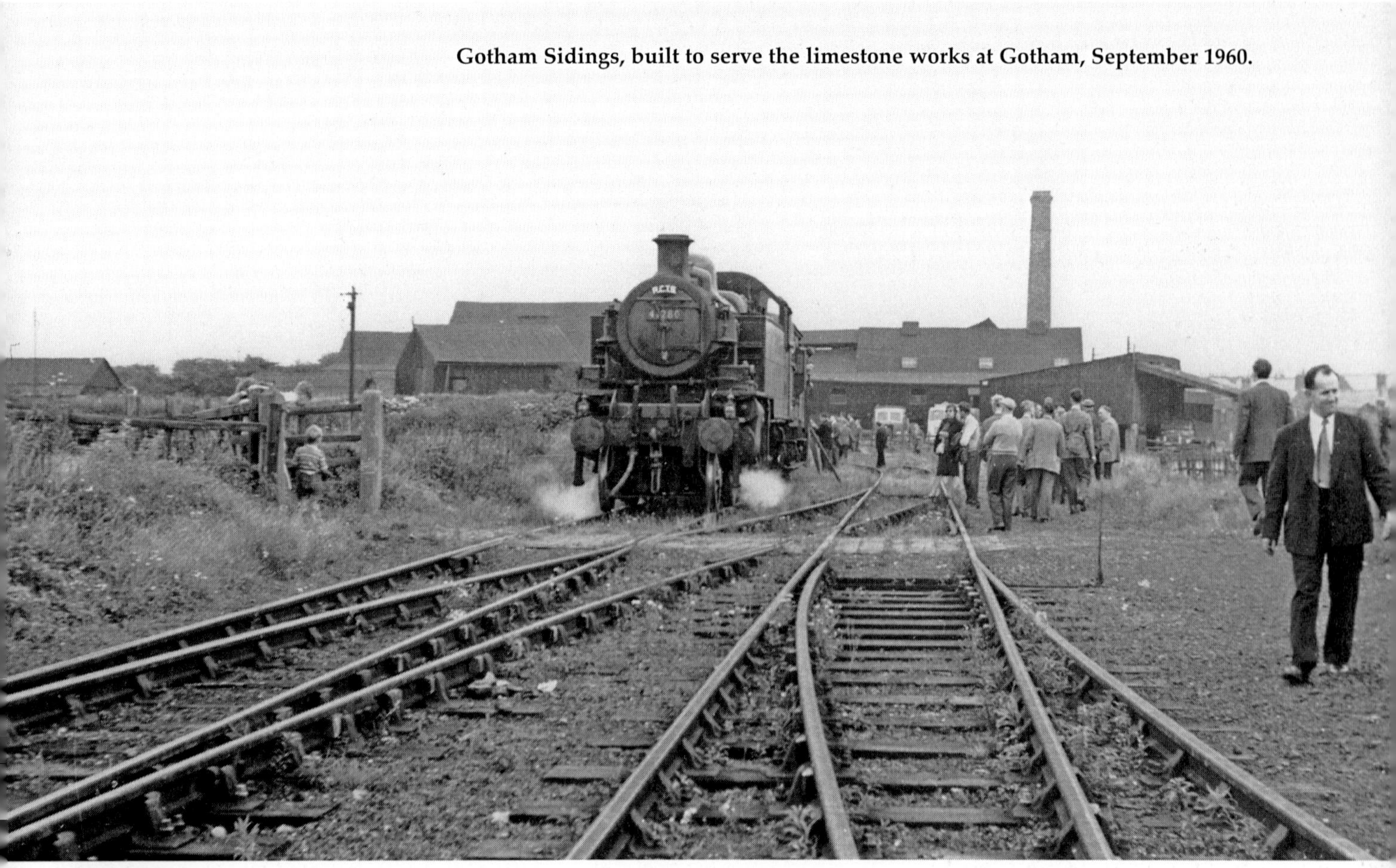

Gotham Sidings, built to serve the limestone works at Gotham, September 1960.

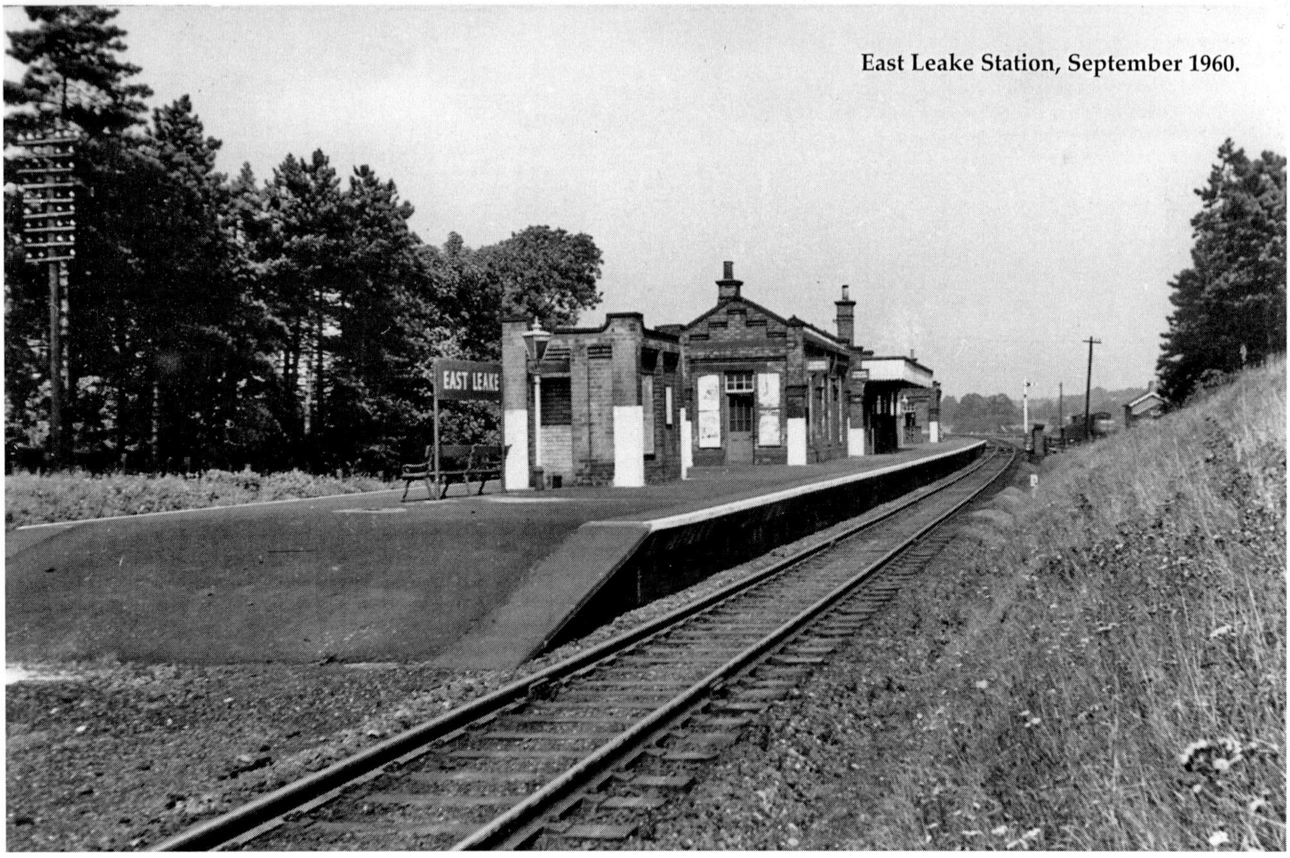


East Leake Station, September 1960.

# Kimberley – Pinxton

| | |
|---|---|
| *Passenger services withdrawn* | 7 January 1963 |
| *Length* | $8^1/_2$ miles |
| *Original owning company* | Great Northern Railway |

| *Stations closed* | *Date of closure* |
|---|---|
| Newthorpe | 7 January 1963 |
| Eastwood & Langley Mill | 7 January 1963 |
| Codnor Park * | 7 January 1963 |
| Pye Hill & Somercotes | 7 January 1963 |
| Pinxton | 7 January 1963 |

* Originally named Codnor Park & Selston until 22 May 1901, then named Codnor Park for Ironville & Jacksdal until 1 July 1950.

Although the town of Pinxton is in Derbyshire, this Great Northern branch off the 'back line' from Kimberley was in Nottinghamshire – including the terminus at Pinxton itself – more or less following the county boundary throughout its length. Coal was the principal reason for building it, but the passenger traffic kept going until the end, goods facilities also being withdrawn on the day the passenger service ceased. The route was duplicated along its whole length by the Midland Railway's Erewash Valley line, though the Great Northern line was credited with having stations which were generally thought to be better placed for the communities they served.

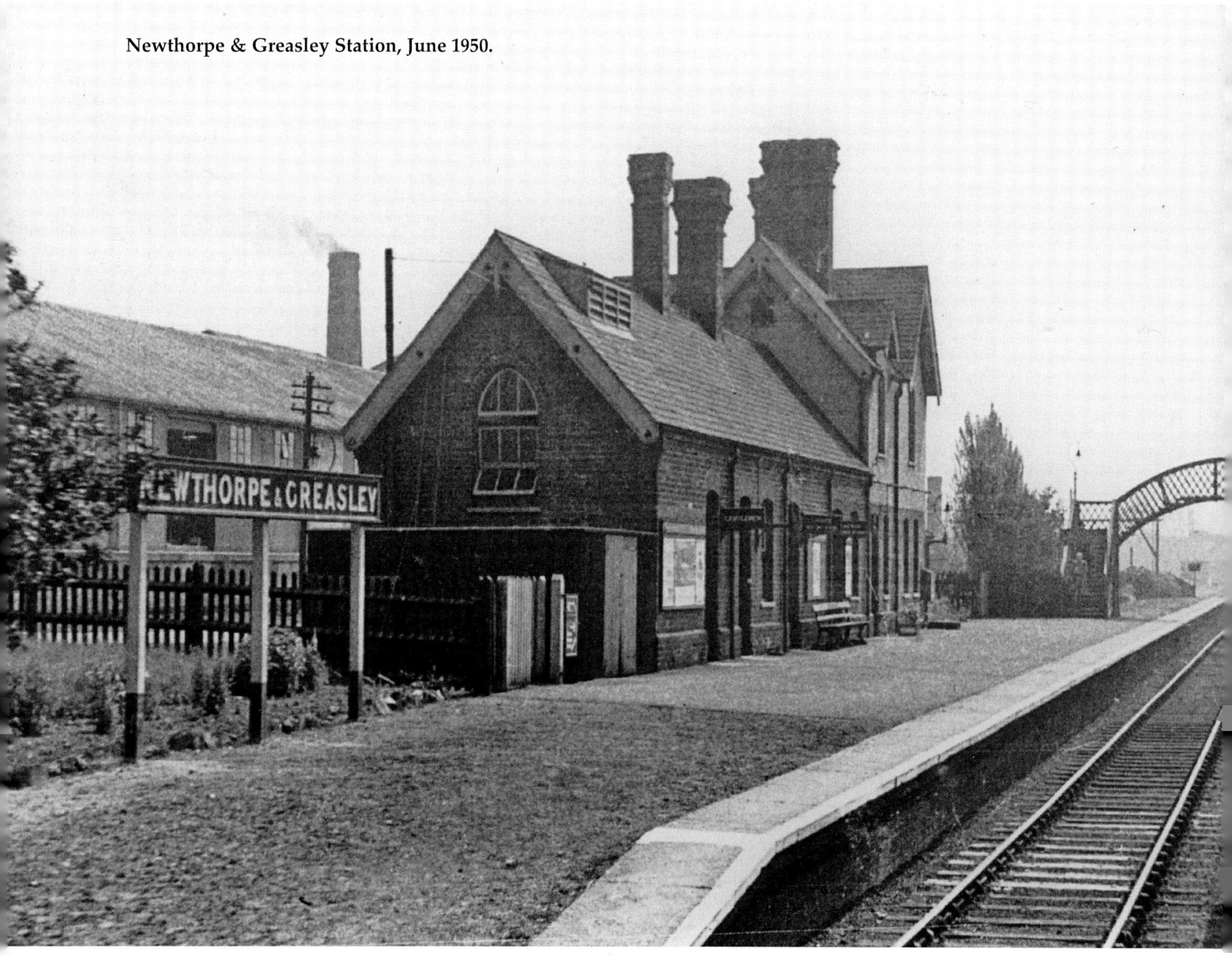


**Newthorpe & Greasley Station, June 1950.**

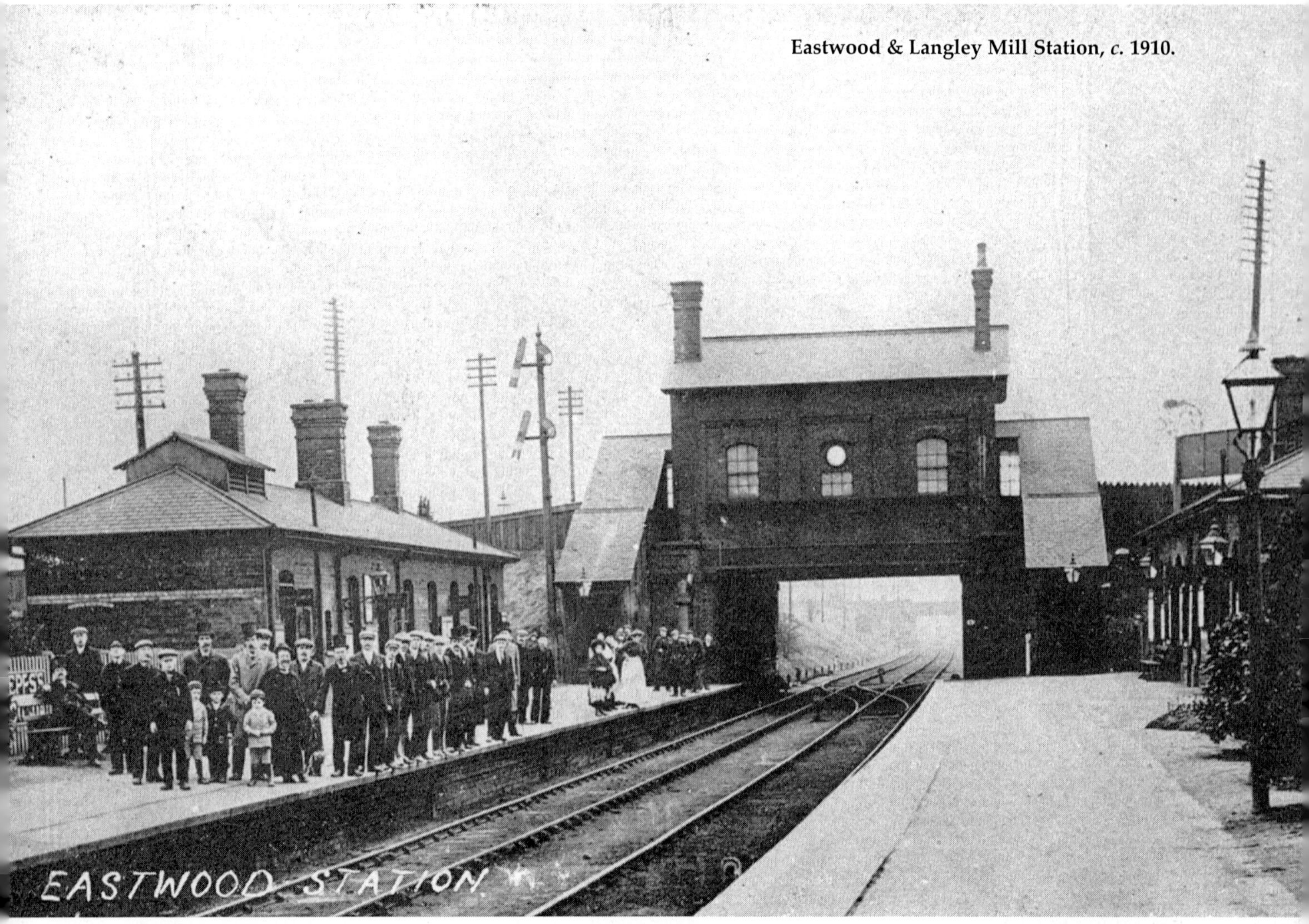


Eastwood & Langley Mill Station, *c.* 1910.

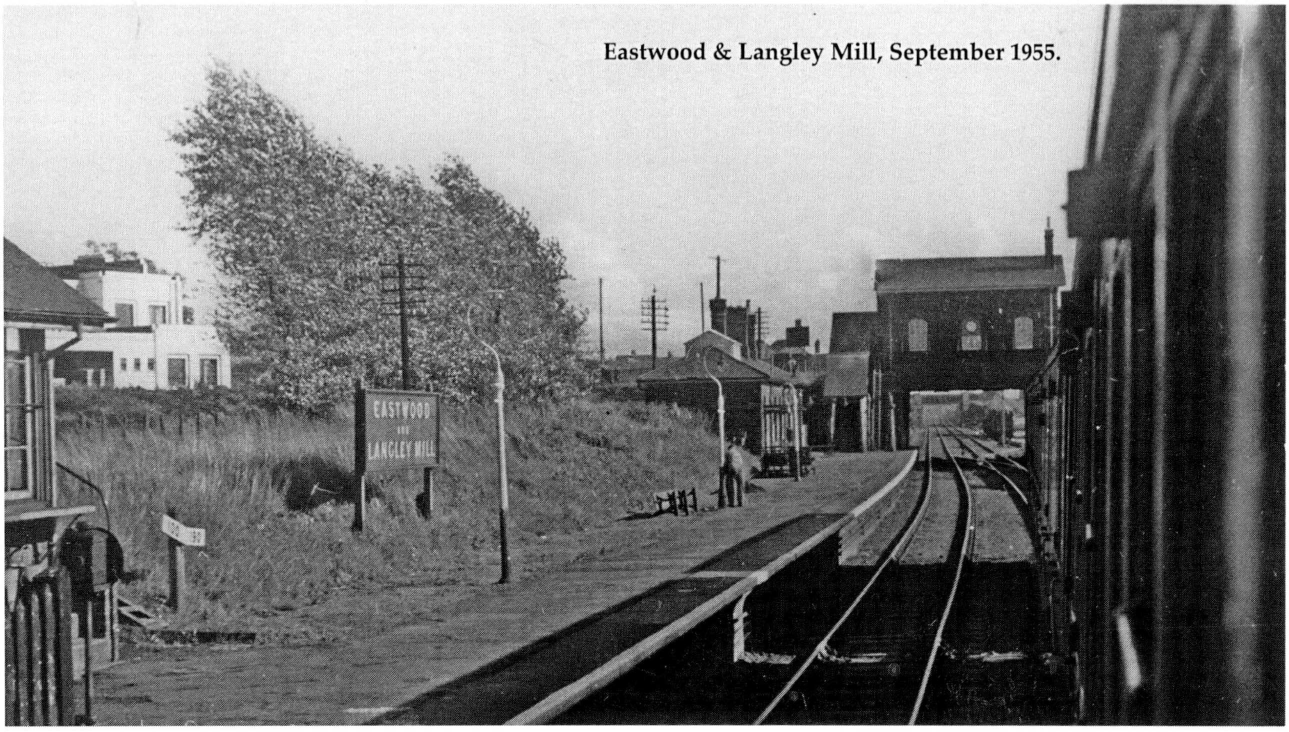


Eastwood & Langley Mill, September 1955.

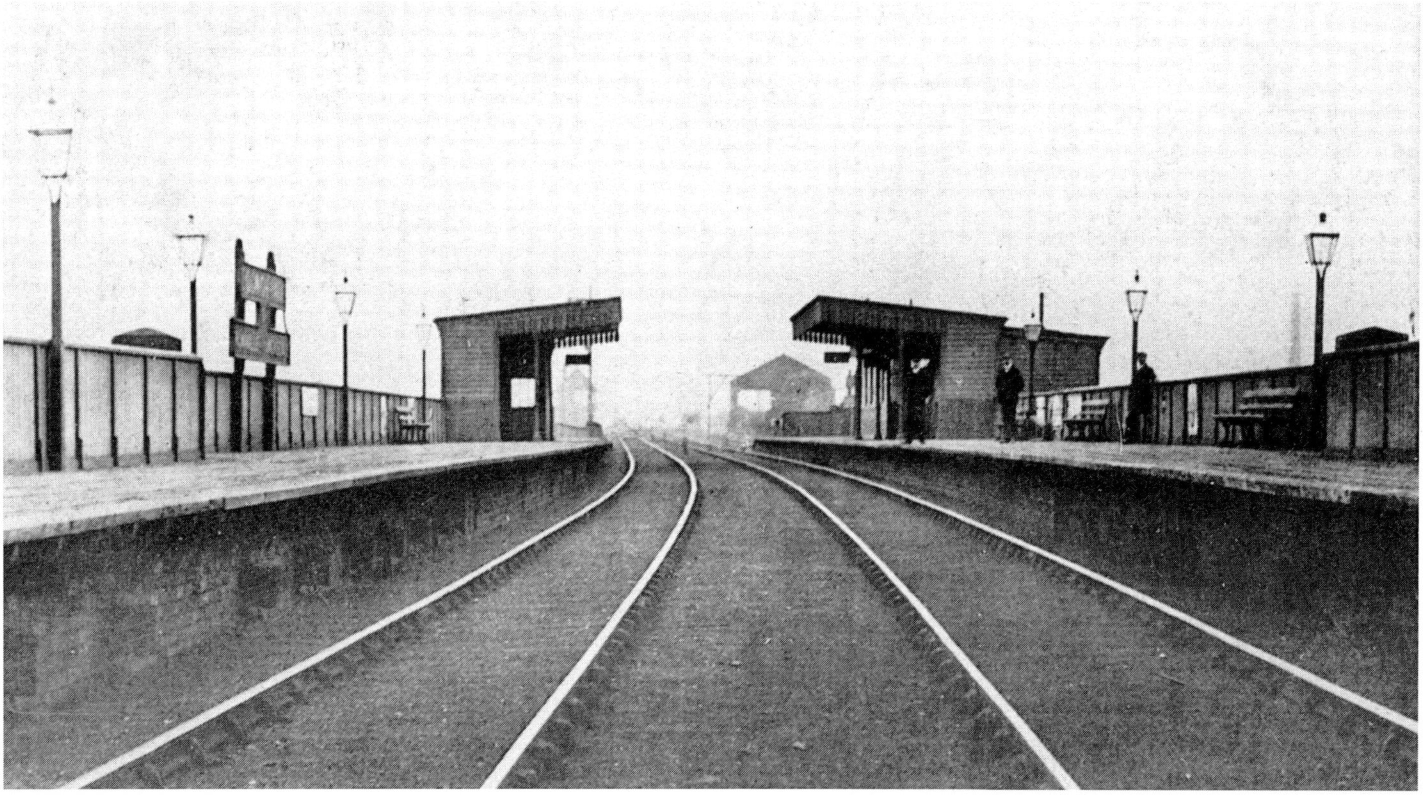

Codnor Park Station was a modest affair at platform level but that hid the considerable engineering work below; both line and station were on top of a substantial viaduct. These pictures are *c.* 1905.

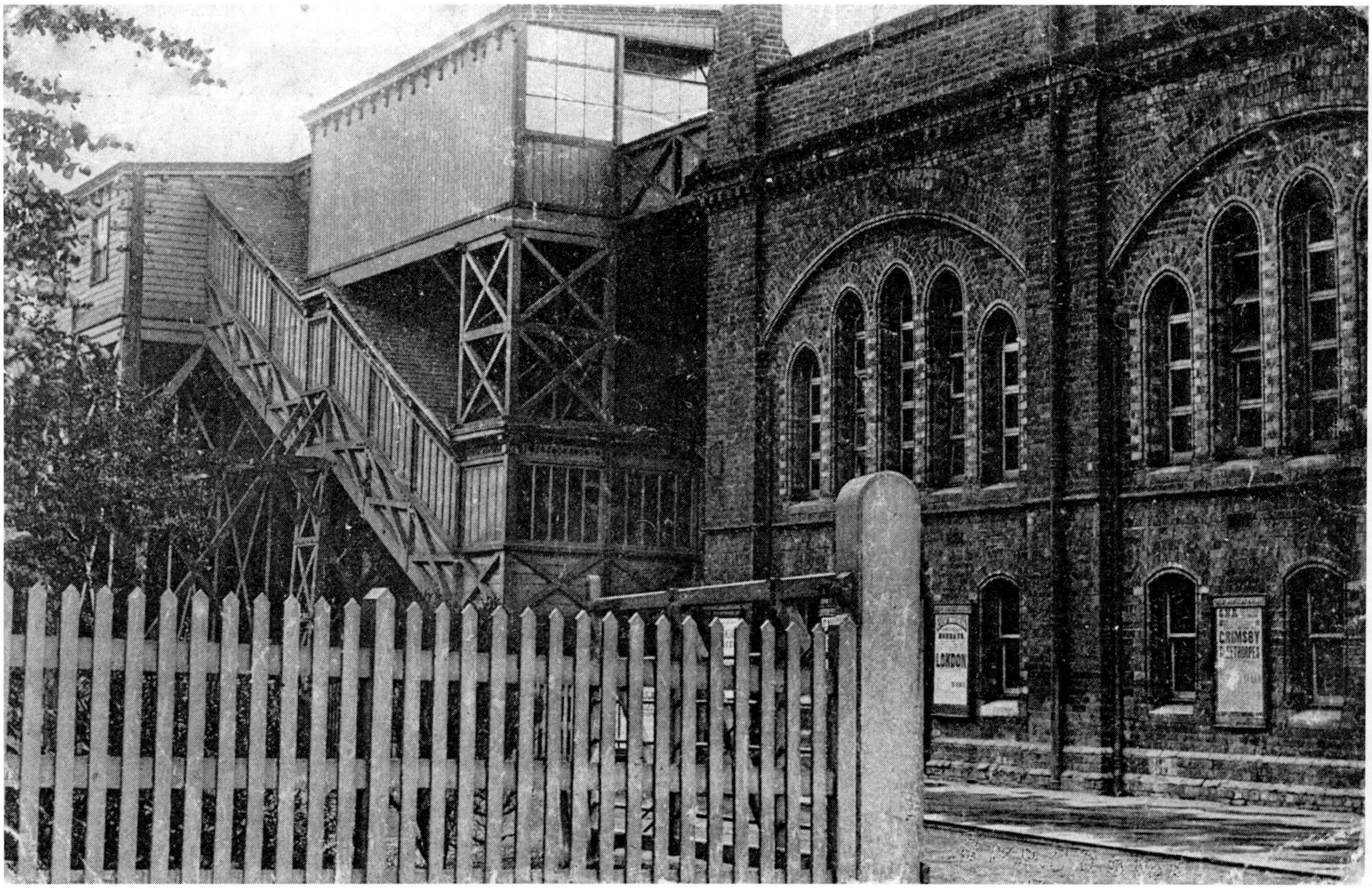

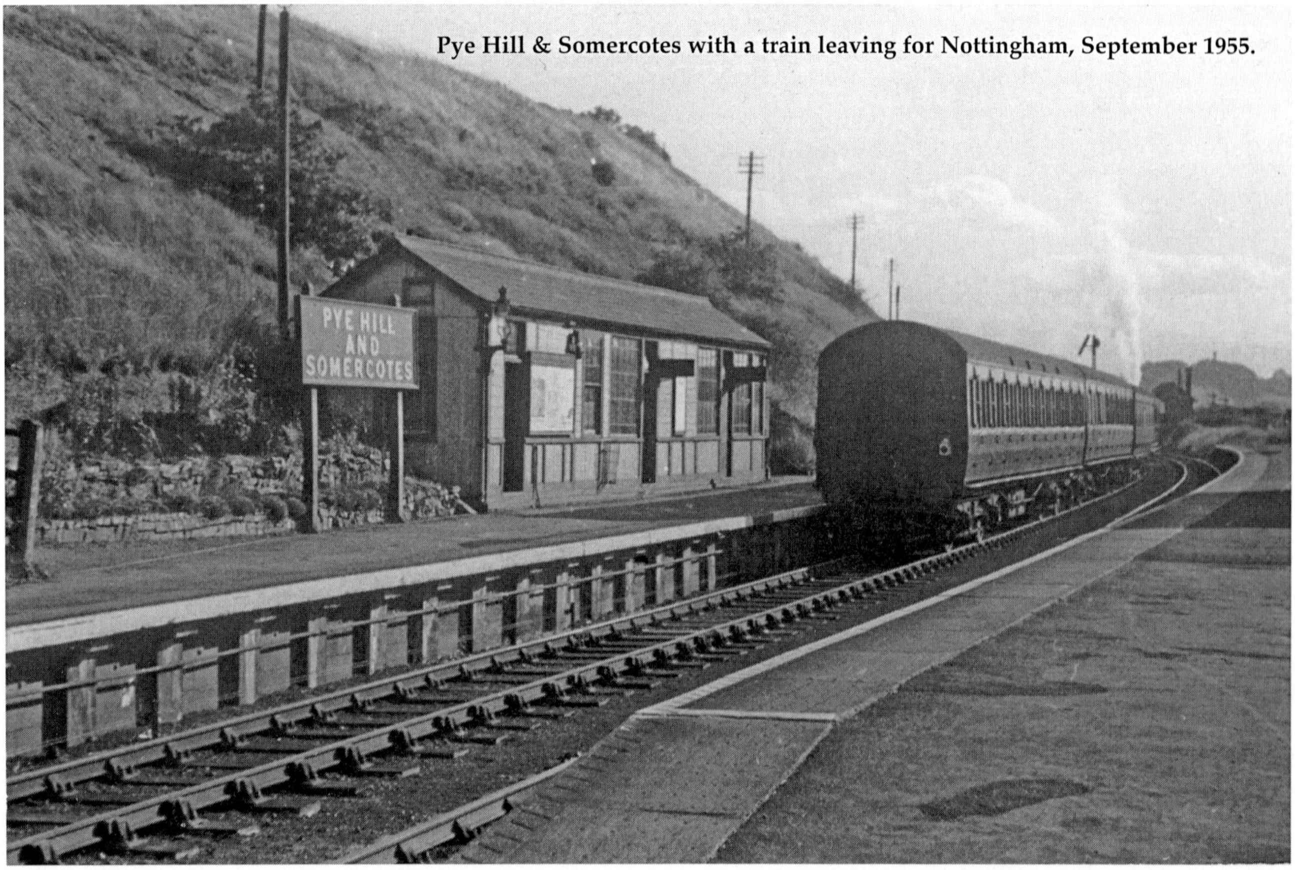

Pye Hill & Somercotes with a train leaving for Nottingham, September 1955.

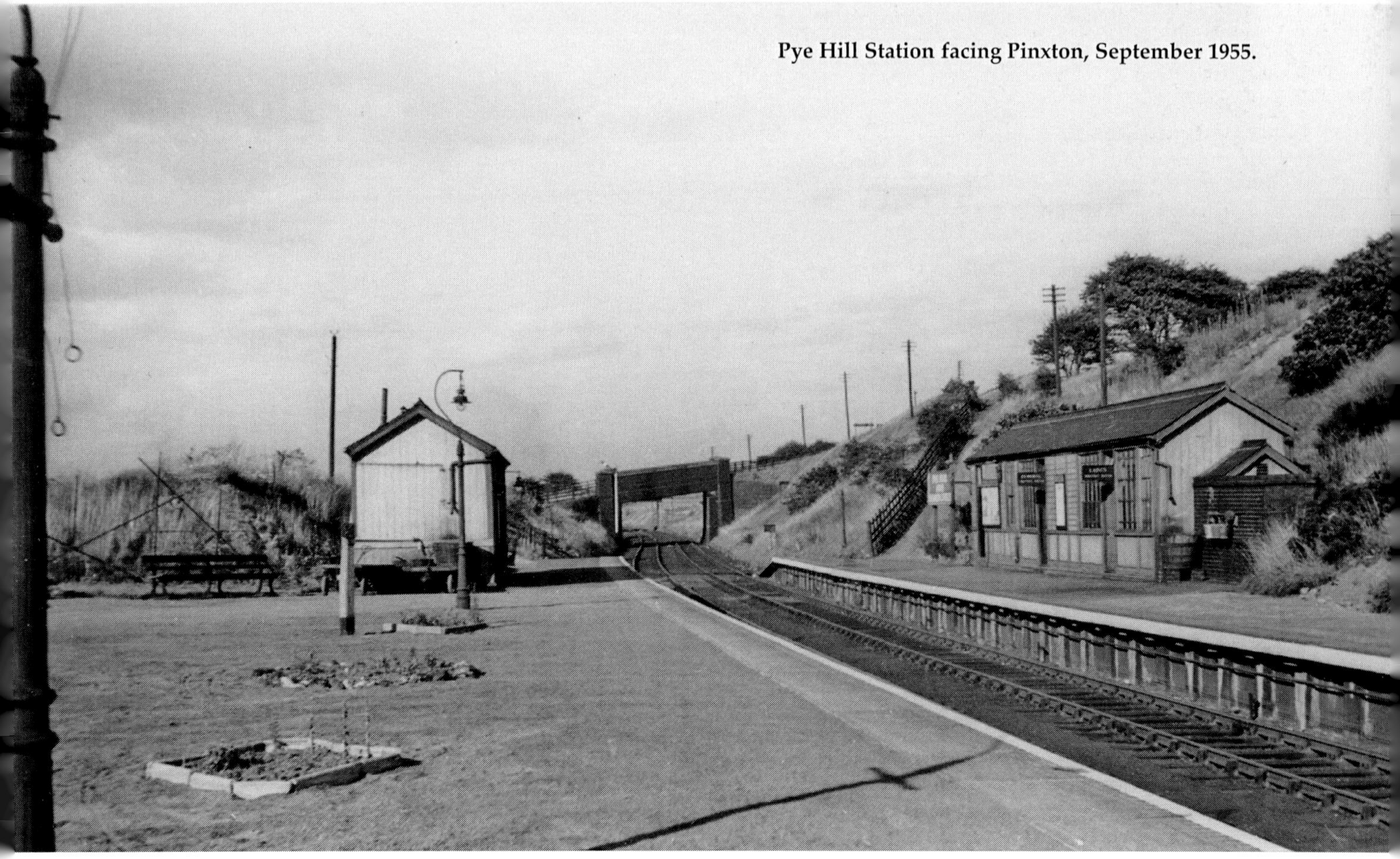
Pye Hill Station facing Pinxton, September 1955.

Pinxton Station with the 5.10 p.m. to Nottingham waiting to depart, September 1955.

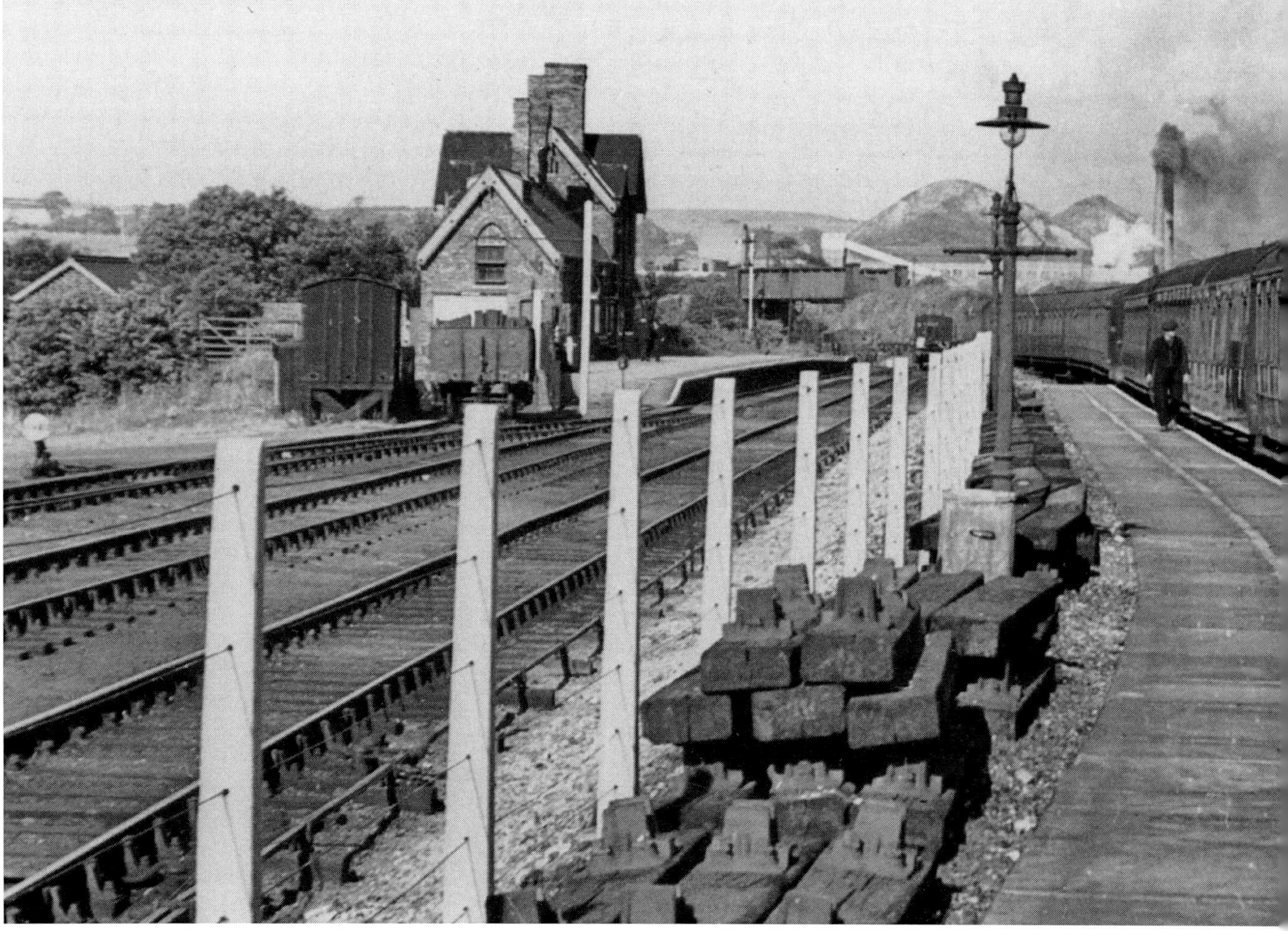

Pixton Station facing the dead end, June 1950.

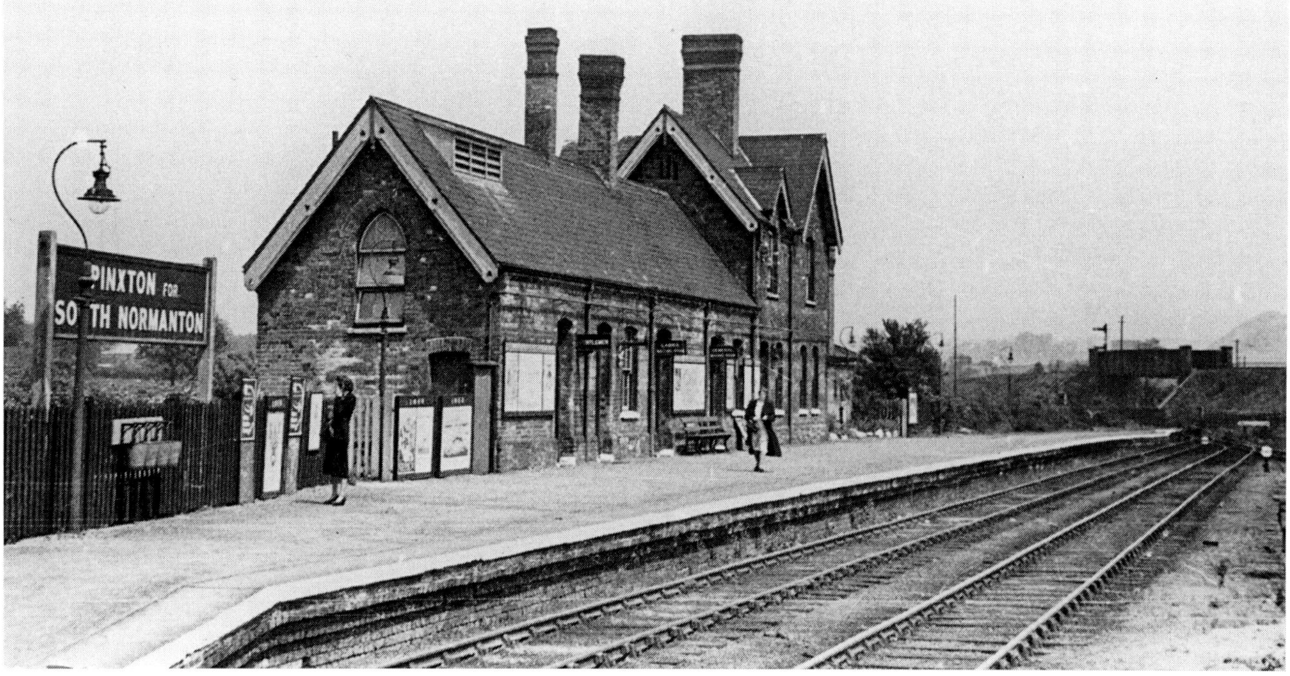

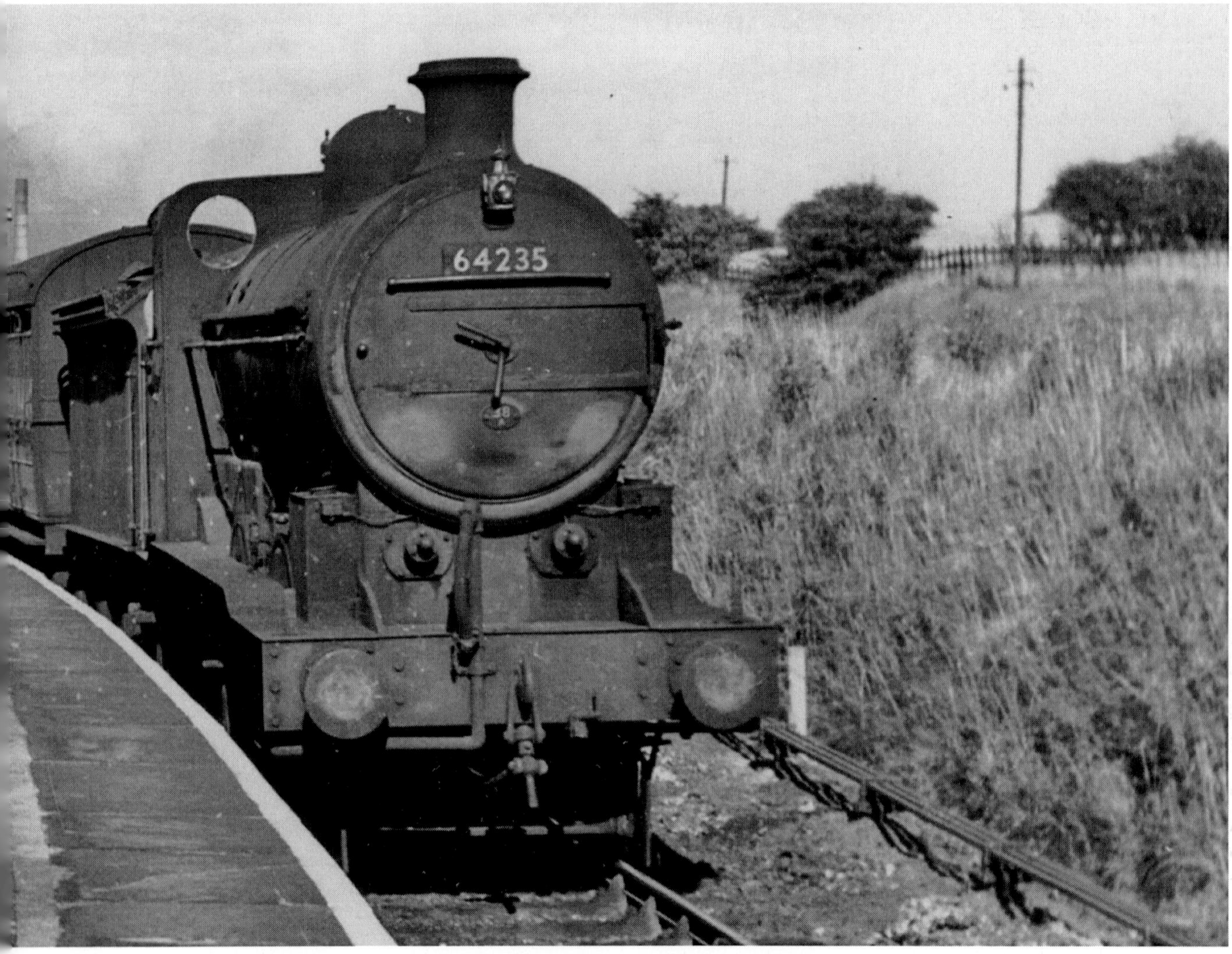


# Kirkby-in-Ashfield – Mansfield – Clipstone

| | |
|---|---|
| *Passenger services withdrawn* | 2 January 1956 |
| *Length* | 10 miles |
| *Original owning company* | Mansfield Railway (operated by the Great Central Railway) |

| *Stations closed* | *Date of closure* |
|---|---|
| Kirkby-in-Ashfield Central * | 2 January 1956 |
| Sutton-in-Ashfield Central ** | 2 January 1956 |
| Mansfield Central *** | 2 January 1956 |

* Originally named Kirkby-in-Ashfield until 1 July 1923.
** Originally named Sutton-in-Ashfield until 1 July 1923.
*** Originally named Mansfield until 1 July 1923.

Although the Nottinghamshire and Derbyshire coalfield was of considerable significance throughout the twentieth century, parts of it were relatively late on the scene. In the early years of last century efforts were made to develop deep mining around Mansfield, including collieries around the town and at the village of Clipstone, which was virtually built by the colliery company. A prerequisite for successful development was a rail connection and so in 1910 the Mansfield Railway was promoted by local people to connect the Great Central line to Kirkby-in-Ashfield with the Lancashire, Derbyshire & East Coast line between Warsop and Edwinstowe. The Mansfield company was one of the last new lines to be promoted in the country and, with the Great Central at either end, it made sense for that company to operate it from the outset. Goods and mineral traffic began running from Mansfield Colliery in 1913, but the Great War delayed the opening of the whole line until 2 April 1917 – just about the same time as other Nottinghamshire lines in this book were losing their passenger services.

The Great Central was energetic in promoting the line and ran a service between Nottingham Victoria and Ollerton on the LD&ECR line, which the LNER expanded to more than a dozen trains each way by the beginning of the Second World War, including a through express from Leeds to Bournemouth. LD&EC line trains also ran down to Mansfield from Sheffield and Chesterfield. After the war the passenger service was curtailed, and eventually withdrawn altogether on 2 January 1956, though coal traffic continued to be worked out along the LD&EC route into the 1980s and beyond, until the collieries closed around the turn of the century.

# Nottingham – Derby Friargate *

| | |
|---|---|
| *Passenger services withdrawn* | 7 September 1964 |
| *Length* | $18^{1}/_{2}$ miles |
| *Original owning company* | Great Northern Railway |

| *Stations closed* | *Date of closure* |
|---|---|
| Nottingham London Road High Level ** | 3 July 1967 |
| Gedling & Carlton | 4 April 1960 |
| Daybrook *** | 4 April 1960 |
| Basford North **** | 7 September 1964 |
| Kimberley East ***** | 7 September 1964 |
| Awsworth East | 7 September 1964 |

* Closed stations on this line that were in Derbyshire were Ilkeston North, West Hallam, Breadsall and Derby Friargate.
** Closed when Nottingham – Grantham services were diverted into the Midland station.
*** Originally named Bestwood & Arnold until 1 March 1876, then named Daybrook for Arnold & Bestwood until 1 August 1876.
**** Originally named New Basford until 1 August 1876, then named Basford & Bulwell until 21 September 1953.
***** Originally named Kimberley until 13 June 1955.

This line – known locally as the 'back line' – also features in *Derbyshire's Lost Railways*, where the story was told of the Great Northern's ambitions to cross the midlands to Stafford, courtesy of running powers over the North Staffordshire Railway's line between Egginton Junction and Bramshall Junction and thence by the Stafford & Uttoxeter line, the latter an originally independent company worked by the Great Northern from 1867 and acquired in 1881. Coal was the prime traffic along the Nottinghamshire/Derbyshire section, the line cutting through the coalfield north of Nottingham and throwing off branches along the Leen Valley to Newstead, and also to Pinxton, both of which are discussed elsewhere.

The line west of Derby lost its passenger service in 1939, just after the outbreak of war, but the line eastwards to Nottingham survived into the mid-1960s, though the collapse of Mapperley tunnel on 23 January 1925 caused services thereafter to be re-routed into Nottingham over the Great Central line via Basford North. Some traces of the 'back line' can still be found, but much in the north Nottingham area has disappeared for ever under redevelopment works.

**Nottingham London Road High Level Station, facing west, August 1956.**

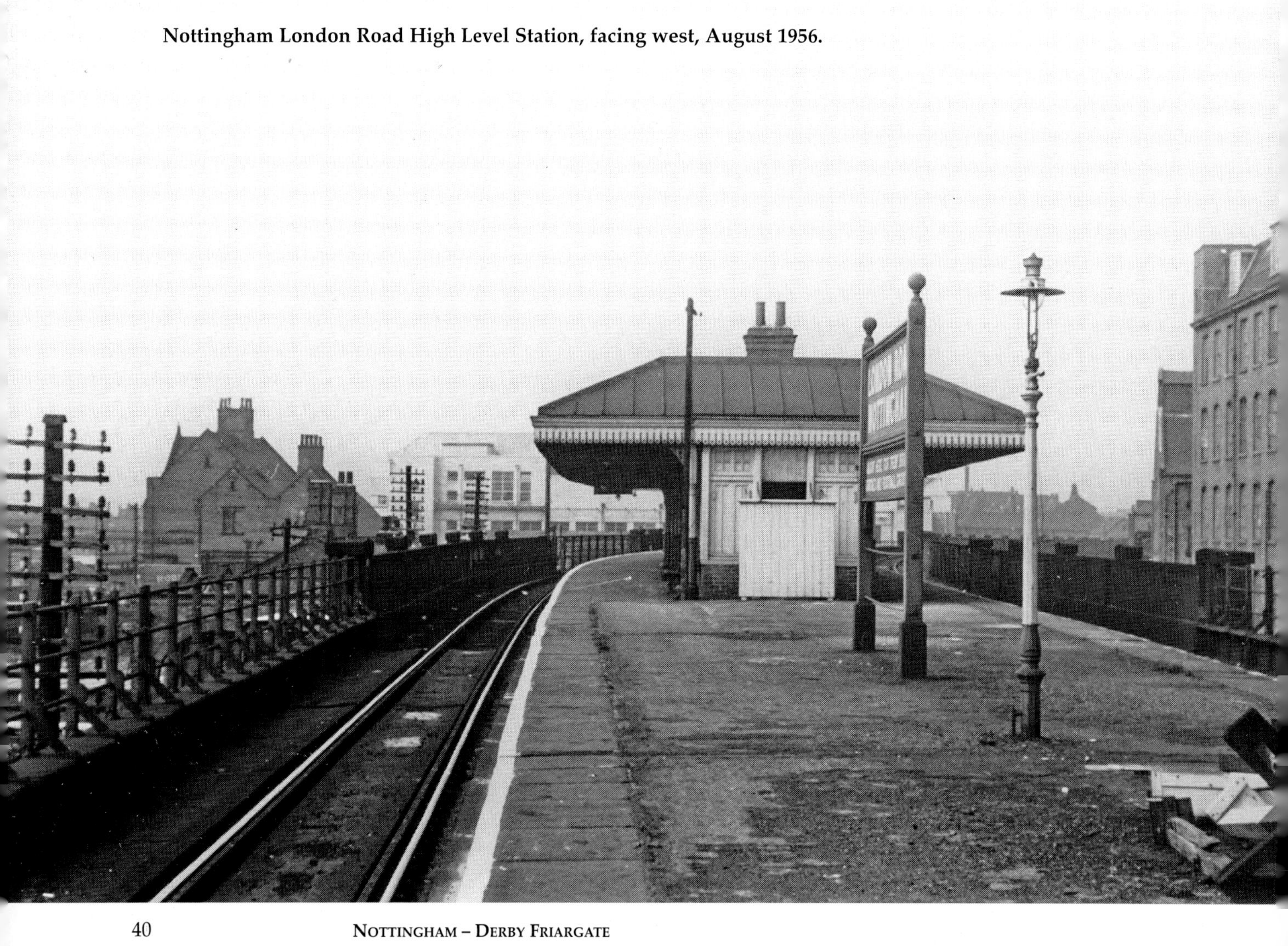

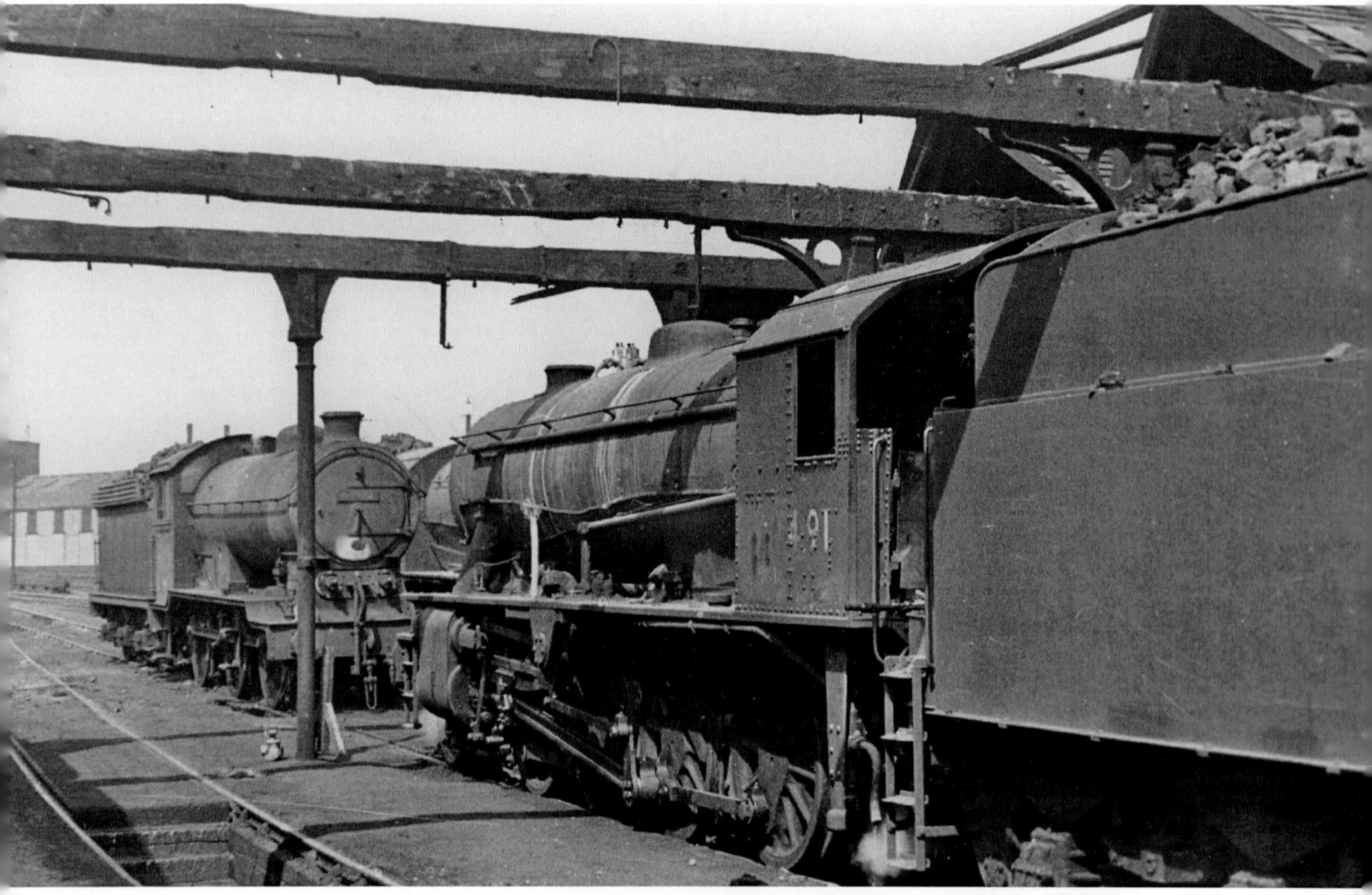

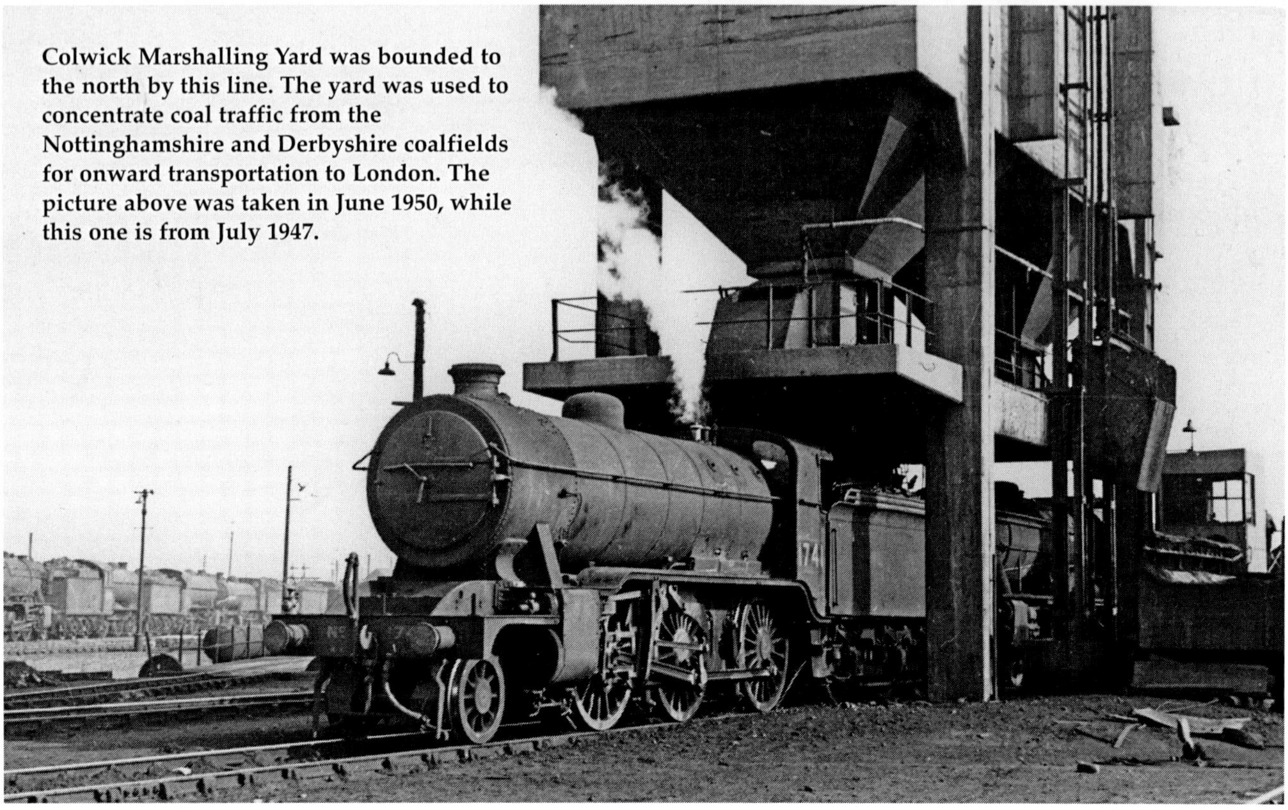

Colwick Marshalling Yard was bounded to the north by this line. The yard was used to concentrate coal traffic from the Nottinghamshire and Derbyshire coalfields for onward transportation to London. The picture above was taken in June 1950, while this one is from July 1947.

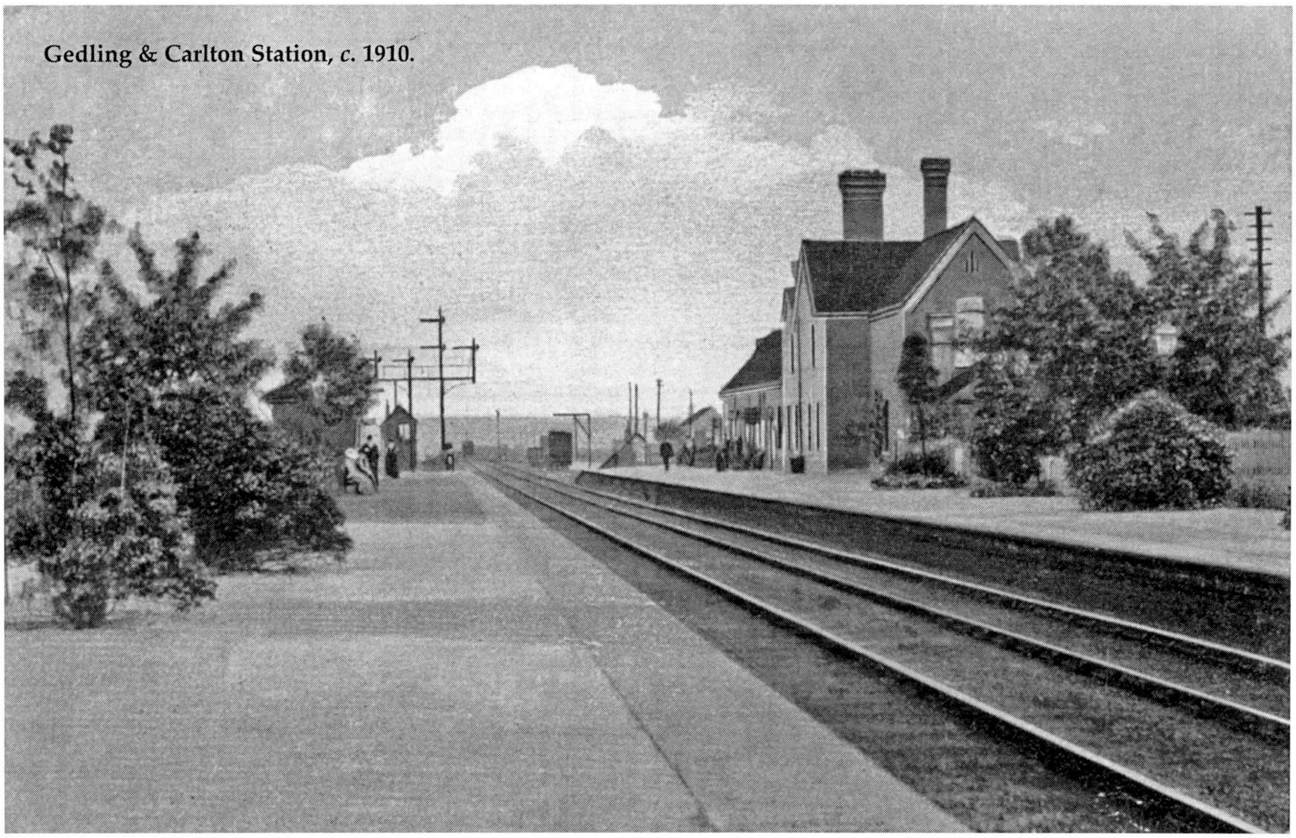

Gedling & Carlton Station, *c.* 1910.

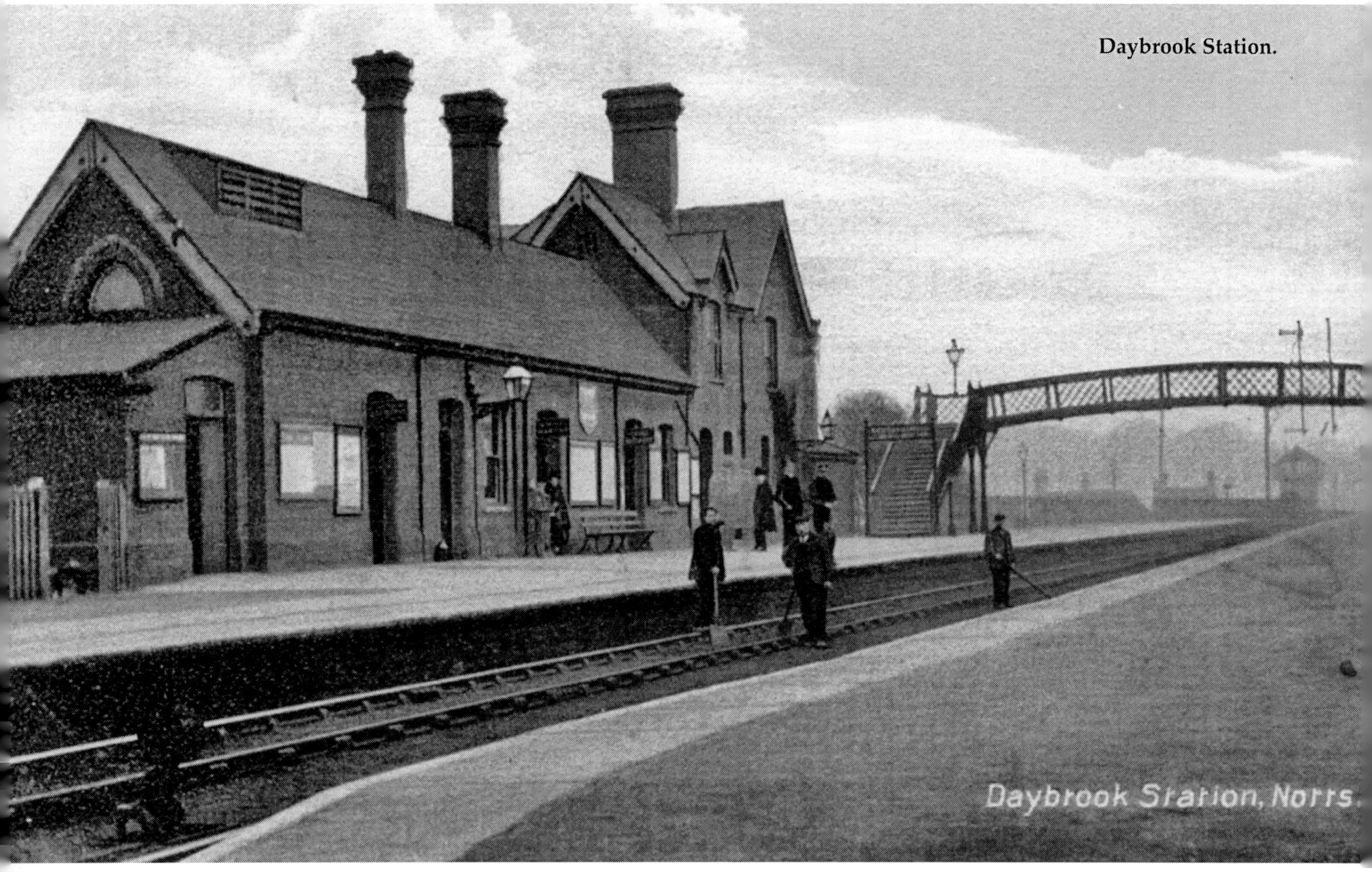


Daybrook Station.

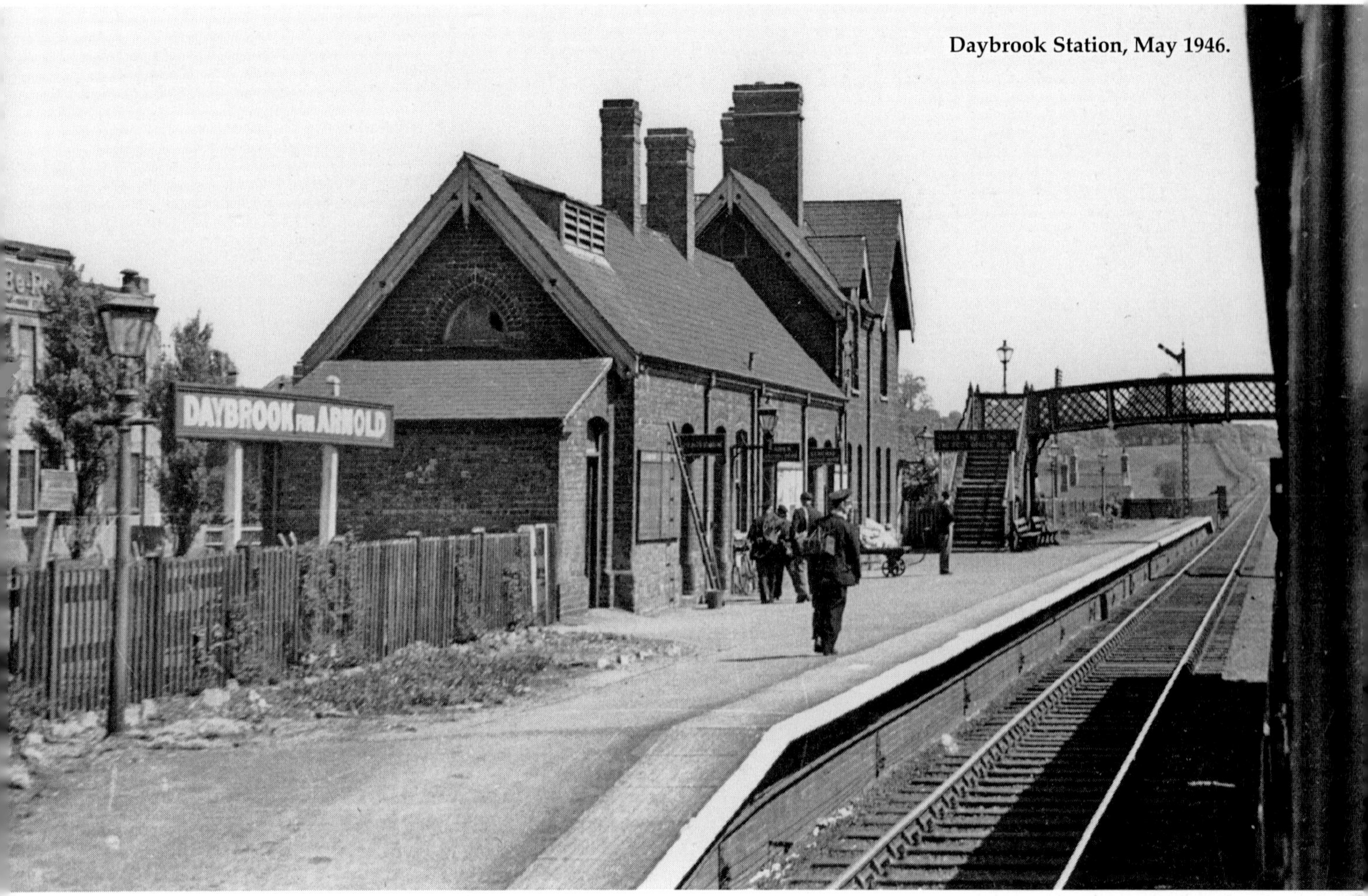


Daybrook Station, May 1946.

GNR No. 1306 at Basford North Station en route to Nottingham Victoria Station.

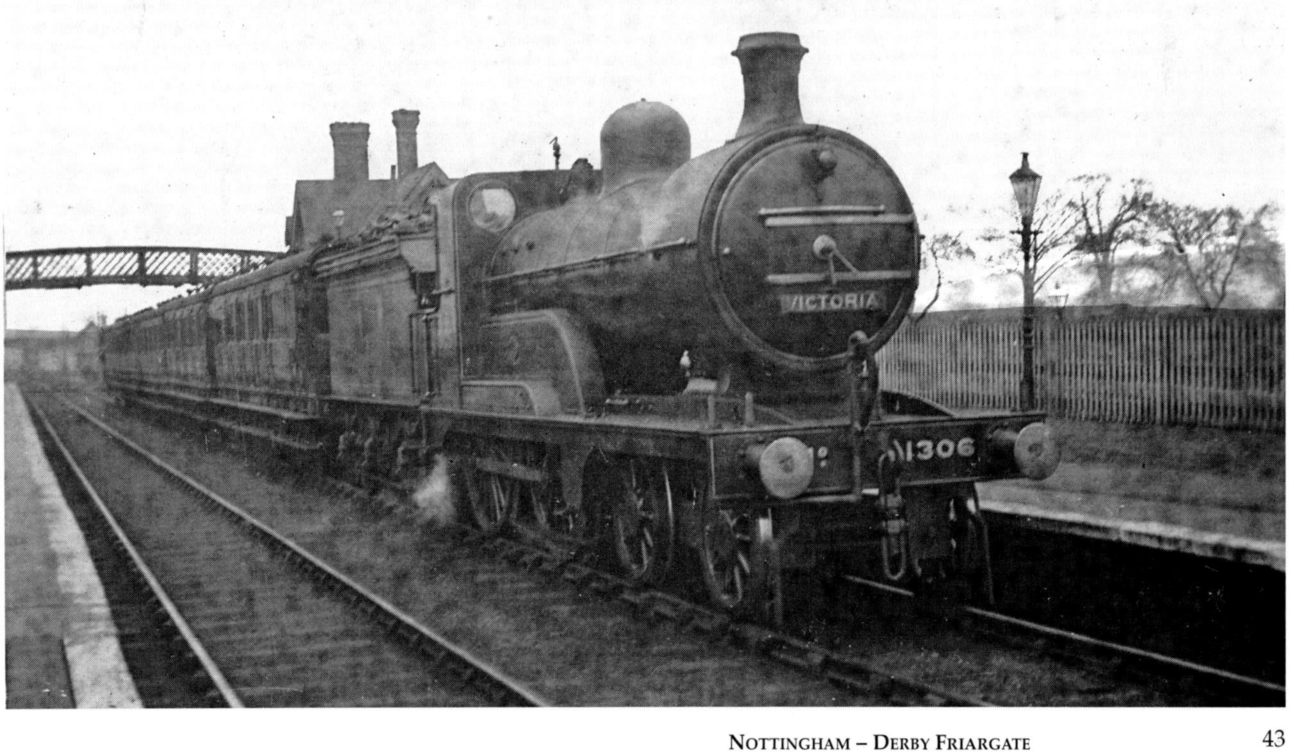

Kimberley Station.

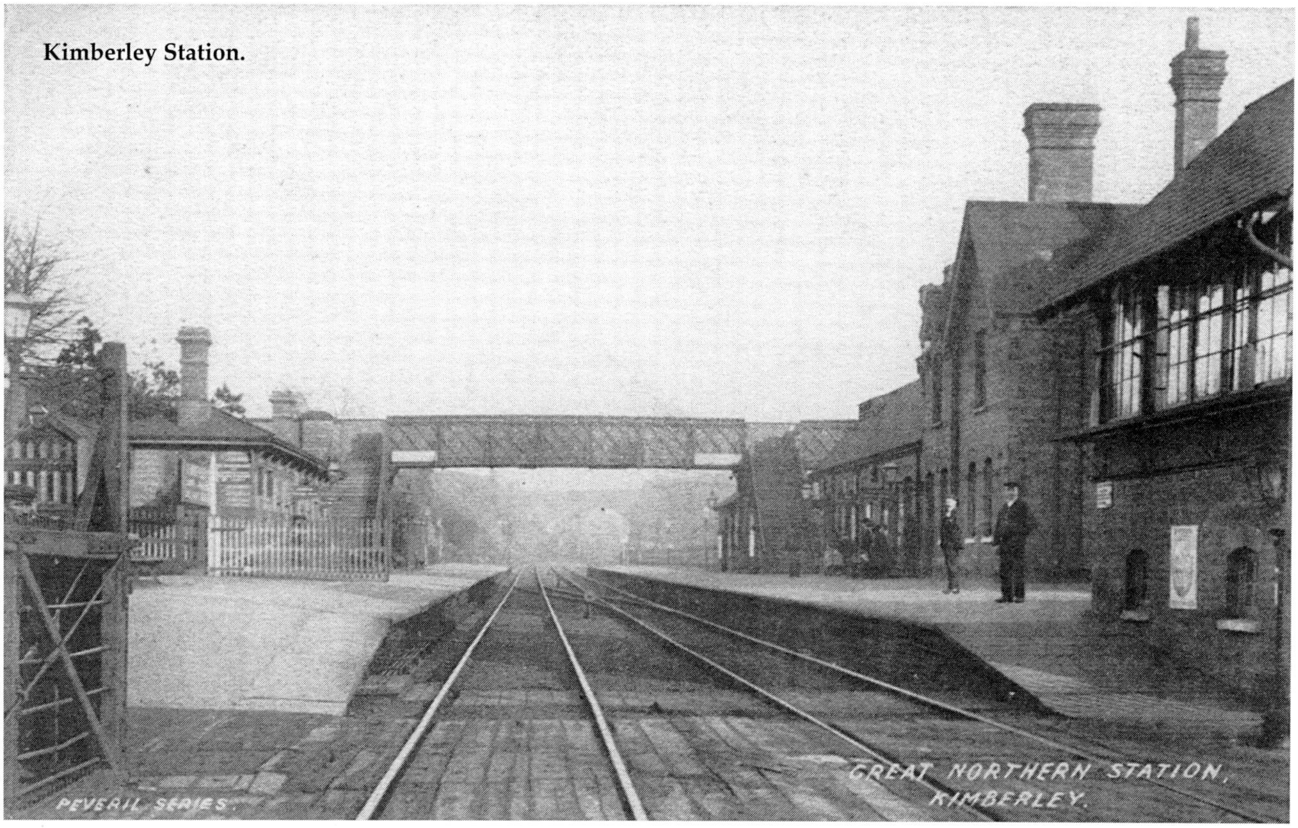


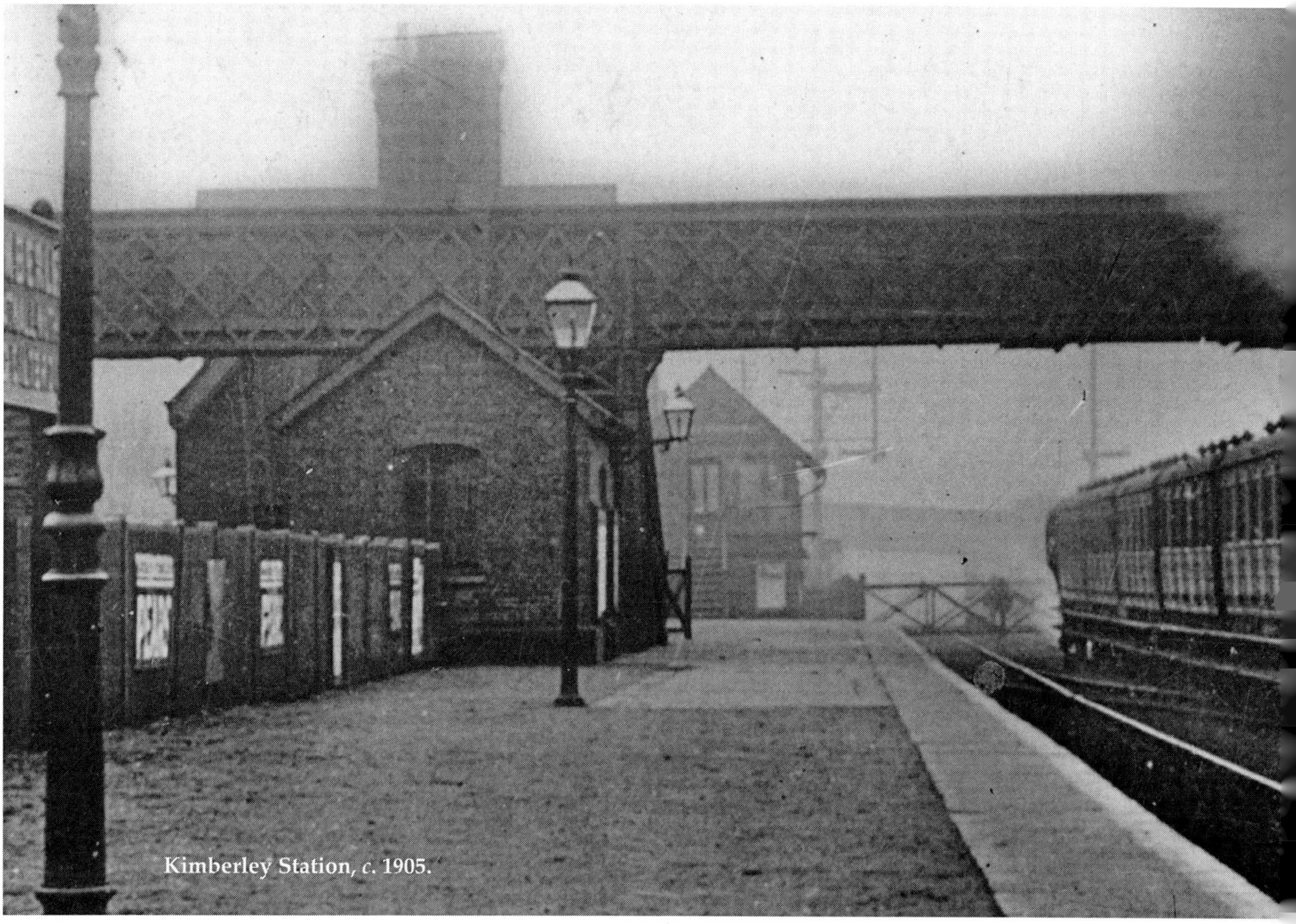

Kimberley Station, *c.* 1905.

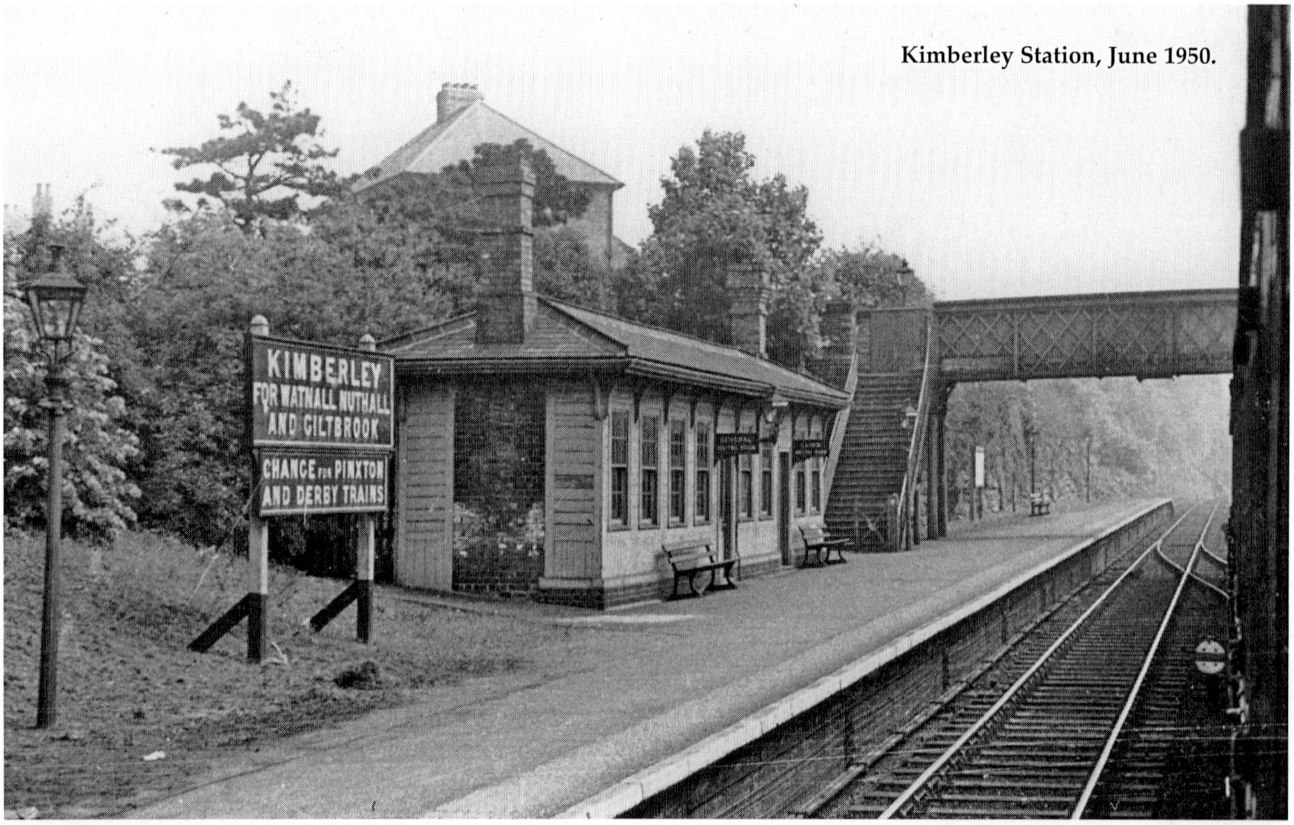

Kimberley Station, June 1950.

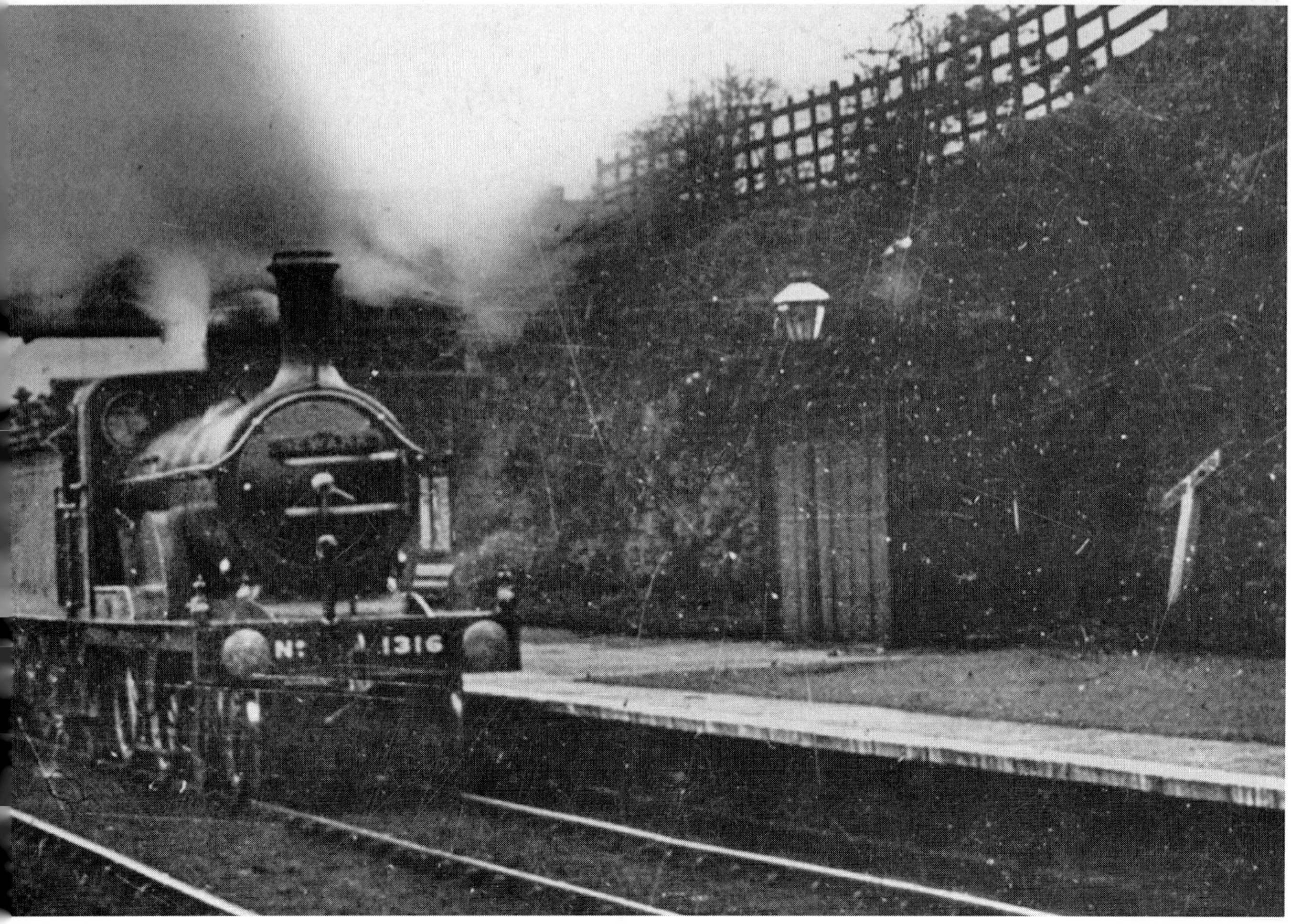

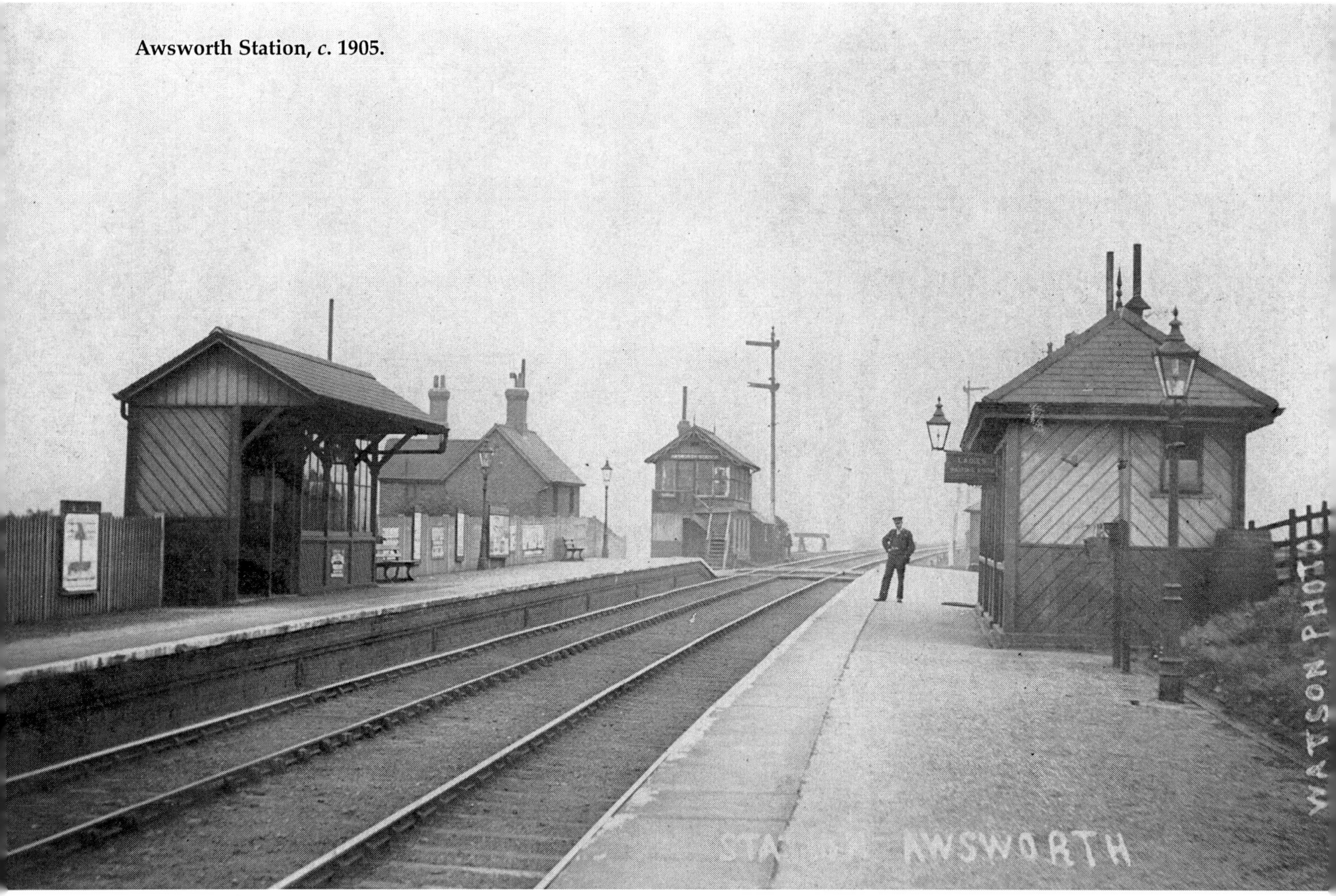

Awsworth Station, *c.* 1905.

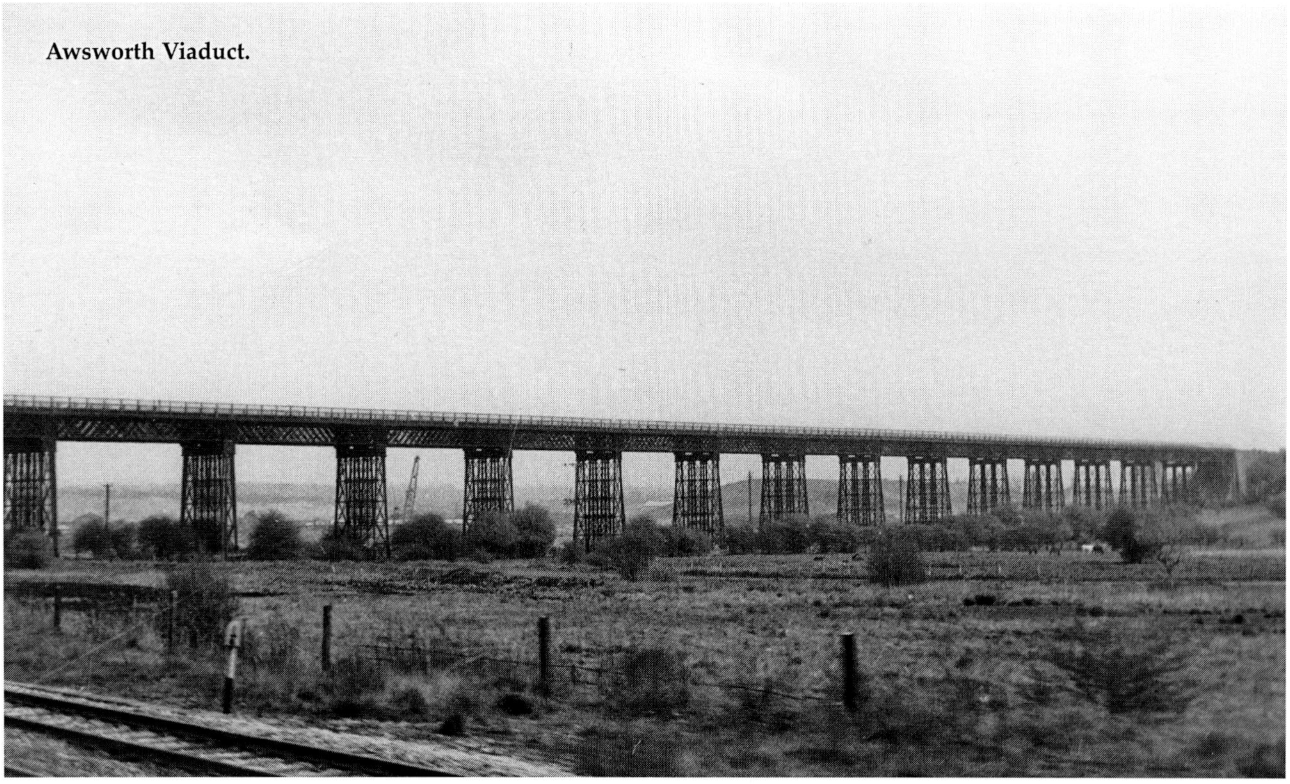
Awsworth Viaduct.

# Nottingham – Melton Mowbray

| | |
|---|---|
| *Passenger services withdrawn* | 29 April 1967 |
| *Length* | $18^1/_4$ miles |
| *Original owning company* | Midland Railway |

| *Stations closed* | *Date of closure* |
|---|---|
| Edwalton | 28 July 1941 |
| Plumtree | 28 February 1949 |
| Widmerpool | 28 February 1949 |
| Upper Broughton | 31 May 1948 |

* Closed stations on this line that were in Leicestershire were Old Dalby and Grimston.

The Midland Railway was one of the earliest companies to operate in the east midlands and from its early days operated lines serving the major towns and cities in the region. Not surprisingly these tended to be constructed between adjacent centres of population, so places like Chesterfield, Derby, Nottingham, Loughborough, Leicester and Market Harborough were on the original north-south axes of its system. In due course, during the 1860s, this route was developed by the company's London extension and today is the route taken by trains from Derby and Nottingham to the capital.

One of the problems faced by railways in the latter part of the nineteenth century was that their facilities and routes were regularly becoming congested as traffic grew beyond the expectations of the original promoters. Between Nottingham and Derby the difficulties centred on Trent, the junction between the Erewash Valley line, down which came vast quantities of coal, and the line from Nottingham to London. The solution was to route the slower-moving traffic along the original line, which was eventually quadrupled as far as Leicester, and to construct a new and faster route into Nottingham from the south-east. Thus it was that the new route came up from Melton Mowbray and entered the city through Edwalton, crossing the Trent by a three-span bowstring bridge at Lady Bay. South of Melton trains for London travelled through Oakham, Manton, over the great viaduct spanning the valley of the Welland at Harringworth, eventually joining the original London line at Glendon South Junction.

The new route was certainly a great advantage, but it was mainly useful for through traffic, since the country it crossed was predominantly rural with no large centres of population. The intermediate stations between Melton and Nottingham succumbed during the 1940s, apart from Old Dalby, which continued to be served by stopping passenger services until 1966. The line, designated by the Beeching Report of 1963 as a duplicate route for the original line to London, was closed between Nottingham and Melton in 1967, though trains still continue to use the route south of Melton. The Nottinghamshire part of the line has been lifted and Lady Bay bridge converted to carry a road, but the section in Leicestershire still sees periodic rail traffic, since it is the test track for the experimental rail testing centre at Derby. Over the years the ill-fated Advanced Passenger Train [APT] and its successor, the Virgin Pendolino, have been tested there; one of the most spectacular tests was the staged collision of a Sulzer diesel, No. 46009, and a three-coach train with a nuclear flask, on 17 July 1984.

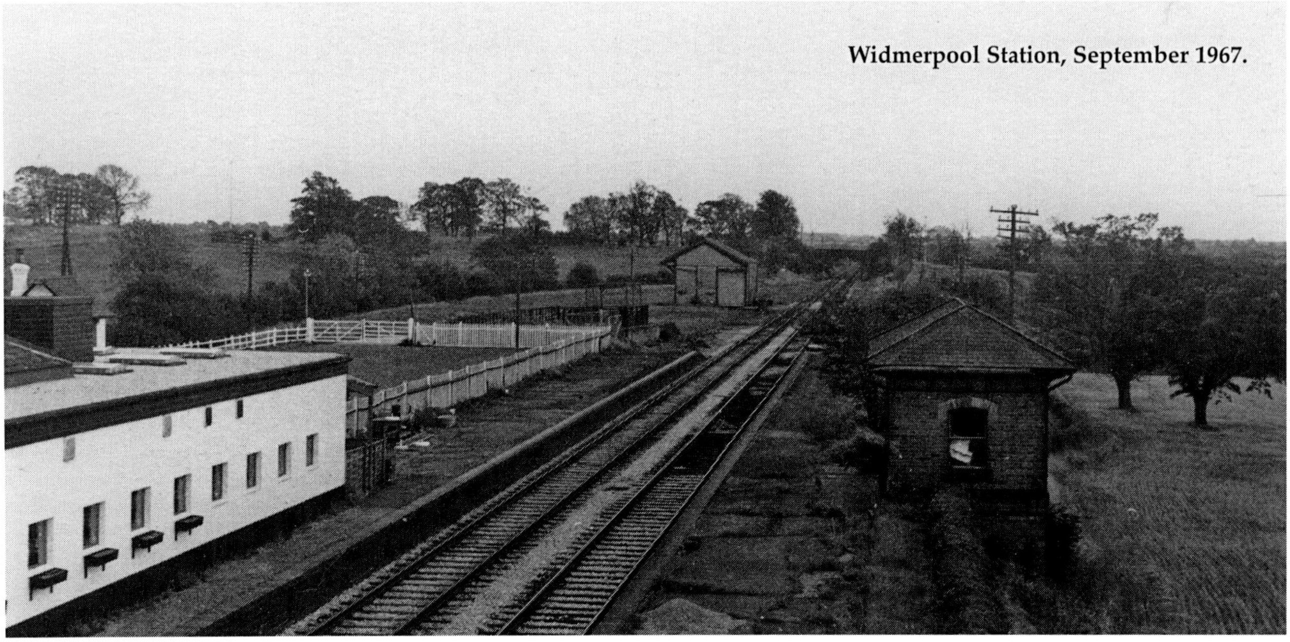

**Widmerpool Station, September 1967.**

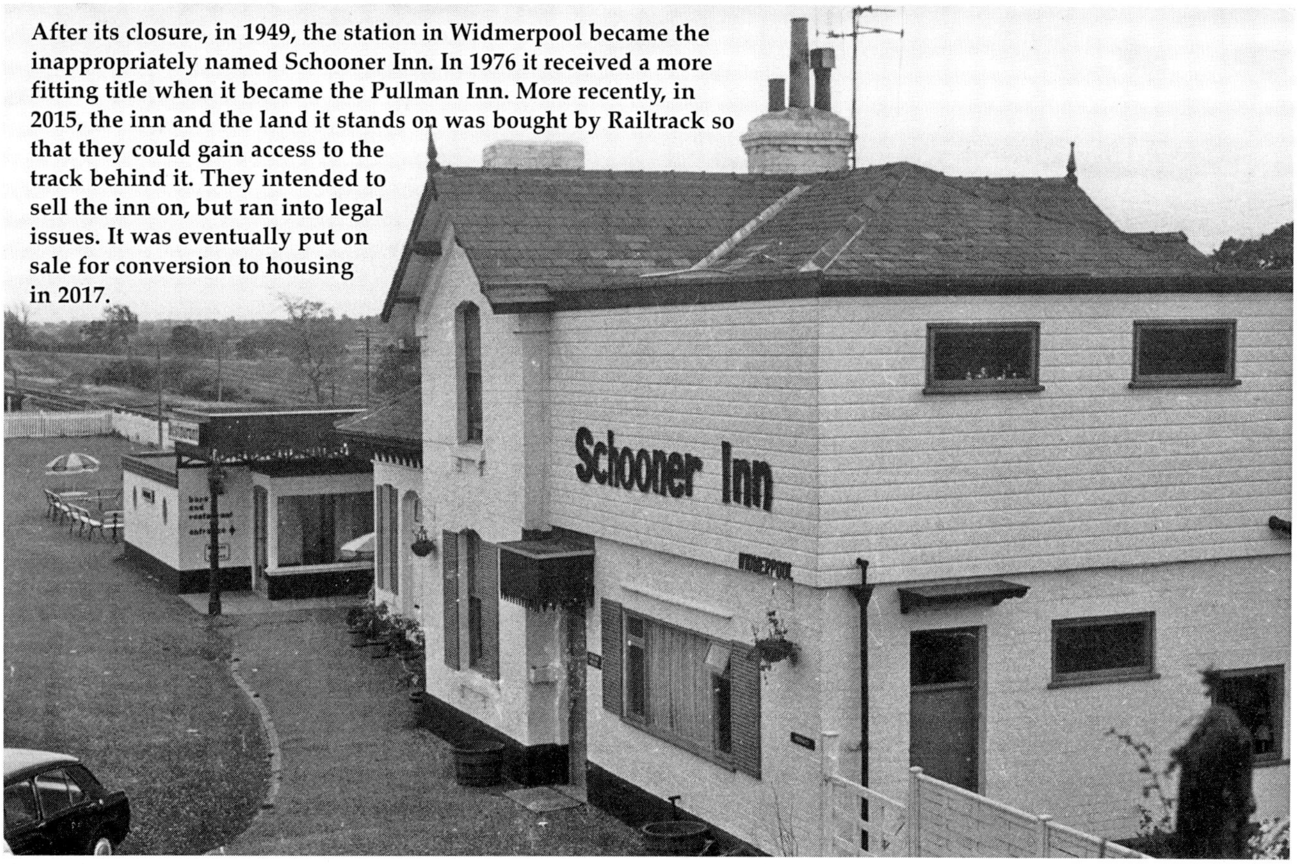


After its closure, in 1949, the station in Widmerpool became the inappropriately named Schooner Inn. In 1976 it received a more fitting title when it became the Pullman Inn. More recently, in 2015, the inn and the land it stands on was bought by Railtrack so that they could gain access to the track behind it. They intended to sell the inn on, but ran into legal issues. It was eventually put on sale for conversion to housing in 2017.

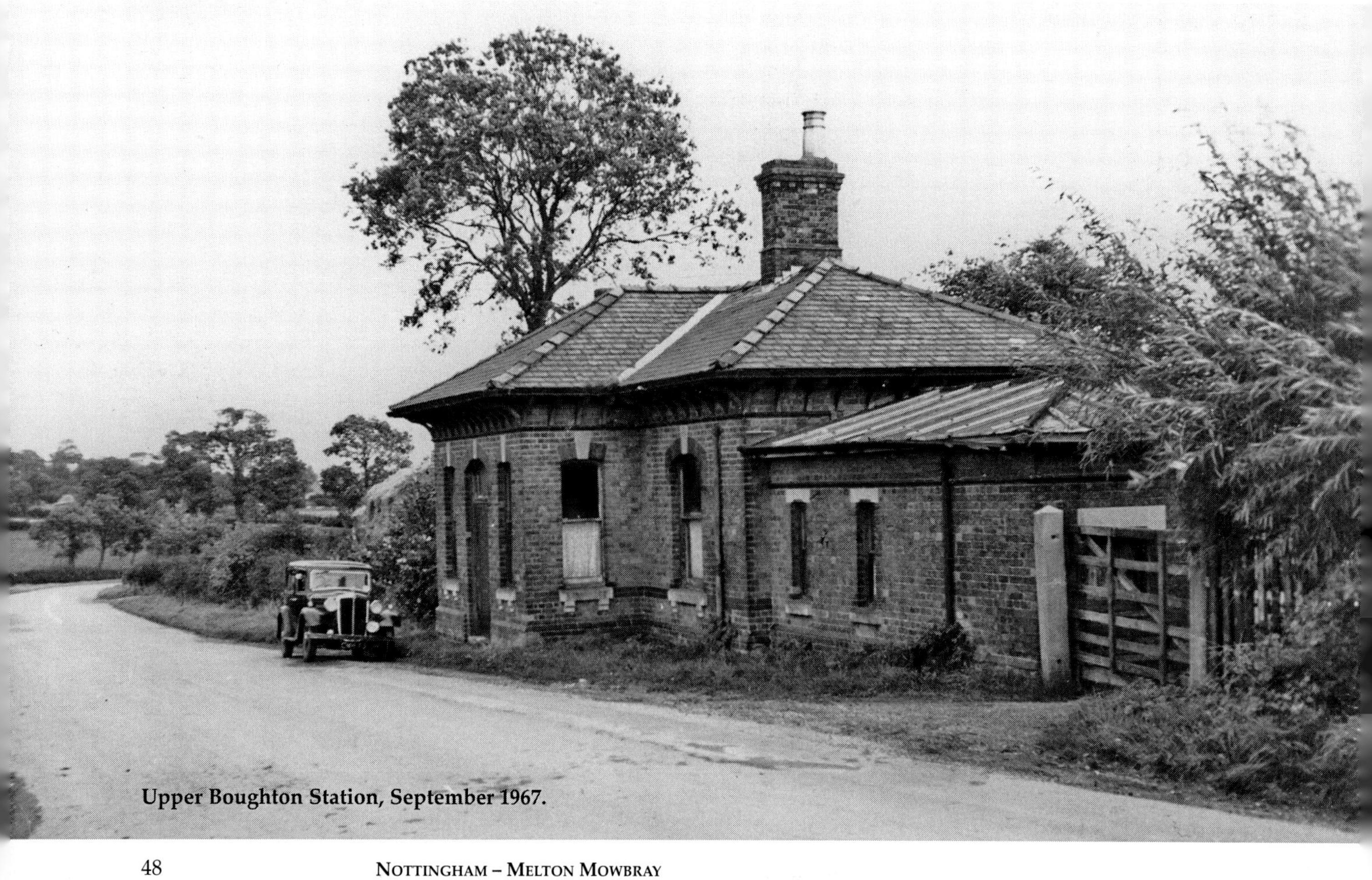

Upper Boughton Station, September 1967.

# Nottingham Victoria – Daybrook: The Nottingham Suburban Railway

| | |
|---|---|
| *Passenger services withdrawn* | 29 April 1967 |
| *Length* | $3^3/_4$ miles |
| *Original owning company* | Nottingham Suburban Railway (worked by the Great Northern from opening) |

| *Stations closed* | *Date of closure* |
|---|---|
| Nottingham Victoria * | 4 September 1967 |
| Nottingham London Road High Level ** | 3 July 1967 |
| Nottingham London Road Low Level *** | 22 May 1944 |
| Thorneywood | 1 July 1916 |
| St Ann's Well | 1 July 1916 |
| Sherwood | 1 July 1916 |

* Originally named Nottingham Joint by the Great Northern until 12 June 1900 (it was known as Nottingham Central by the Great Central). Closed along with the Great Central Railway's London Extension.
** Closed when Nottingham – Grantham services were diverted into the Midland station.
*** Originally named Nottingham London Road until 15 March 1899.

Nottingham's suburban development began during the second half of the nineteenth century as the city pushed out beyond its mediaeval boundaries to absorb many places which had hitherto been separate villages. Like other cities before the development of the electric street tramway the railway was the best method of passenger transport, whether for long or short distances, and accordingly the Nottingham Suburban Railway was promoted by local businessmen during the 1880s. The line ran within the arc of the Great Northern's line from Nottingham to Derby, connecting with it at both ends, so it made sense for the independent company to look to the larger one to operate its line; this was the arrangement from the opening on 2 December 1889.

Nottingham is built on hills and the route involved a total of four tunnels, along with other significant earthworks such as embankments and cuttings, while the stations were generously proportioned, no doubt in the expectation of a large volume of traffic. Although its title suggests a primarily passenger line, the promoters included Robert Mellors, whose brickworks at Mapperley was served by a short spur off the main route. Indeed, this was in the end to become the line's principal source of revenue, since in the early years of the twentieth century the electric tramway spread its routes out into the north-eastern suburbs, offering a level of competition the railway found itself unable to withstand. The passenger services were temporarily suspended in the summer of 1916, coincidentally on the disastrous first day of the Battle of the Somme, just as the domestic economies required by the Great War were beginning to bite. A very limited through passenger service continued to use the line, but the stations were never re-opened and closure was confirmed in 1930. Then, overnight on 8/9 May 1941, during Nottingham's worst night of bombing, the bridge carrying the line over the Midland Railway's Nottingham – Lincoln route was damaged. This resulted in the complete closure of the Suburban line south of Thorneywood, trains from Daybrook serving the brickworks and delivering domestic coal. The stump of the line soldiered on for another decade until total closure on 1 August 1951, so ending the short and disappointing career of the Nottingham Suburban Railway. Though much of the route has been erased, it is still possible to trace parts of it and the station house at St Ann's Well remains as a private house.

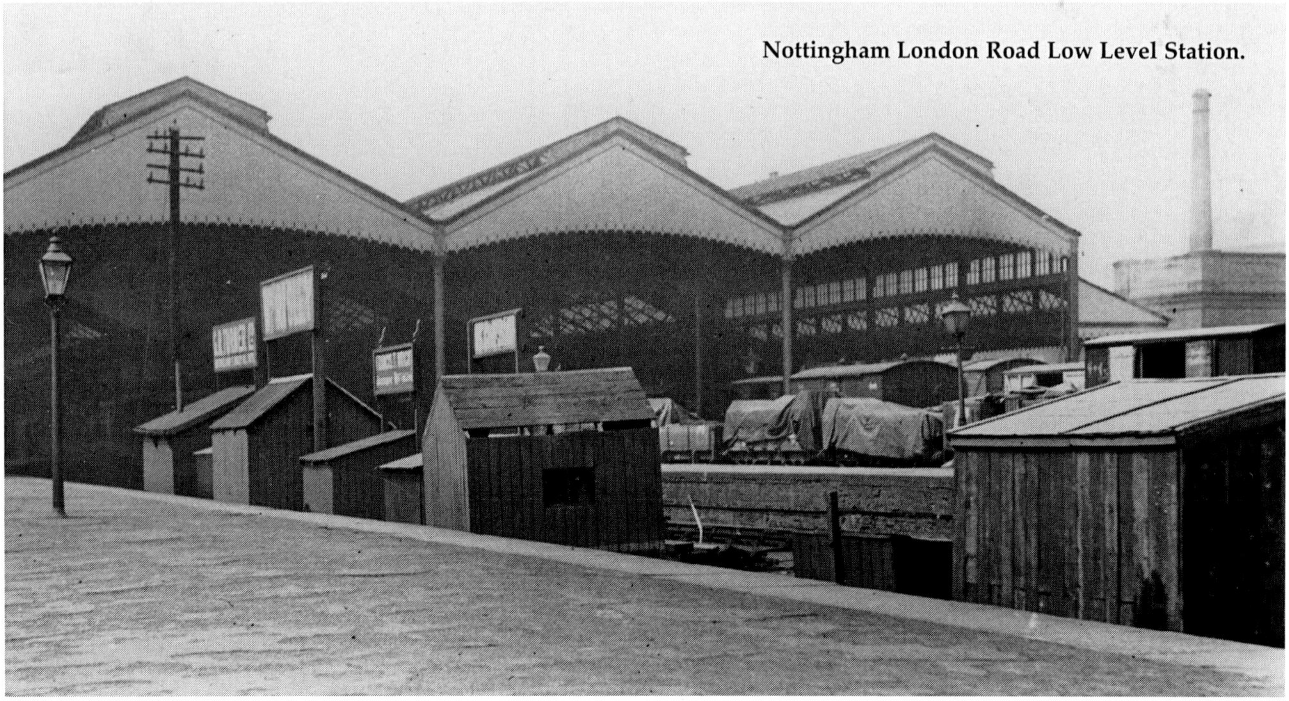

Nottingham London Road Low Level Station.

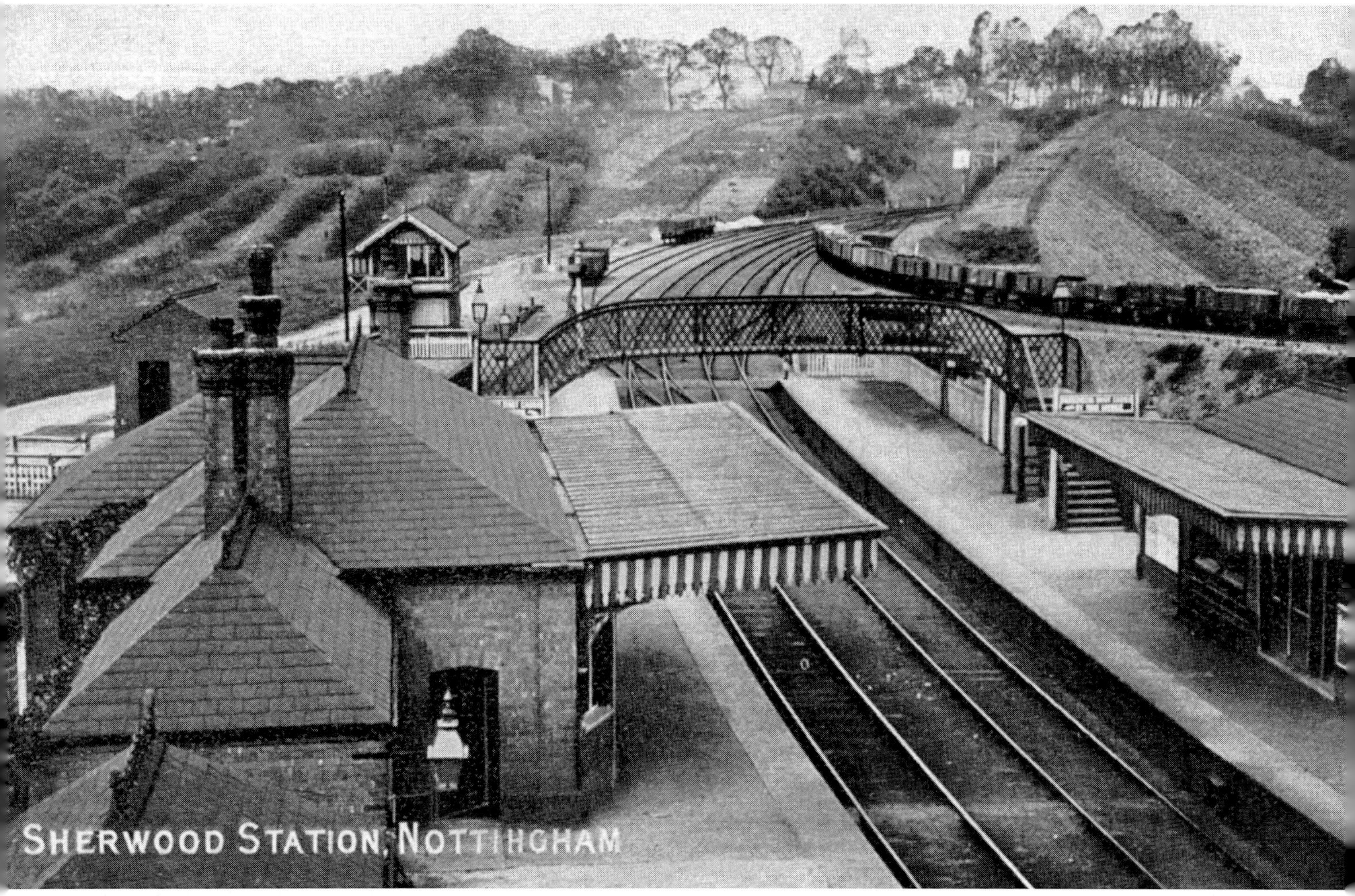


Sherwood Station was located between two tunnels. The upper picture looks north to the shorter of the two, which is pictured below. On the right of the upper picture wagons are waiting on the incline that led to Mapperley Brick Works.

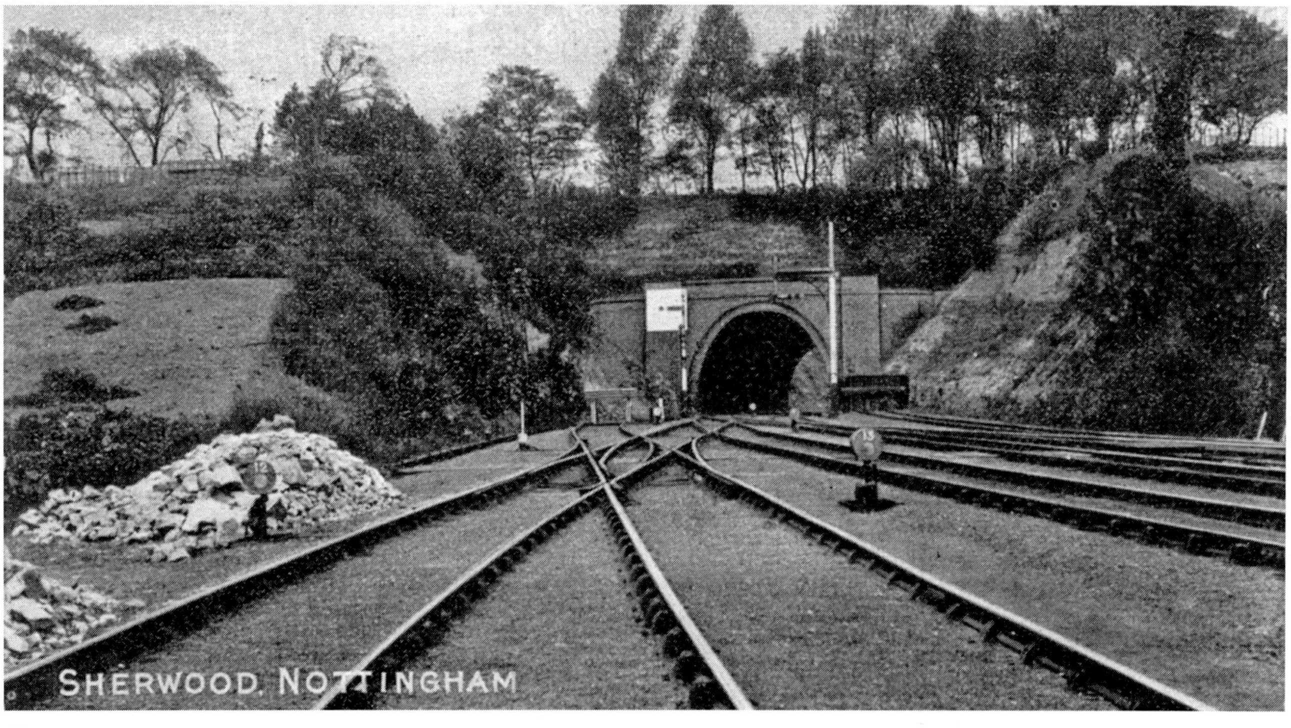

# Retford – Lincoln

| | |
|---|---|
| *Passenger services withdrawn* | 2 November 1959 |
| *Length* | 8 miles |
| *Original owning company* | Manchester, Sheffield & Lincolnshire Railway (Great Central Railway from 1899) |

| *Stations closed* | *Date of closure* |
|---|---|
| Leverton | 2 November 1959 |
| Cottam | 2 November 1959 |

* The closed station on this line that was in Lincolnshire was Torksey.

This line was featured in *Lincolnshire's Lost Railways* and was the original Manchester, Sheffield & Lincolnshire Railway's route to Lincoln from Sheffield. Indeed for a time the Great Northern used it as a way of gaining access to Yorkshire before its own route through Gainsborough to Doncaster was constructed. The line crossed the Trent on an elegant bridge and it was the need to effect significant repairs to this which prompted the decision to close the line as a through route: paradoxically the bridge still survives half a century later! Thus the line became two separate branches, one from Sykes Junction on the line just north of Saxilby to Torksey, to serve an oil terminal, and the other from Clarborough, on the MS&LR line from Retford through Gainsborough to Grimsby, to Cottam Power Station, for use by merry-go-round coal trains. The Torksey section closed in the late 1980s, but the section to the power station still remains in use.

**Leverton Station looking towards North Leverton Windmill, *c.* 1900.**

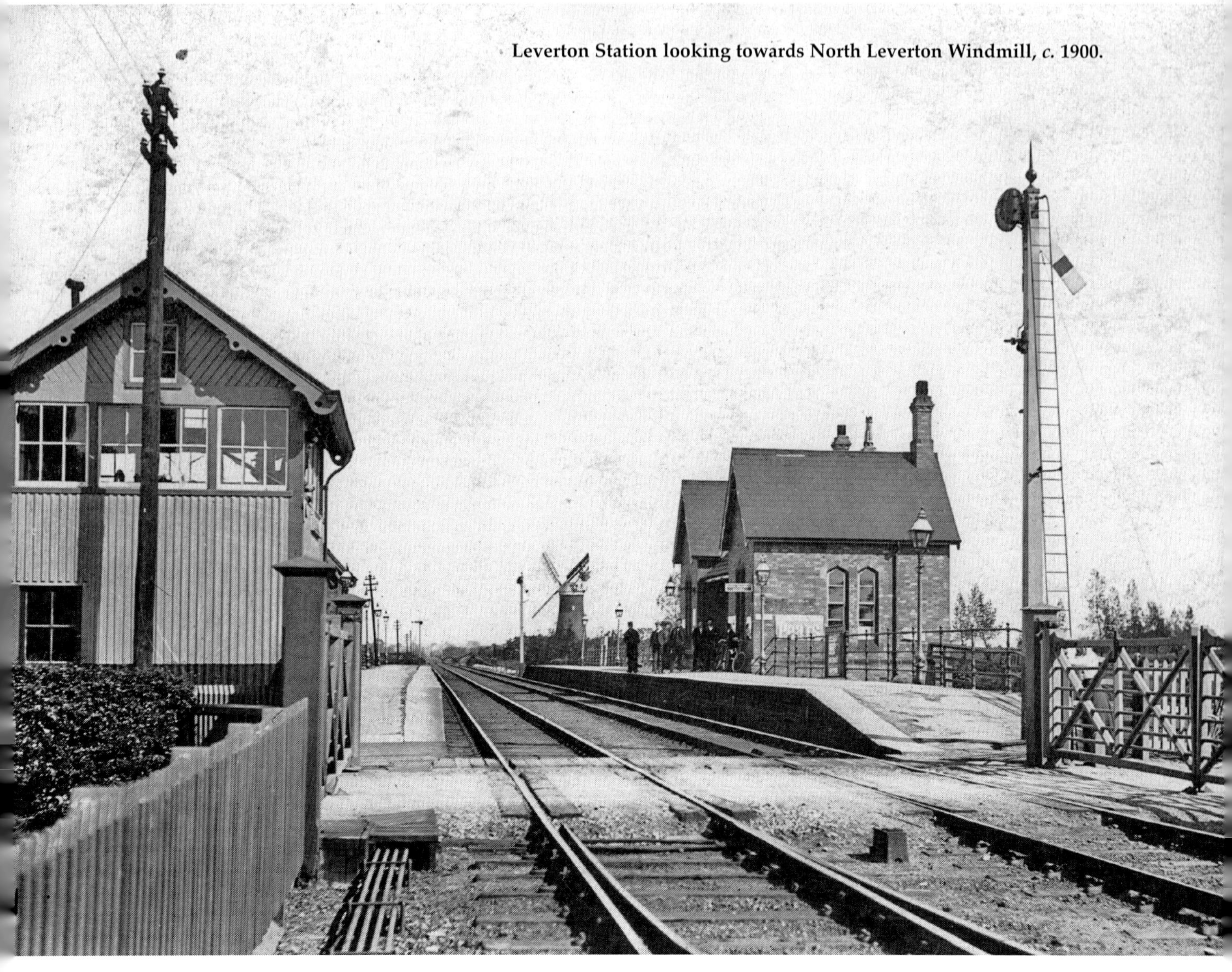

# Rolleston Junction – Mansfield

| | |
|---|---|
| *Passenger services withdrawn* | see text |
| *Length* | 15 miles |
| *Original owning company* | Midland Railway |

| *Stations closed* | *Date of closure* |
|---|---|
| Southwell | 15 June 1959 |
| Kirklington | 12 August 1929 |
| Farnsfield | 12 August 1929 |
| Rainworth | 12 August 1929 |
| Mansfield | 12 October 1964 |

The line from Nottingham to Lincoln was built by the Midland Railway and opened in 1846, the first to enter the latter city. The following year, in July 1847, a short branch was opened from Rolleston, then called Southwell Junction, to Southwell itself, a distance of $2\frac{1}{2}$ miles. The line seems to have had little commercial success and even went though a period in which steam locomotives were replaced by horses as motive power. The growth of the Nottinghamshire coalfield stimulated a plan to extend the line to Mansfield and, after some hesitation, the Midland opened the through route on 3 April 1871.

The country between Mansfield and Newark was predominantly rural throughout the nineteenth century, though the coalfield continued to create pockets of industrialisation in the form of mining villages, somewhat incongruously surrounded by fields. As a through route the Mansfield – Rolleston line was a significant artery for the movement of coal, though local traffic was sparse and generally agricultural. By the 1920s the London, Midland & Scottish Railway, as successors to the Midland, decided that passenger receipts had gone lower than they could tolerate and regular passenger services were withdrawn north of Southwell. However, freight traffic continued and occasional passenger trains, particularly excursions bound for the east coast resorts of Skegness, Mablethorpe and Sutton-on-Sea, continued to call at the stations. A third section, the West Curve, was added to make Rolleston a triangular junction in April 1929 allowing through running from Mansfield to Nottingham without reversal at Rolleston, underlining the importance of the line as a route for goods and particularly mineral traffic.

On the remainder of the route, the passenger service between Rolleston and Southwell was retained and operated for much of the twentieth century by 'push-pull' trains, avoiding the need for the engine to run round its solitary coach at each end of the short journey. The 'Southwell Paddy' became renowned locally, but succumbed to closure in June 1959. Rolleston, without its title 'junction' remains open for trains on the Nottingham – Lincoln line and several stations and other structures can still be seen. Parts of the route have been converted to a cycle and walking path, the 'Southwell Trail'.

**Southwell Station.**

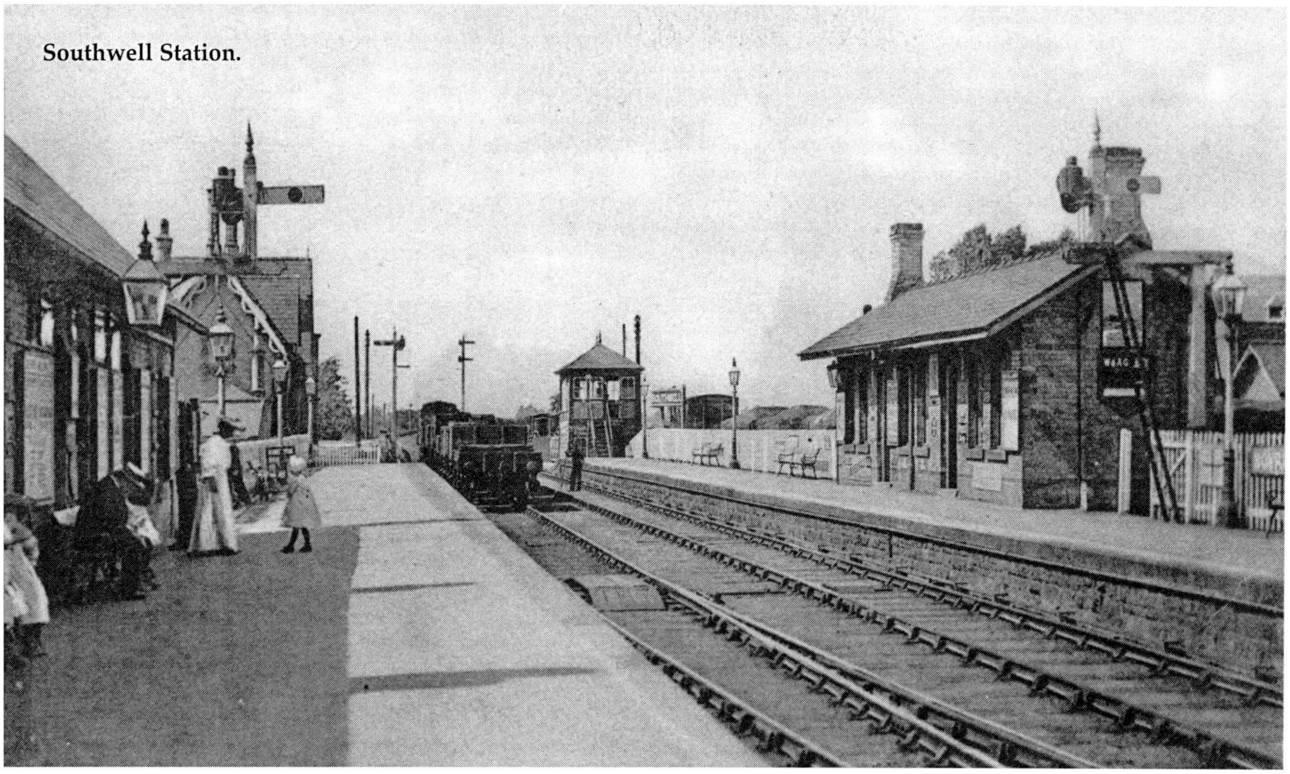

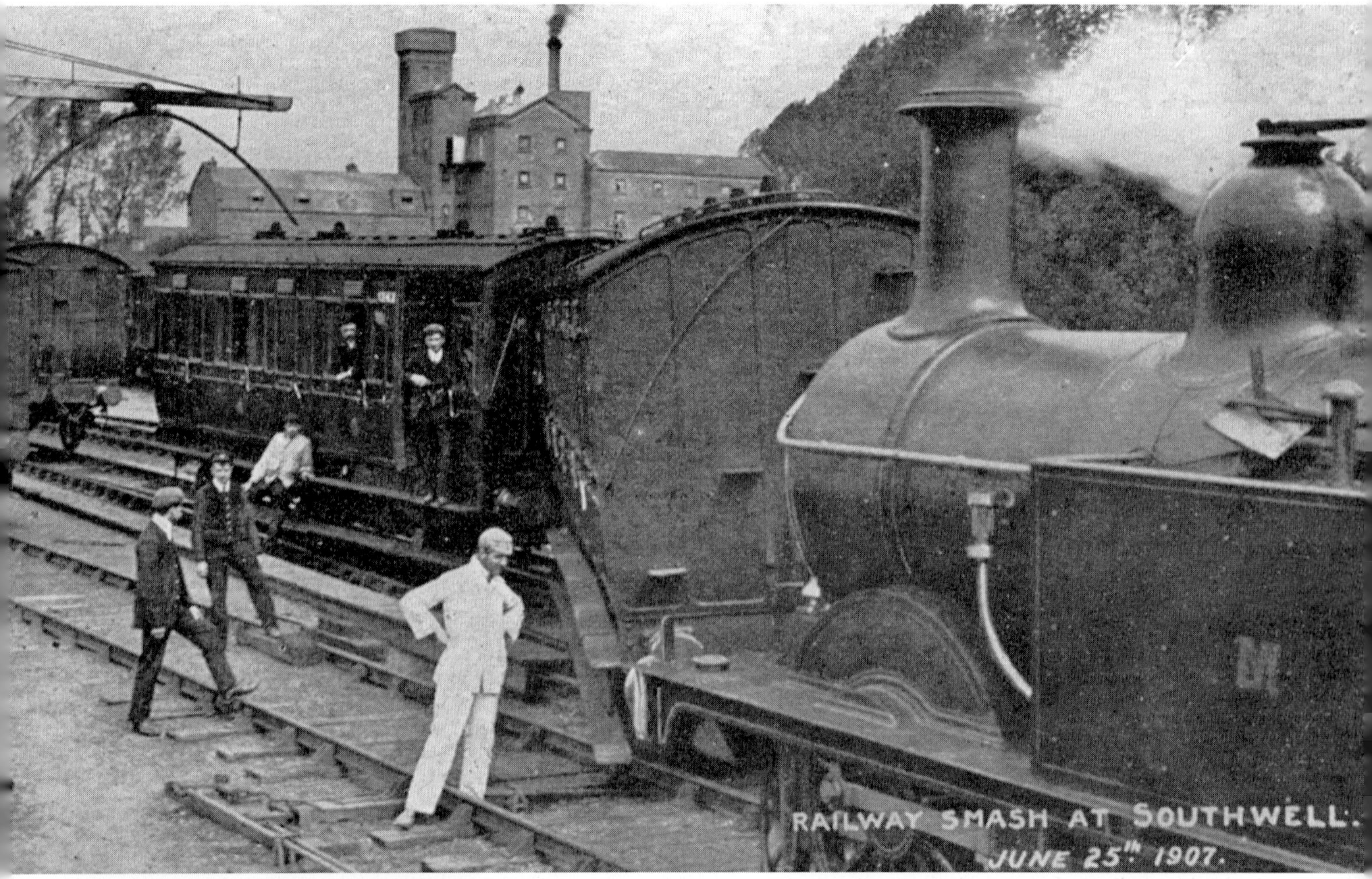


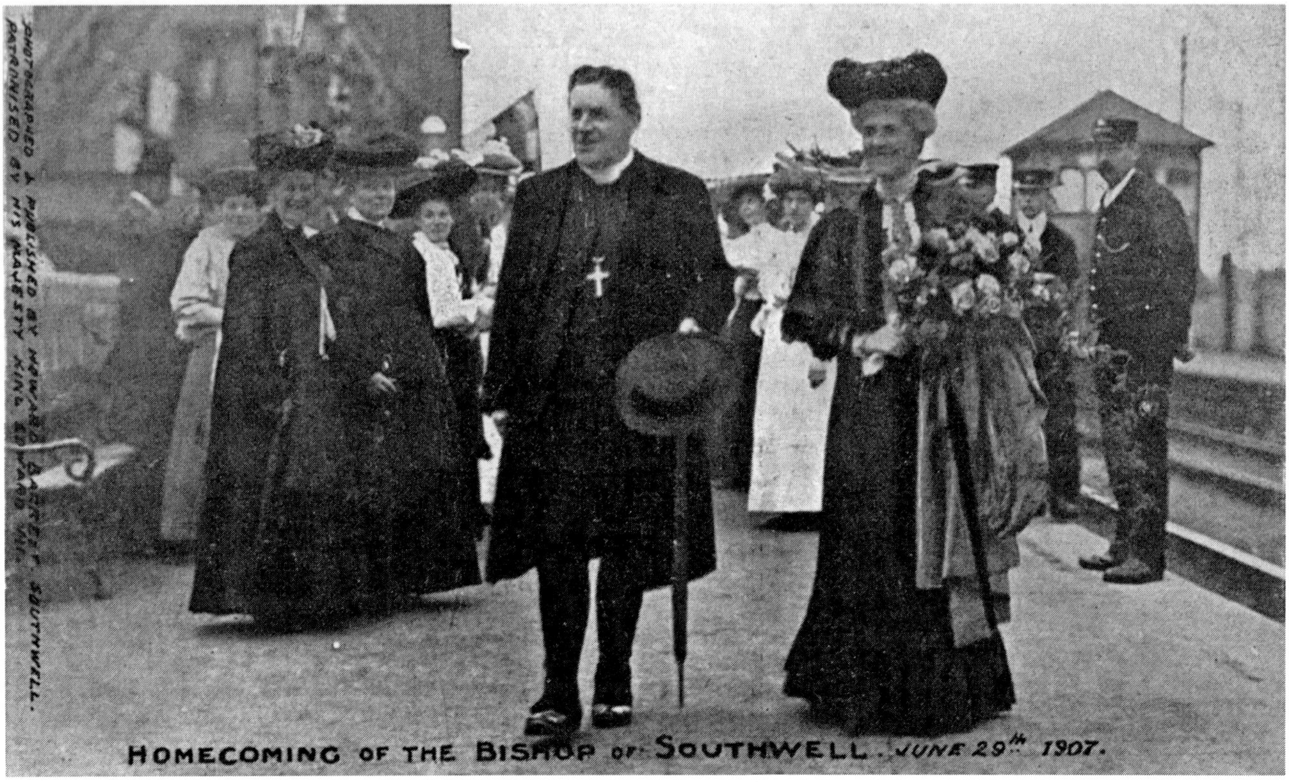


**Two events at Southwell Station a few days apart in June 1907.**

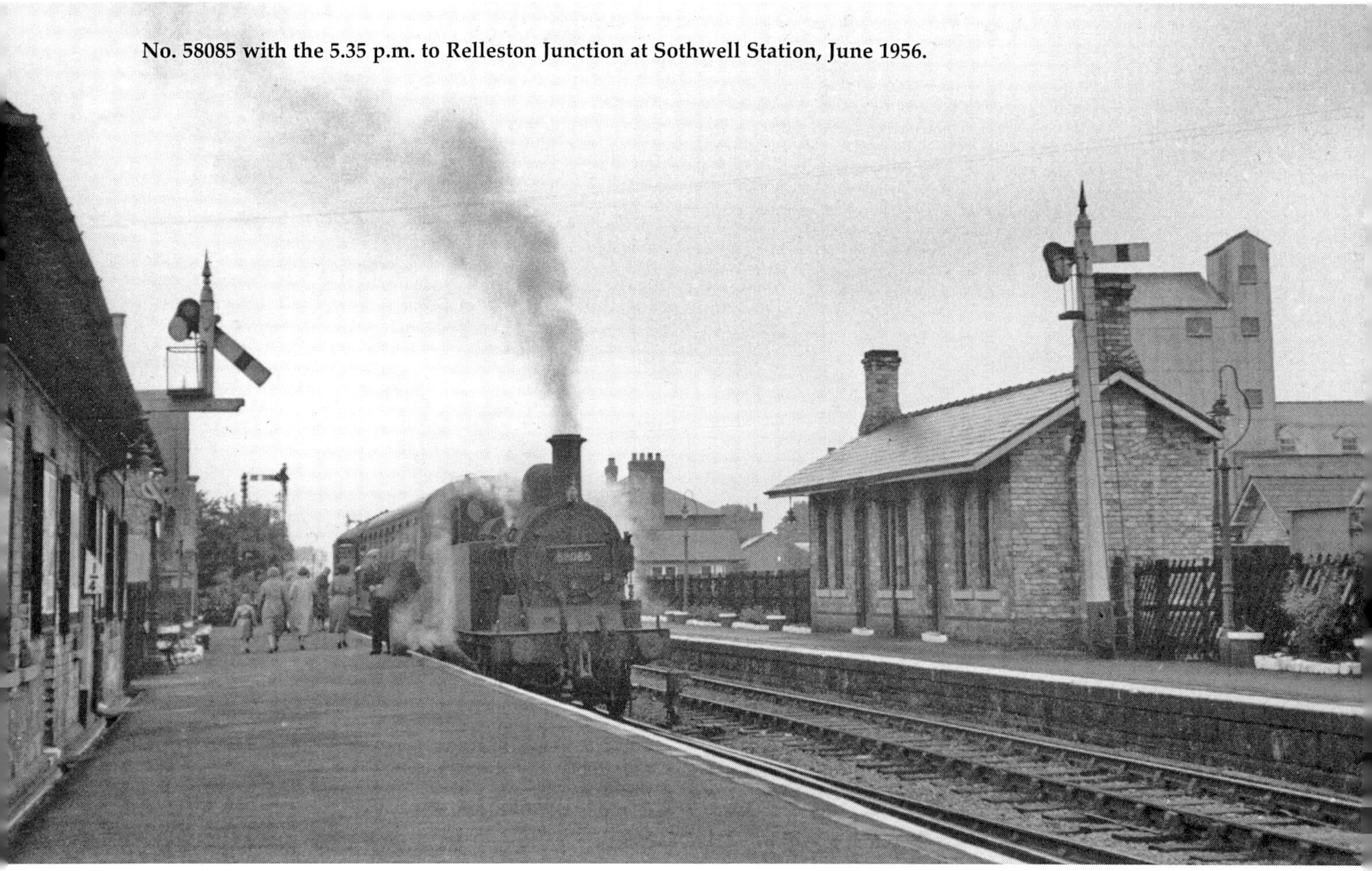

No. 58085 with the 5.35 p.m. to Relleston Junction at Sothwell Station, June 1956.

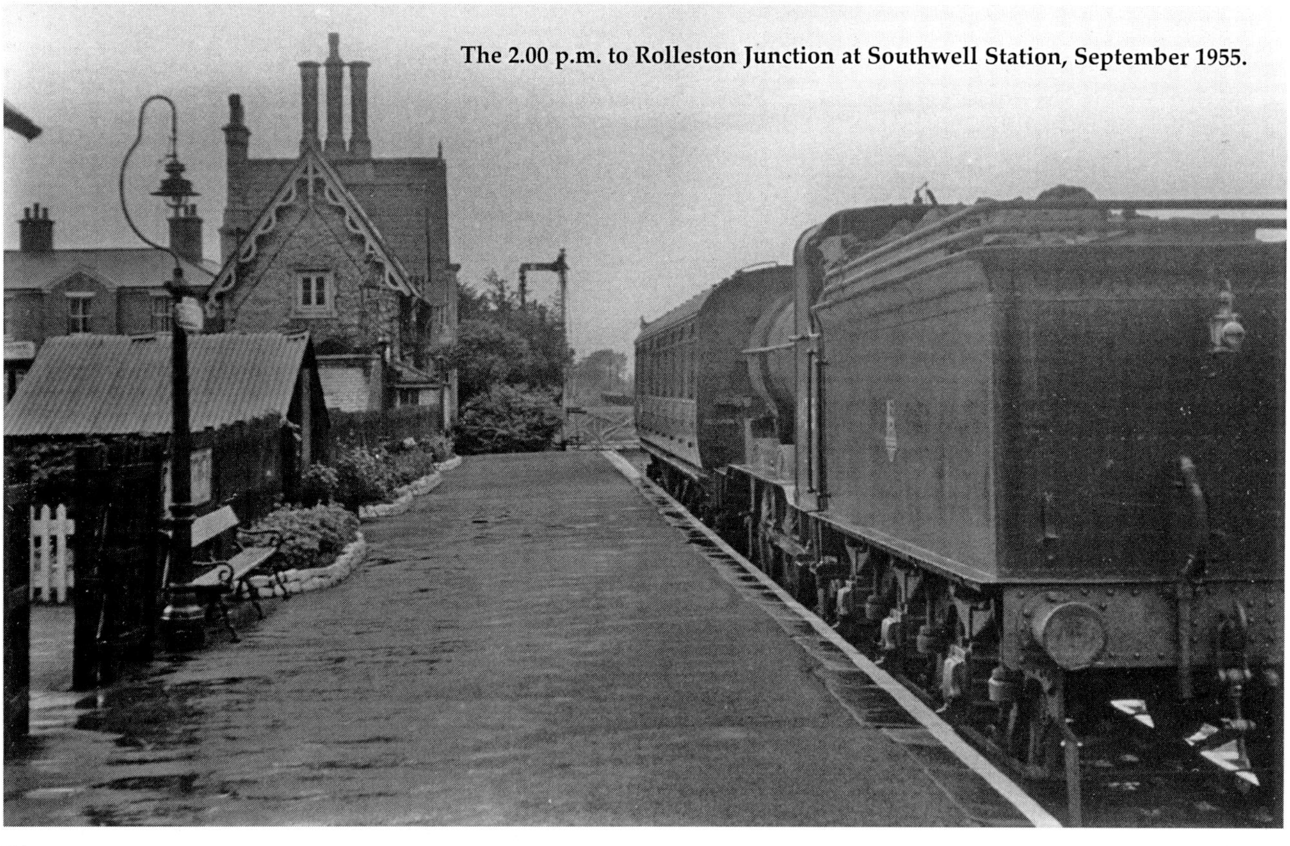

The 2.00 p.m. to Rolleston Junction at Southwell Station, September 1955.

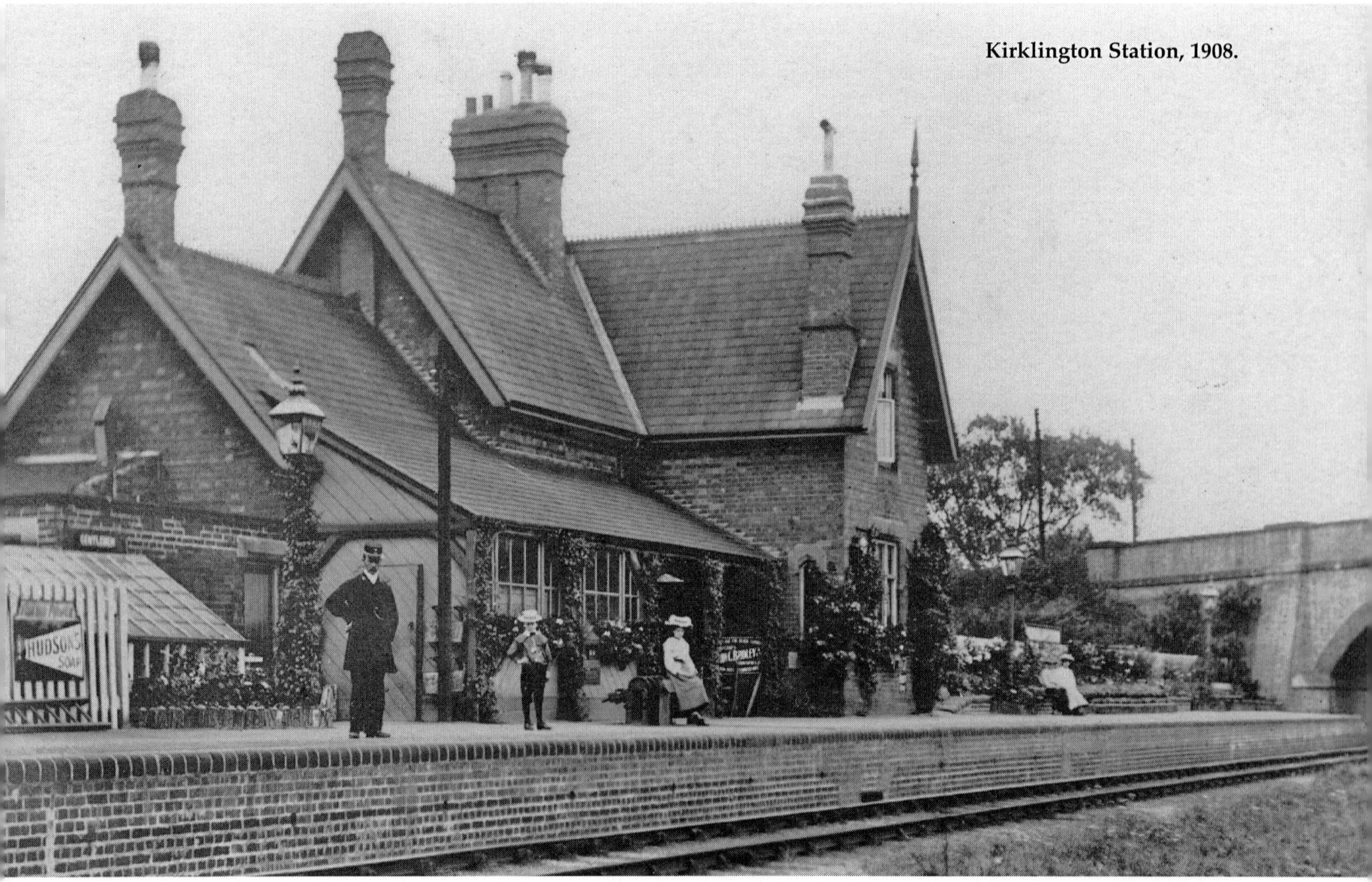


Kirklington Station, 1908.

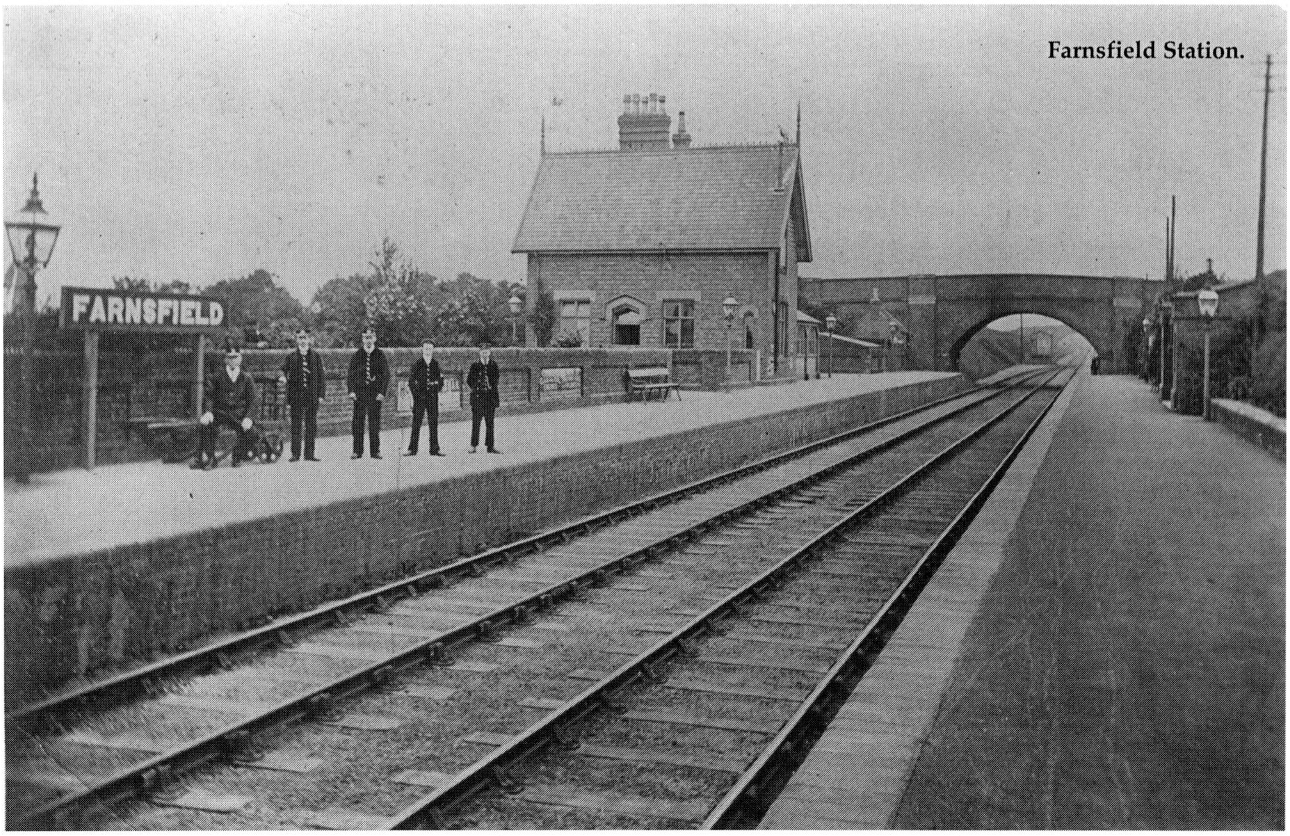


Farnsfield Station.

# The Sutton-in-Ashfield Branch

| | |
|---|---|
| *Passenger services withdrawn* | 26 September 1949 (but see text) |
| *Length* | 1 mile |
| *Original owning company* | Midland Railway |

| | |
|---|---|
| *Stations closed* | *Date of closure* |
| Sutton-in-Ashfield General * | 1 October 1951 |

* Originally named Sutton-in-Ashfield until 1 January 1908, then named Sutton-in-Ashfield for Huwthwaite until closed on 1 January 1917. Reopened and renamed Sutton-in-Ashfield Town on 9 July 1923 (closed between 4 May and 20 September 1926), taking its last name on 1 July 1950.

It is often remarked that Victorian railways tended to miss centres of population along their routes, either because the need to follow land contours made it difficult to engineer a route through towns, or because the economic realities which had promoted the line dictated that this was the preferable course. In many ways our ancestors, unaccustomed to the notion that transport should always run door-to-door, were less concerned at this state of affairs than we might be today; they were glad there was a railway to serve them at all. Also people travelled less, and less frequently, than today, generally living within walking distance of their work, everyday supplies and pleasures. When the Midland Railway opened its Leen Valley line in 1849, it came within a mile or so of Sutton-in-Ashfield, a station named 'Sutton' being provided to serve the town, a situation very similar to that at Ilkeston on the Erewash Valley line. But whereas Ilkeston was soon provided with a short branch line, Sutton was only given this facility in July 1892, when a mile-long branch from the original Sutton station, now renamed Sutton Junction, was opened. The branch train became something of a local institution, gaining the nickname 'the Penny Emma' – possibly a reflection of the original fare – and enjoyed a frequent service, trains running to and from Mansfield in the early days, with over 25 return journeys daily in 1910. However, like many other short urban branches it fell victim to road competition and the last public service ran on 26 September 1949. Unadvertised workmen's trains continued until 1951, when the line closed completely.

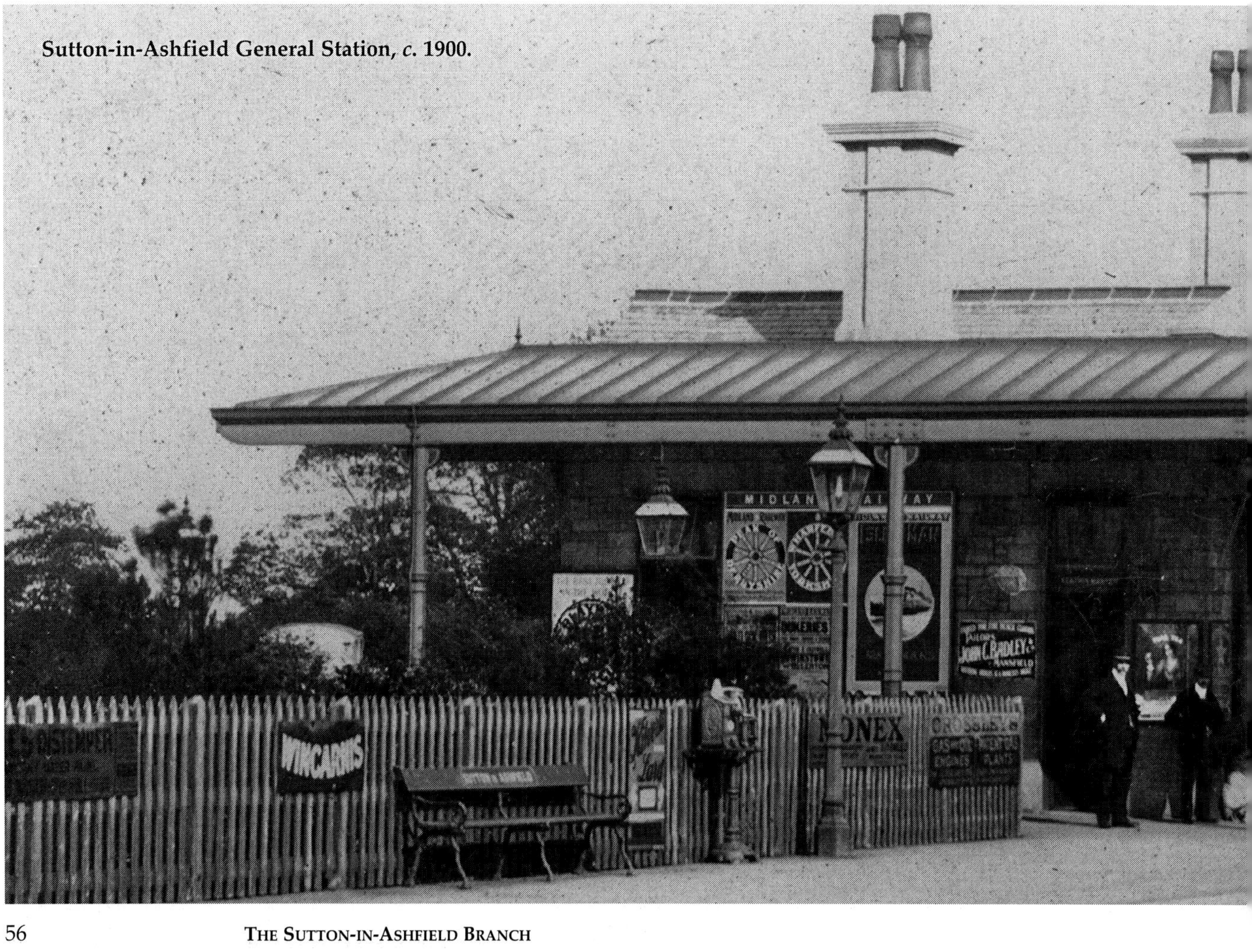


**Sutton-in-Ashfield General Station, *c.* 1900.**

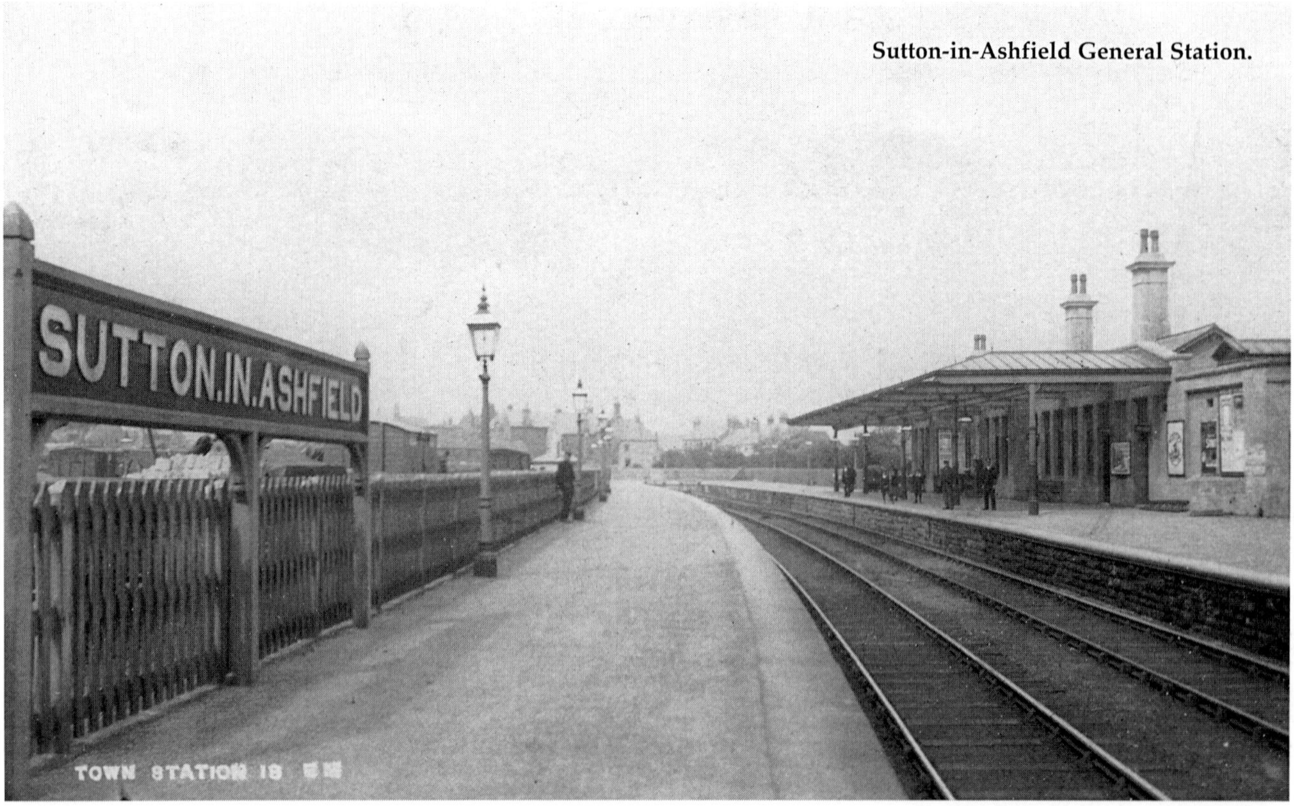

Sutton-in-Ashfield General Station.

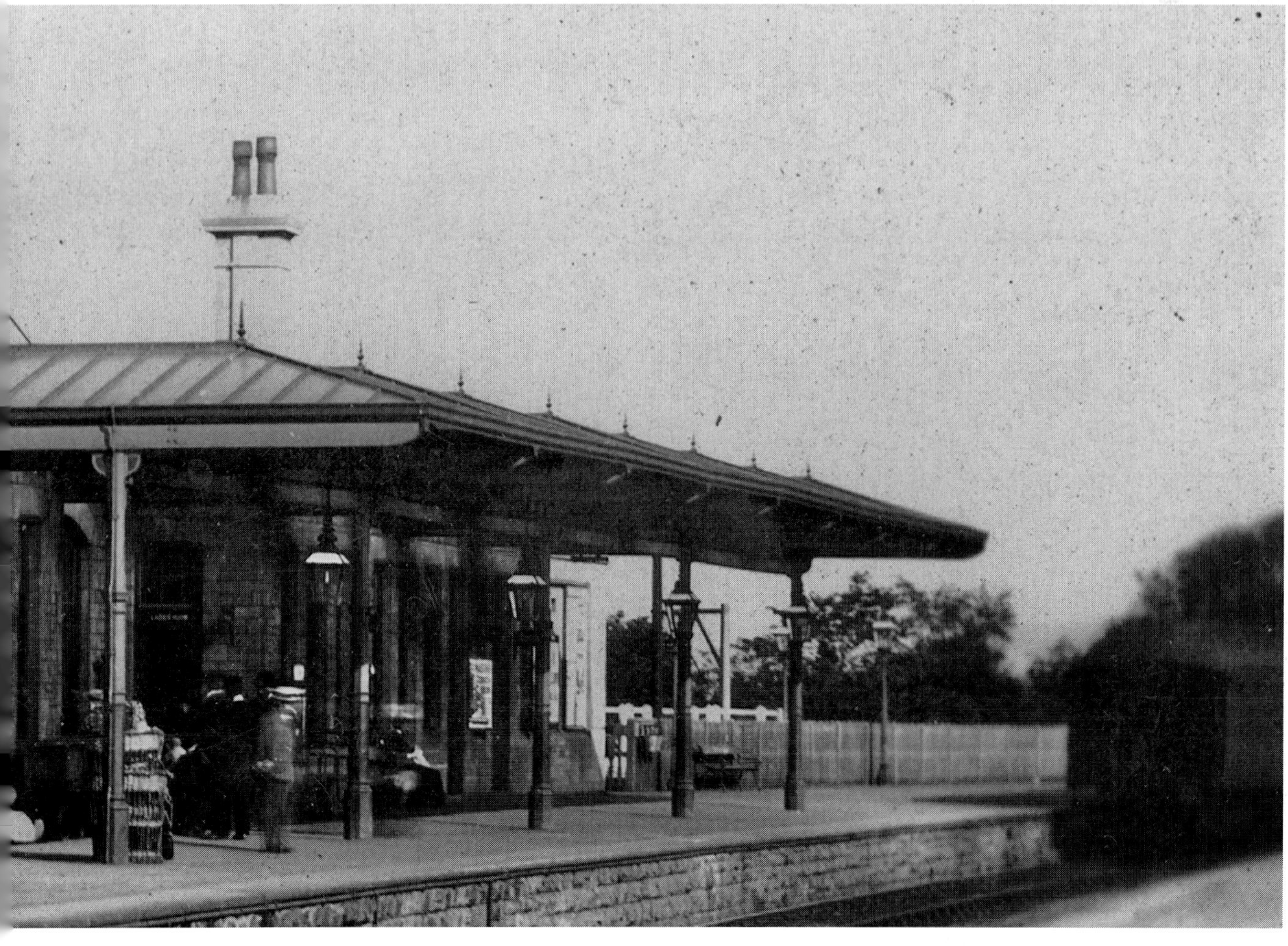

# Lines in the Leen Valley

The River Leen may not be one of Britain's great waterways, but it, or at least the valley through which it flows, has played an important part in Nottinghamshire's industrial history. Like the valley of the Erewash to the west, the Leen Valley was the location of many collieries in the Nottinghamshire coalfield and the valley's floor became an important route for the railways built to serve them. The Midland was first, its line running between the Nottingham – Derby route at Lenton Junction to Kirkby-in-Ashfield, opening in October 1848; one of its first tests as a passenger route was to convey large number of excursionists to Nottingham for the annual Goose Fair, held in that month. Over the years the line threw off a number of branches to collieries along the route, the most recent being that to Calverton Colliery, opened by British Railways in 1952.

It was to be expected that the Great Northern's drive to capture some of the coalfield's traffic would result in its construction of a line into the Leen Valley. This materialised in 1882 with a branch off the Nottingham – Derby loop at Leen Valley Junction, just to the west of Daybrook, up through Newstead, seat of Lord Byron, to Sutton-in-Ashfield. A further line, the Leen Valley Extension Railway of 1898, took the Great Northern through Shirebrook and on to make a junction with the Lancashire, Derbyshire & East Coast line at Langwith Junction.

This meant that several of the towns in the valley were served by two stations, but, as related elsewhere, after 1899 the Great Central Railway's London Extension added a third line and still more stations. The lines crossed and re-crossed each other as they made their way northwards. At Bulwell, the Midland line was to the west, then the Great Central, then the Great Northern; by Hucknall it was Great Central, Great Northern, Midland; while at Newstead the latter order was reversed.

It was only a matter of time before such a concentration of railways was likely to run into financial difficulties. These related mainly to passenger traffic, since this was relatively expensive to provide and, in the early twentieth century, vulnerable to competition from road transport in the forms of electric tram and motor buses: the Midland station at Lenton was an early casualty, closing in 1911. Then the whole Great Northern line succumbed, losing its passenger trains in 1931, its new owners – the London & North Eastern Railway – no doubt judging that the Great Central line was a better proposition for passengers anyway. The Great Central line lost its intermediate stations in 1963 and the Midland route lasted another year. Coal traffic, always attractive to the railways because of its bulk and the fact that they had responsibilities for neither loading nor unloading it, remained for as long as the collieries, which closed one by one into the 1980s.

In the era of the Beeching cuts of the mid 1960s, it was assumed that cars and buses were the answer to urban transport in all but the largest cities. By the time the Nottinghamshire collieries were disappearing, a new realisation had dawned on transport planners; that cars caused such levels of congestion that other forms of road transport would be unable to function effectively. They began to look with renewed interest at the very forms of rail-guided transport that had seemed obsolete in the 1960s – trains and trams. Moreover, there was a long-standing grievance that Mansfield was one of the few towns in Britain with a population over 60,000 which was not connected directly to the national rail network. Discussions began in 1982, but after a survey by Nottinghamshire County Council in 1988, agreement was reached with British Rail a line could be reopened for passengers provided local authorities along the route were willing to provide subsidies.

The resulting railway has been named the 'Robin Hood Line' and was reopened in stages from Nottingham northwards. The majority of the route follows the Midland's Leen Valley line as far as Sutton-in-Ashfield, but thereafter uses the Great Northern route through Kirkby before reverting to the Midland formation. As part of reinstating the route it was necessary to excavate the Midland tunnel at Annesley, which had been filled in after closure. The first section from Nottingham to Newstead opened in 1993, extending to Mansfield Woodhouse in 1995, Kirkby in 1996 and finally through to Worksop on the former MS&LR line from Lincoln to Sheffield in 1998. Thus the wheel of change has come full cycle in the Leen Valley, though it is passengers rather than coal which have provided the staple traffic.

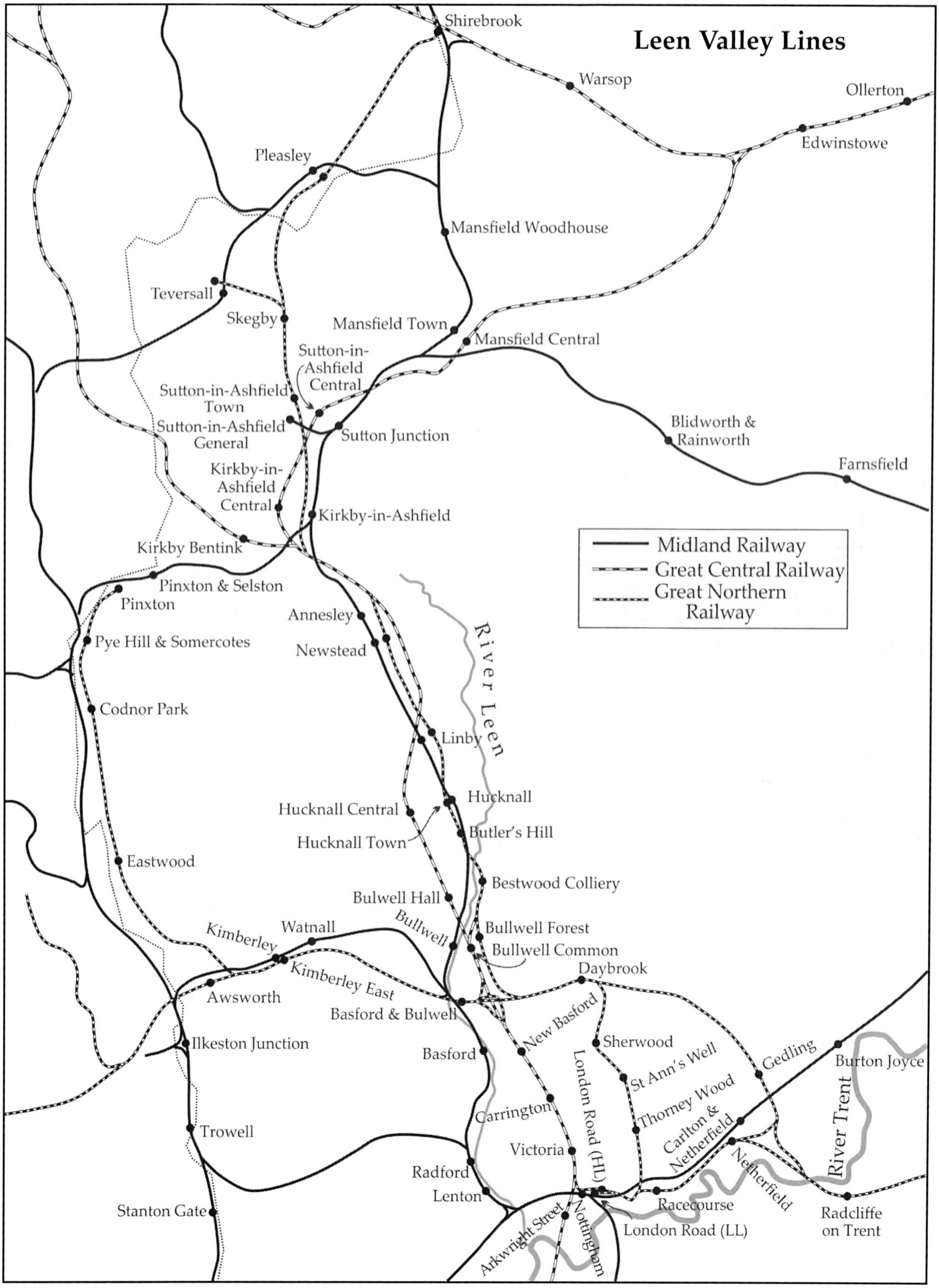
Leen Valley Lines
Midland Railway
Great Central Railway
Great Northern Railway
Shirebrook
Warsop
Ollerton
Edwinstowe
Pleasley
Mansfield Woodhouse
Teversall
Skegby
Mansfield Town
Mansfield Central
Sutton-in-Ashfield Central
Sutton-in-Ashfield Town
Sutton-in-Ashfield General
Sutton Junction
Blidworth & Rainworth
Farnsfield
Kirkby-in-Ashfield Central
Kirkby-in-Ashfield
Kirkby Bentink
Pinxton & Selston
Pinxton
Annesley
Newstead
Pye Hill & Somercotes
River Leen
Codnor Park
Linby
Hucknall
Hucknall Central
Hucknall Town
Butler's Hill
Eastwood
Bestwood Colliery
Bulwell Hall
Bulwell
Bullwell Forest
Bullwell Common
Kimberley
Watnall
Kimberley East
Daybrook
Awsworth
Basford & Bulwell
New Basford
Ilkeston Junction
Sherwood
Basford
St Ann's Well
Gedling
Burton Joyce
London Road (HL)
Thorney Wood
Carrington
Carlton & Netherfield
River Trent
Trowell
Victoria
Netherfield
Radford
Lenton
Racecourse
Radcliffe on Trent
Stanton Gate
Arkwright Street
Nottingham
London Road (LL)

# Leen Valley Junction – Shirebrook

| | |
|---|---|
| *Passenger services withdrawn* | 14 September 1931 |
| *Length* | $17^{1}/_{4}$ miles |
| *Original owning company* | Great Northern Railway |

| *Stations closed* | *Date of closure* |
|---|---|
| Bulwell Forest | 23 September 1929 |
| Bestwood Colliery | 14 September 1931 |
| Butlers Hill | 14 September 1931 |
| Hucknall Town | 14 September 1931 |
| Linby | 1 July 1916 |
| Newstead | 14 September 1931 |
| Sutton-in-Ashfield Town | 17 September 1956 |
| Skegby | 14 September 1931 |
| Pleasley | 14 September 1931 |
| Shirebrook | 14 September 1931 |

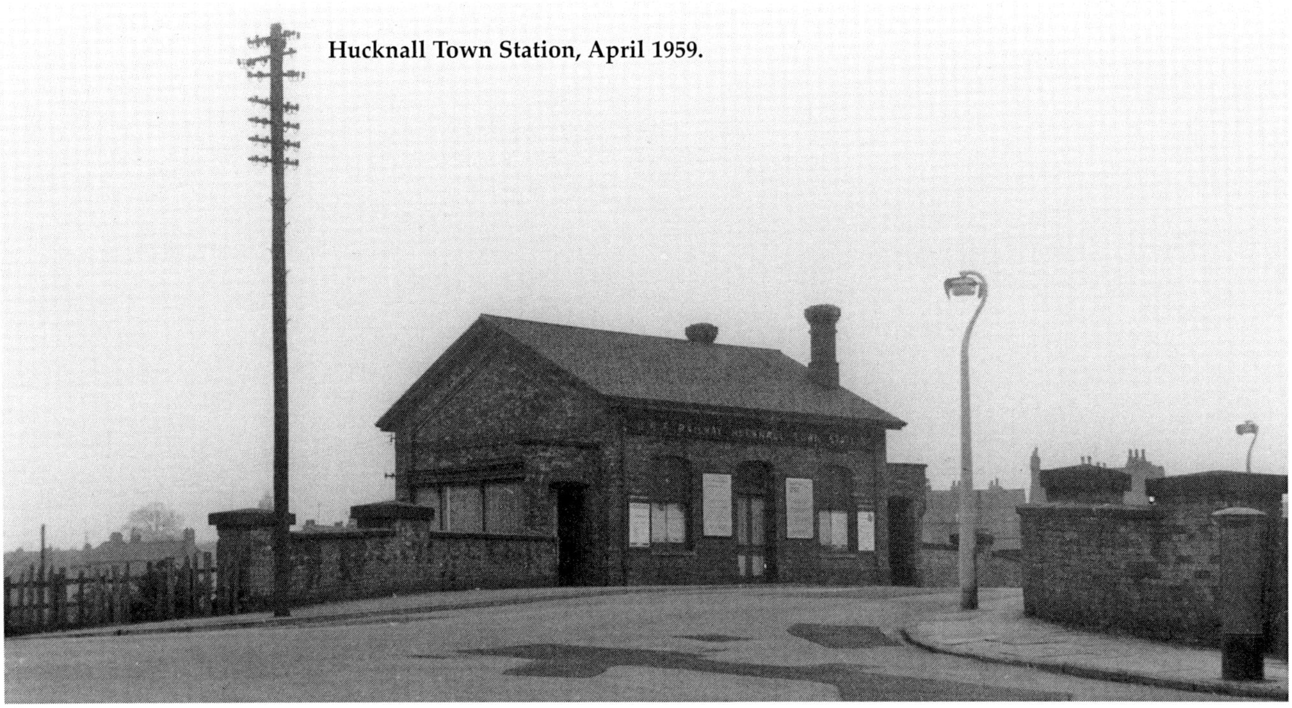

**Hucknall Town Station, April 1959.**

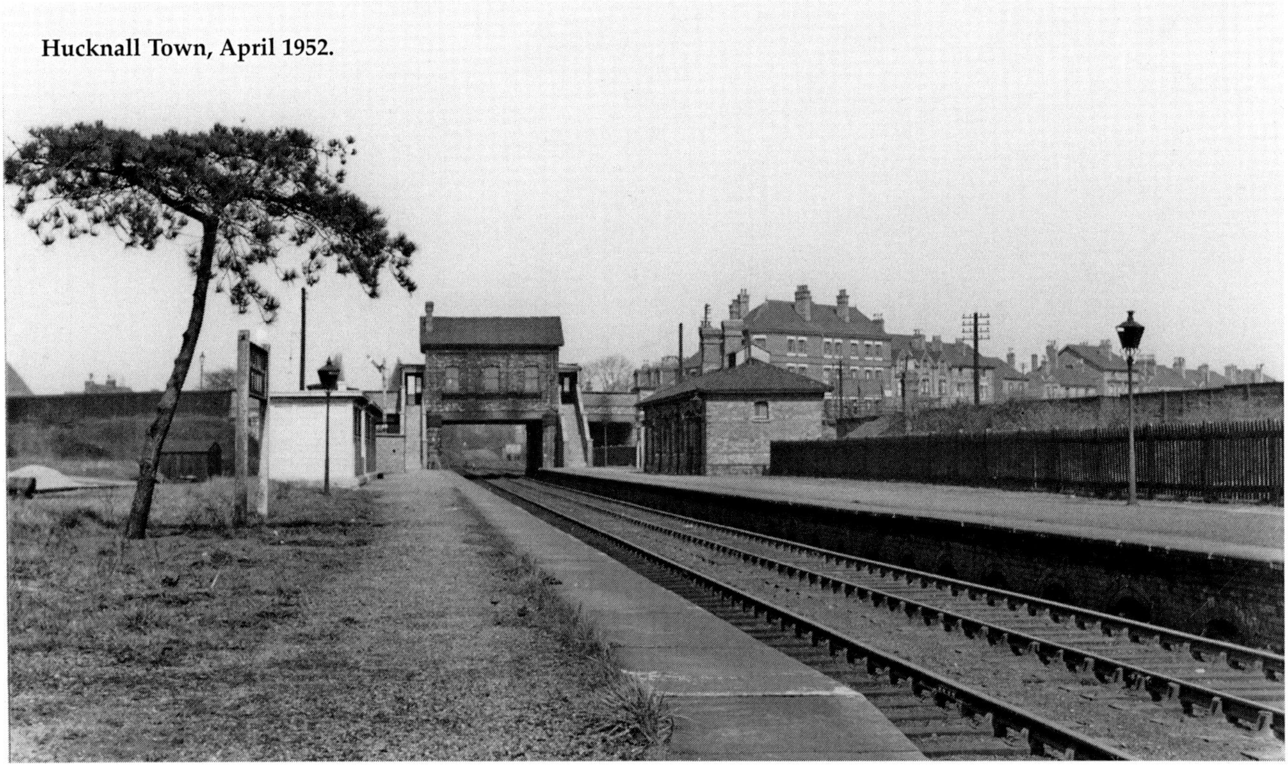

**Hucknall Town, April 1952.**

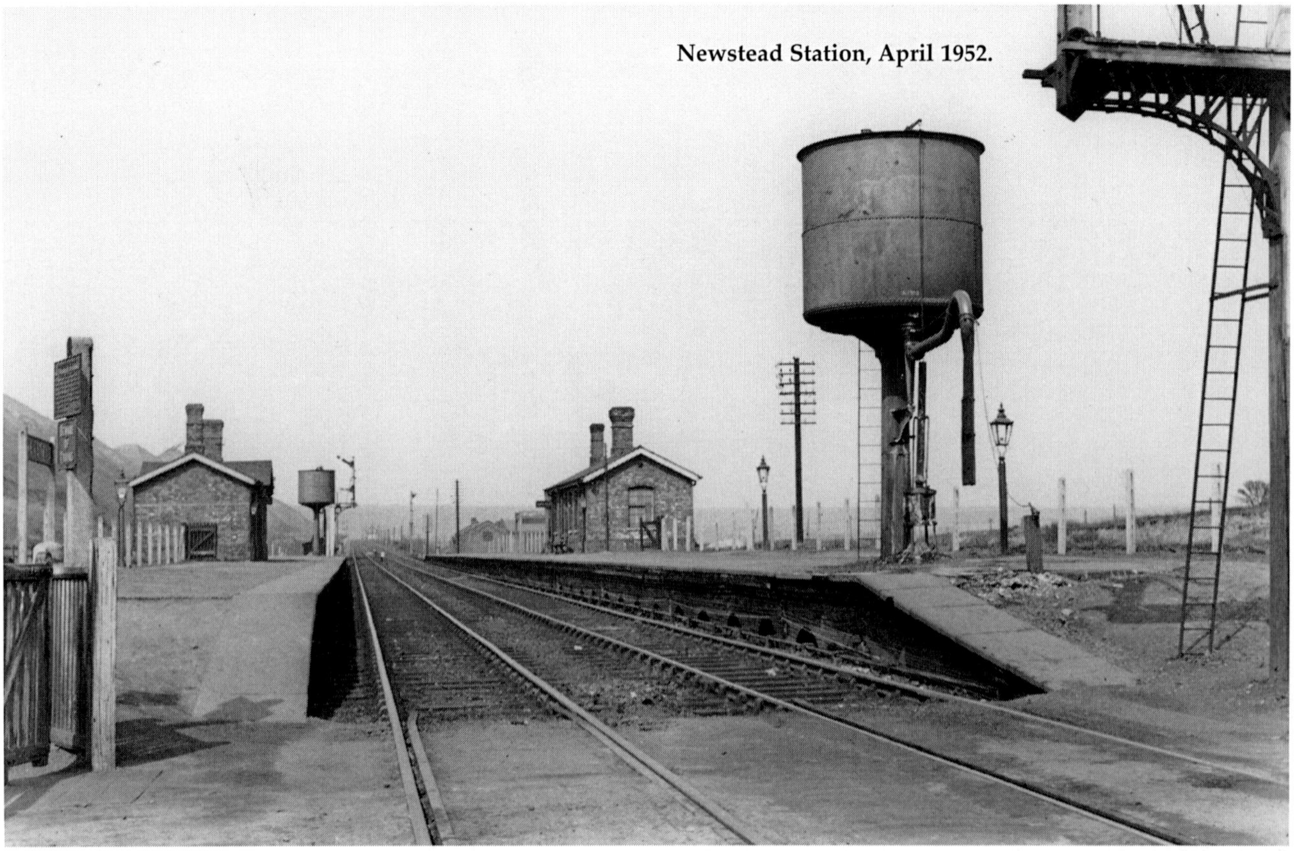

Newstead Station, April 1952.

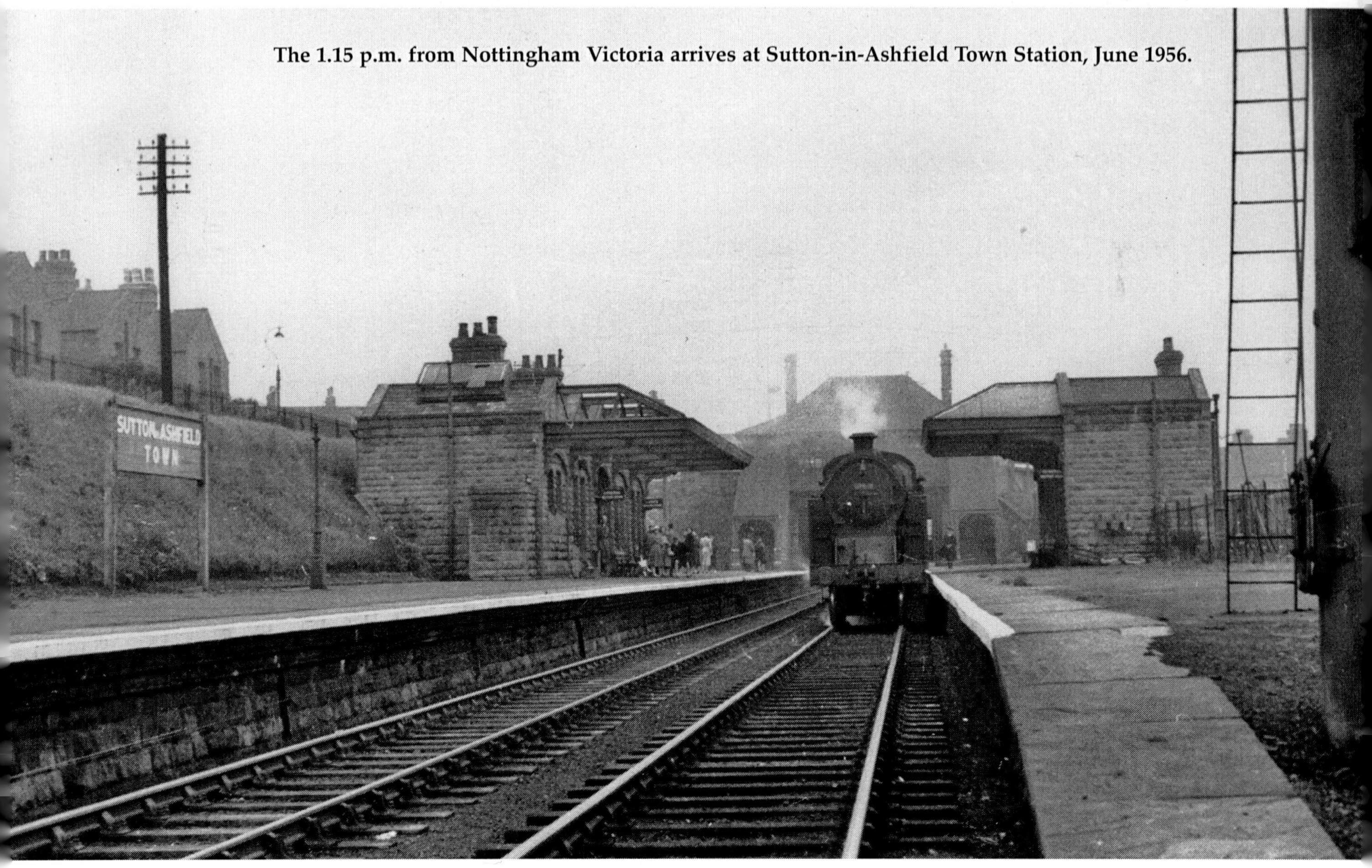


The 1.15 p.m. from Nottingham Victoria arrives at Sutton-in-Ashfield Town Station, June 1956.

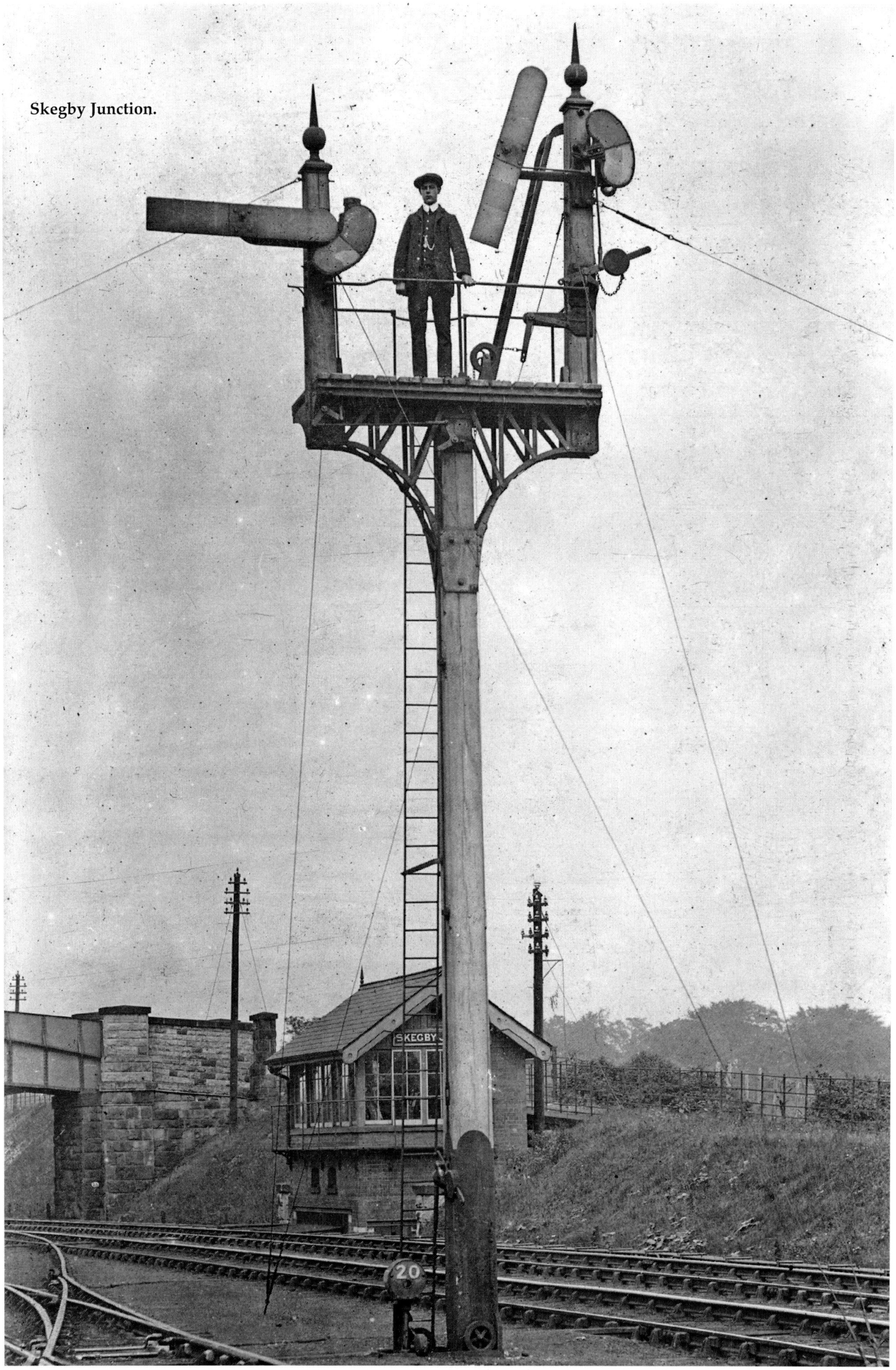


Skegby Junction.

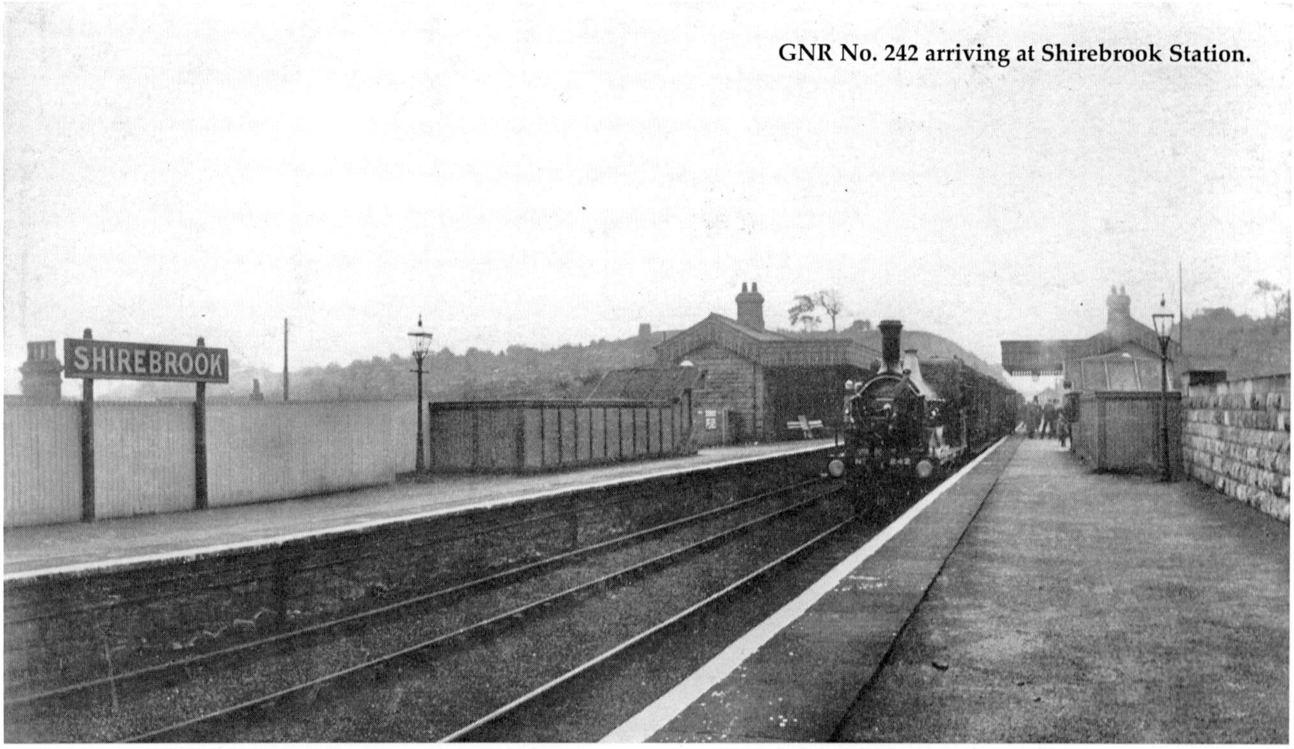

GNR No. 242 arriving at Shirebrook Station.

# Lenton Junction – Kirkby-in-Ashfield

| | |
|---|---|
| *Passenger services withdrawn* | 12 October 1964 |
| *Length* | 13¾ miles |
| *Original owning company* | Midland Railway |

| *Stations closed* | *Date of closure* |
|---|---|
| Lenton | 1 July 1911 |
| Radford * | 12 October 1964 |
| Basford ** | 4 January 1960 |
| Bulwell Market | 12 October 1964 |
| Hucknall *** | 12 October 1964 |
| Linby | 12 October 1964 |
| Newstead † | 12 October 1964 |
| Annesley Colliery Sidings Platform | not recorded |
| Annesley | 6 April 1963 |
| Kirkby-in-Ashfield †† | 12 October 1964 |

* Second station; original station replaced in 1876.
** Renamed Basford Vernon after 1952.
*** Second station; original station replaced in 1895; renamed Hucknall Byron 1952.
† Original station for private use; made public in 1883.
†† Originally 'Kirkby'; suffix 'East' added in 1959.

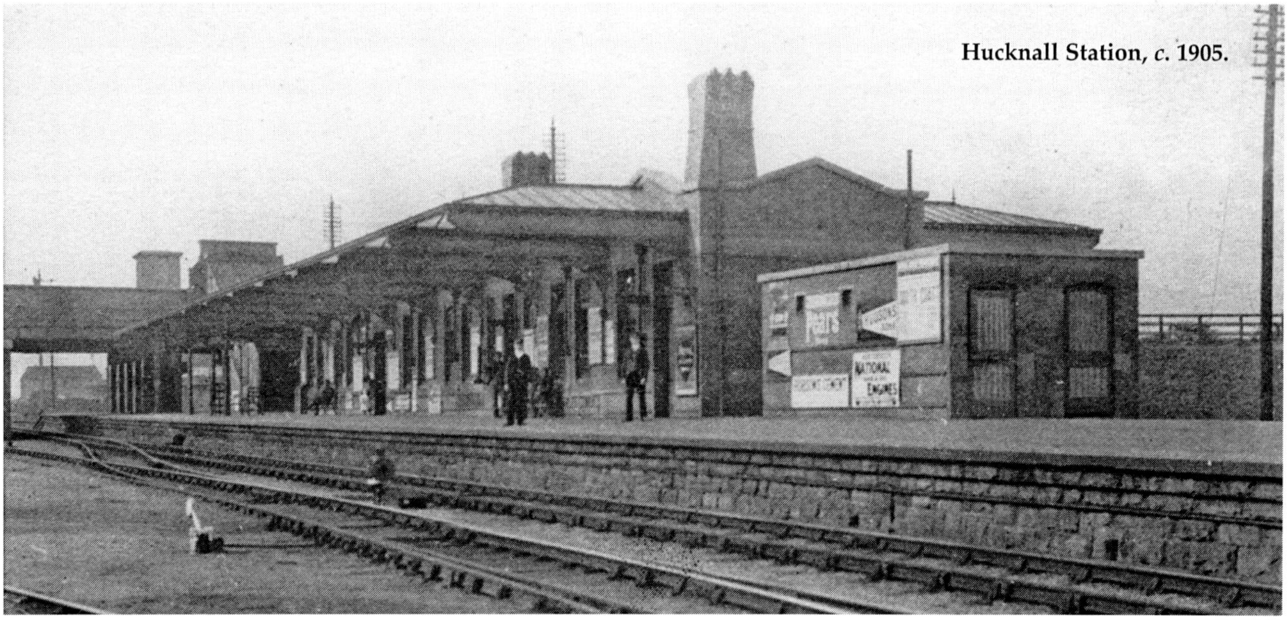
Hucknall Station, *c.* 1905.

Linby Station looking to the spoil heaps of Linby Colliery, April 1952.

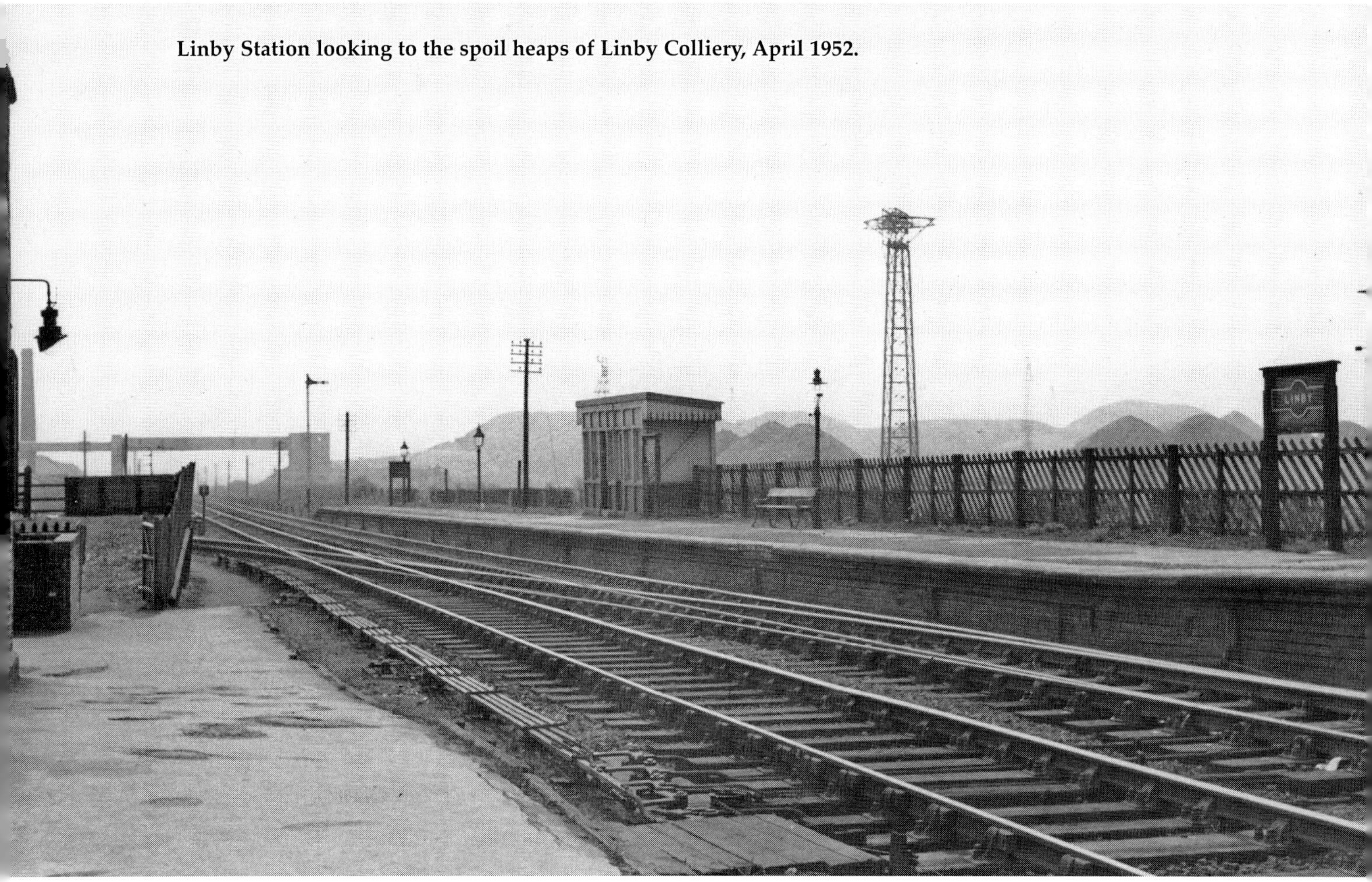


Linby Station, 1954.

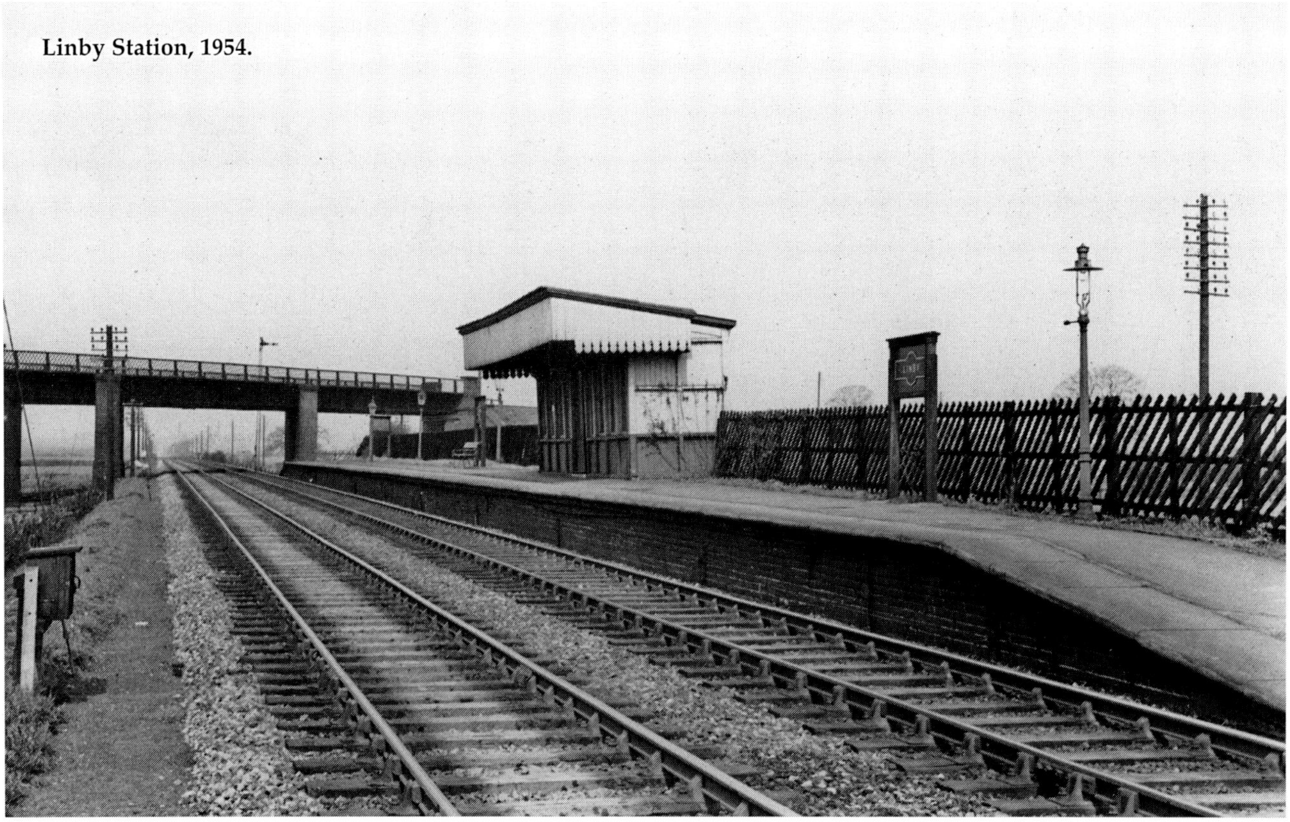

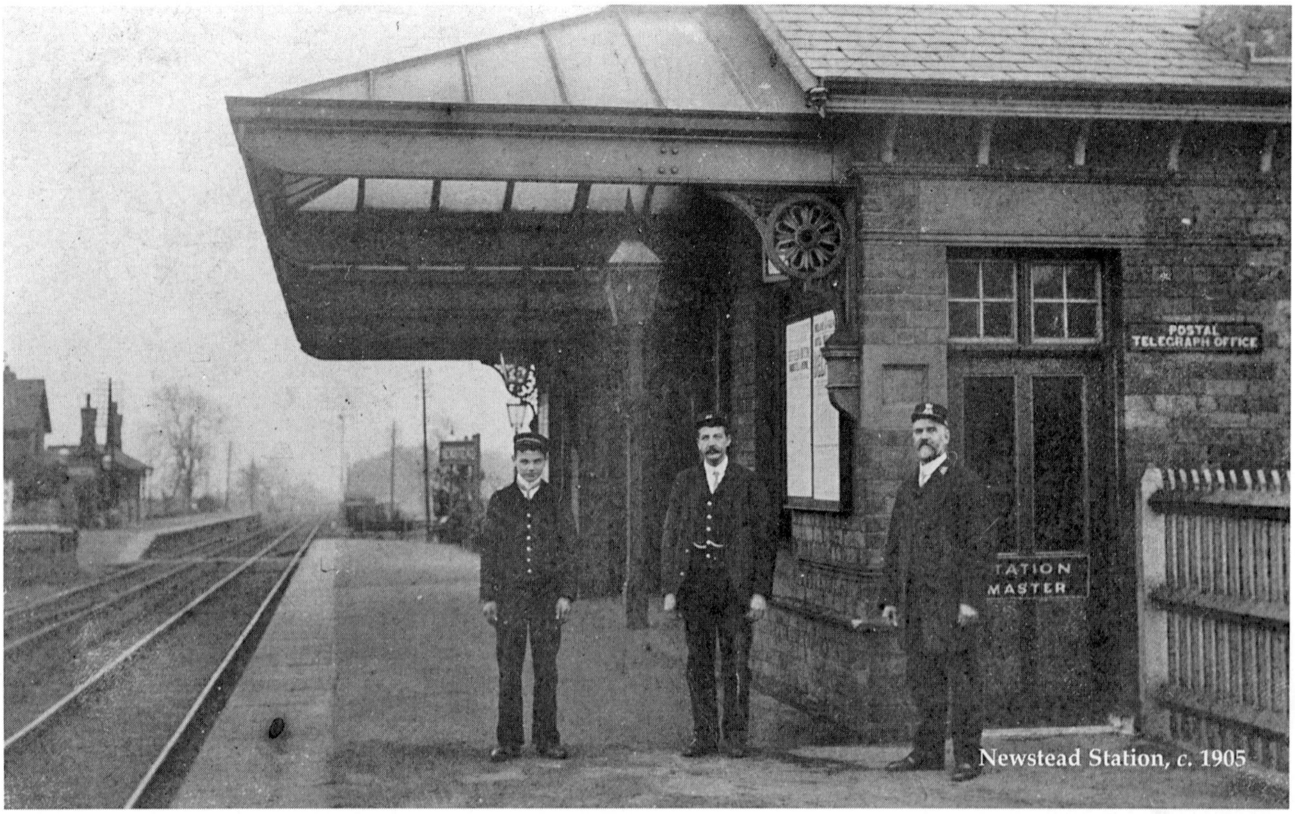

Newstead Station, *c.* 1905

**Newstead Station looking north to Newstead Colliery, April 1952.**

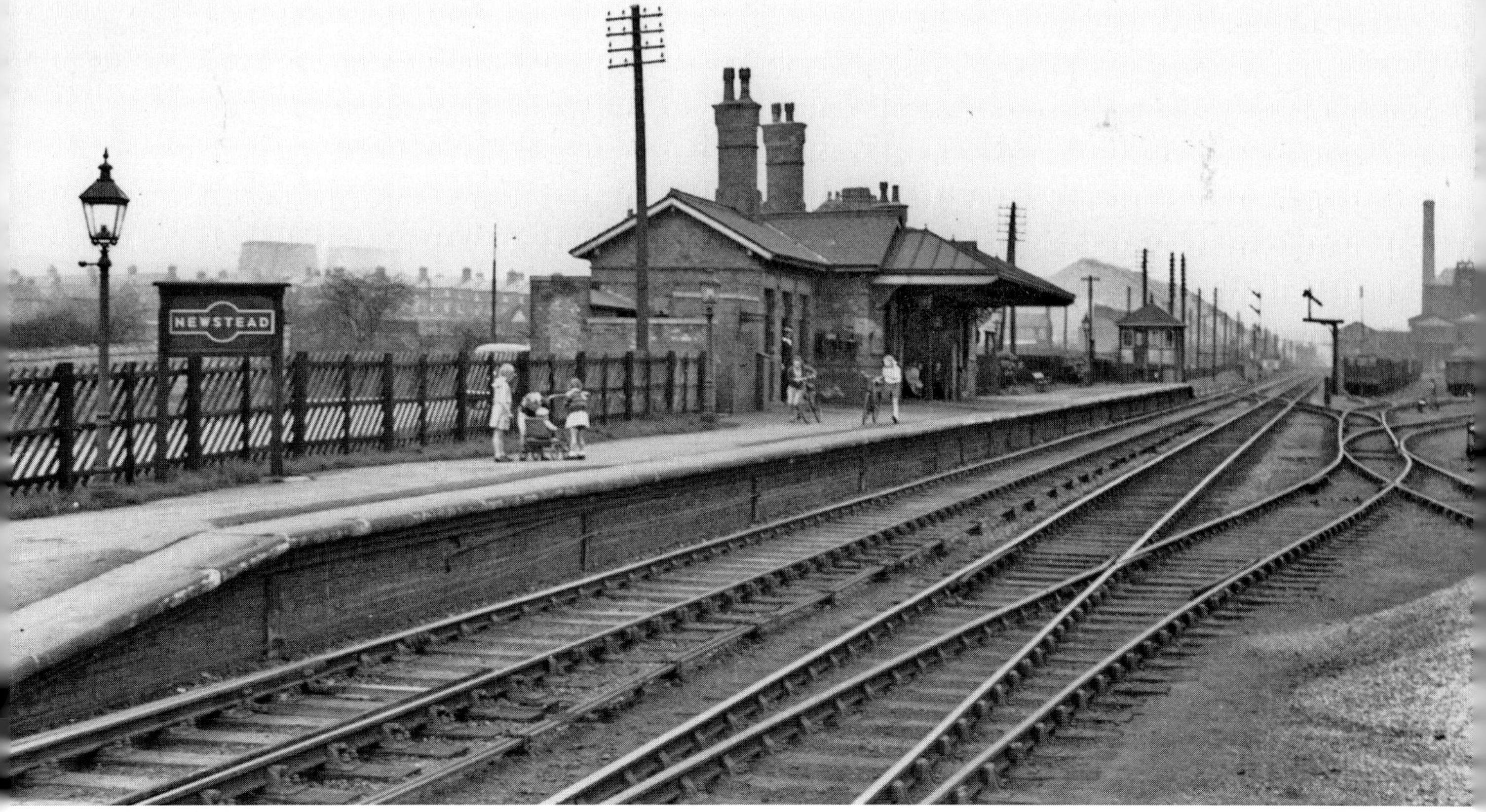

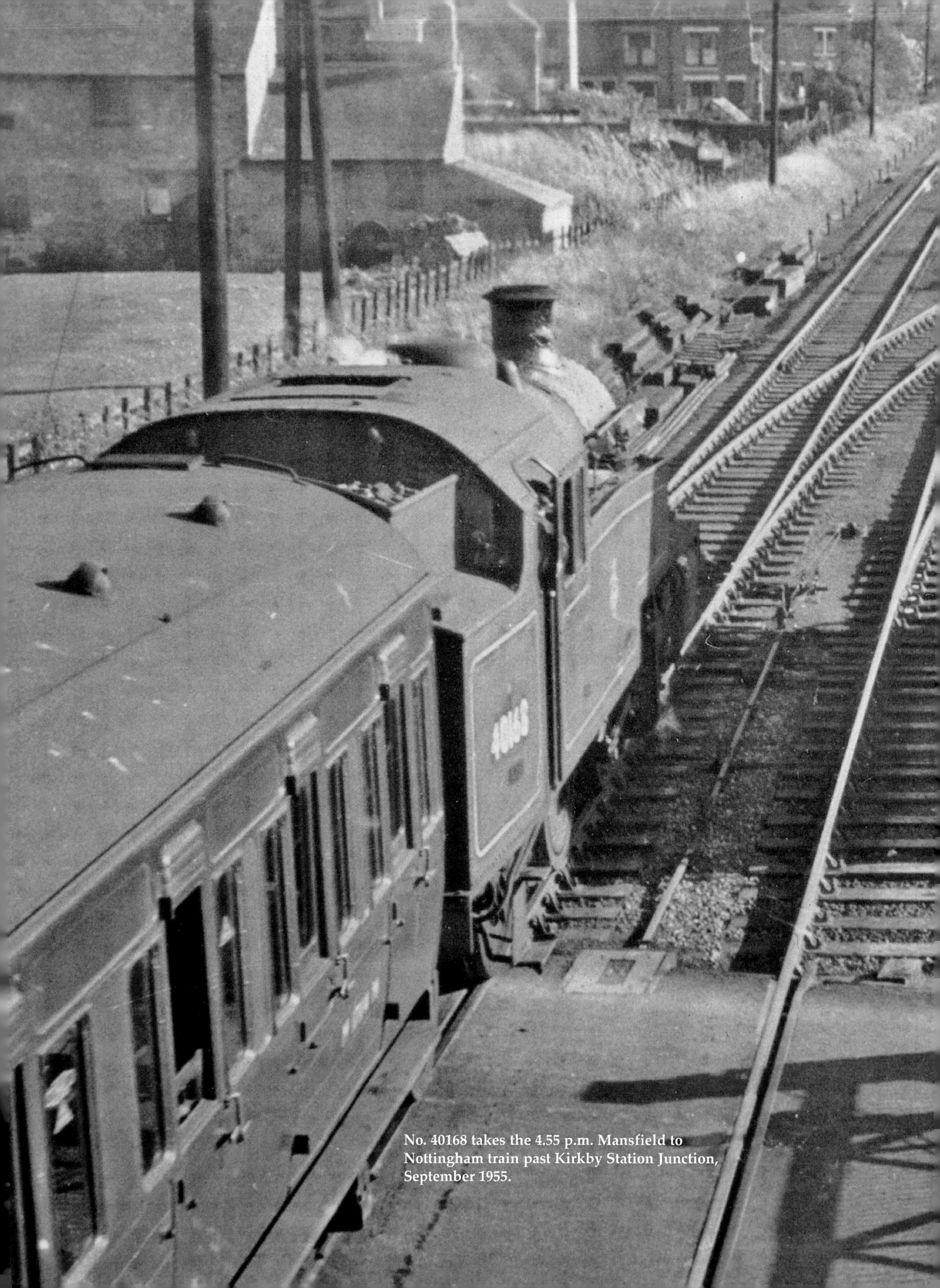

No. 40168 takes the 4.55 p.m. Mansfield to Nottingham train past Kirkby Station Junction, September 1955.

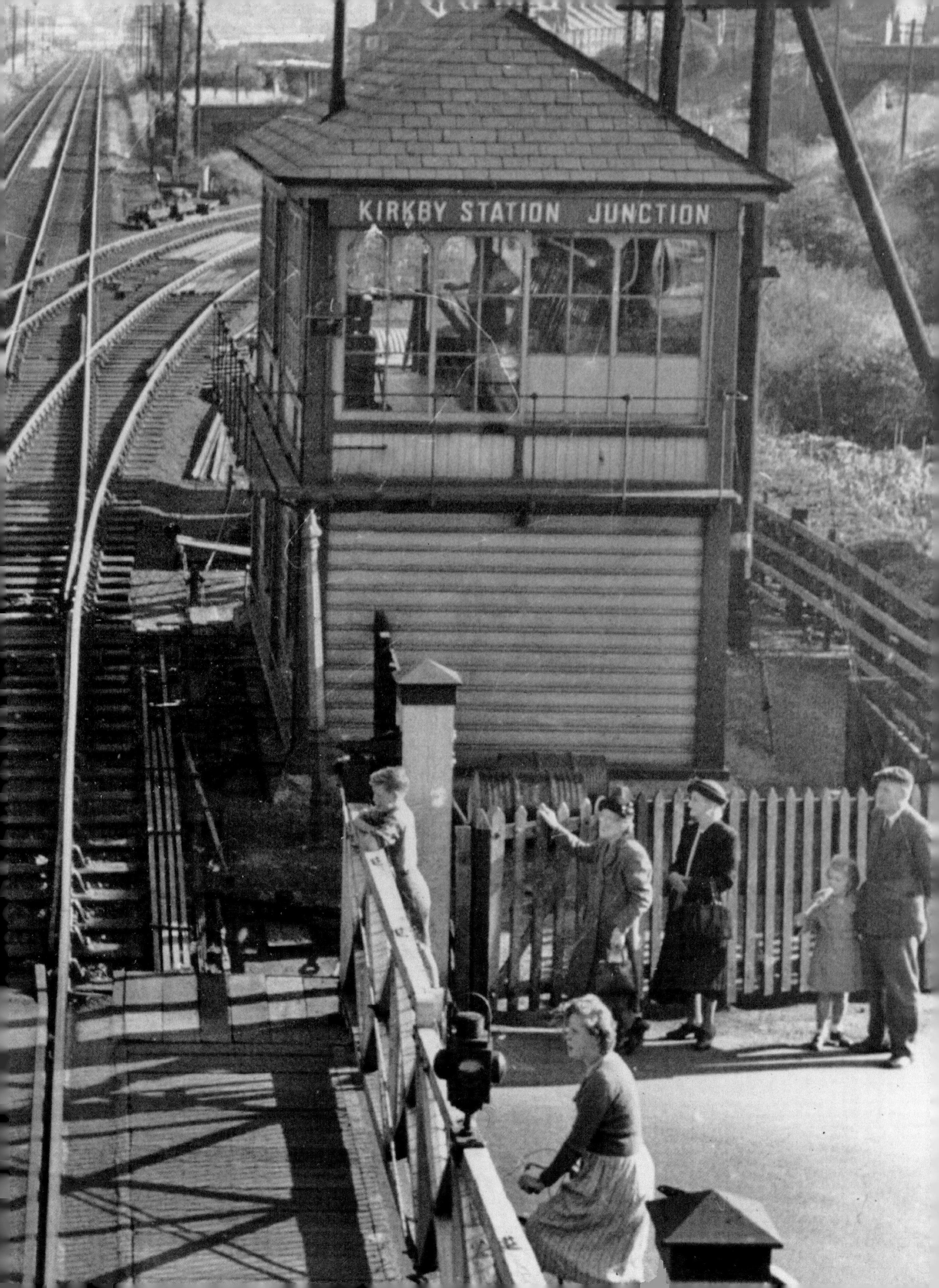
KIRKBY STATION JUNCTION

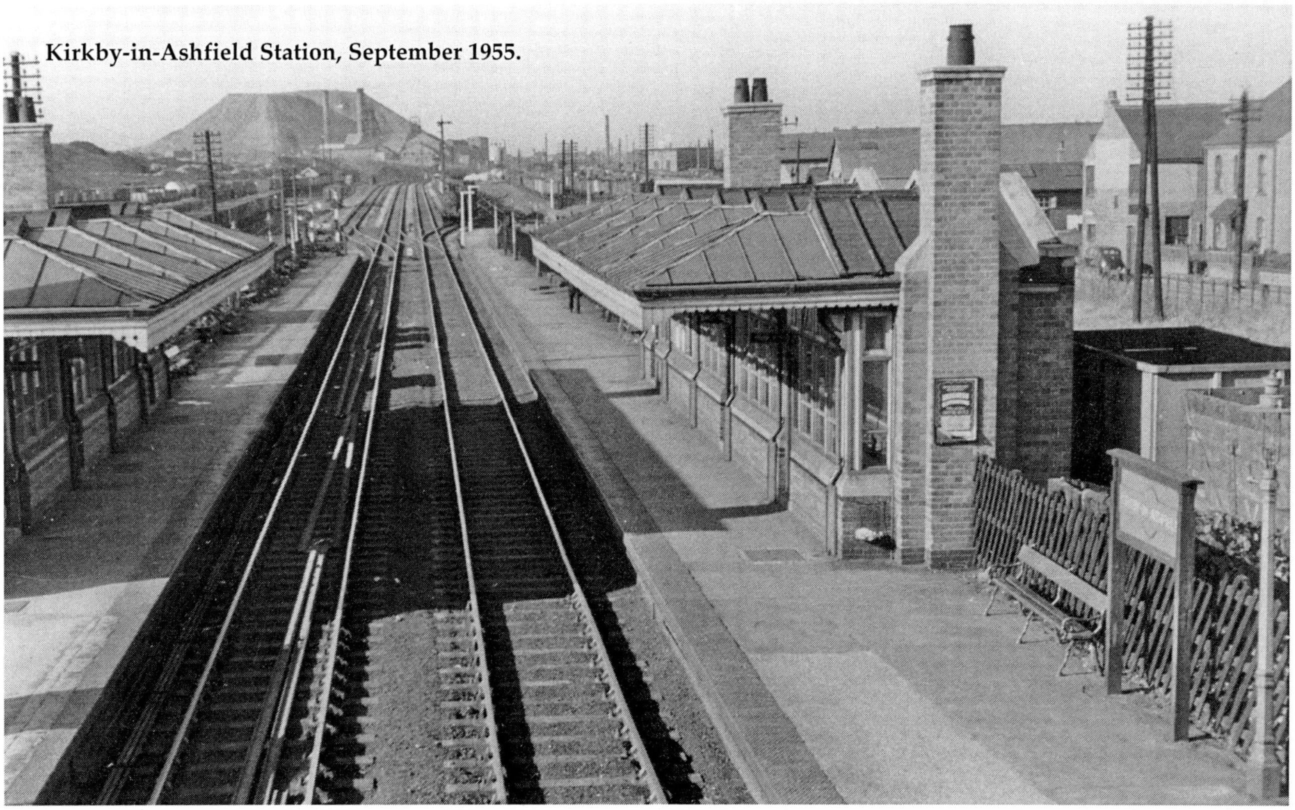

Kirkby-in-Ashfield Station, September 1955.

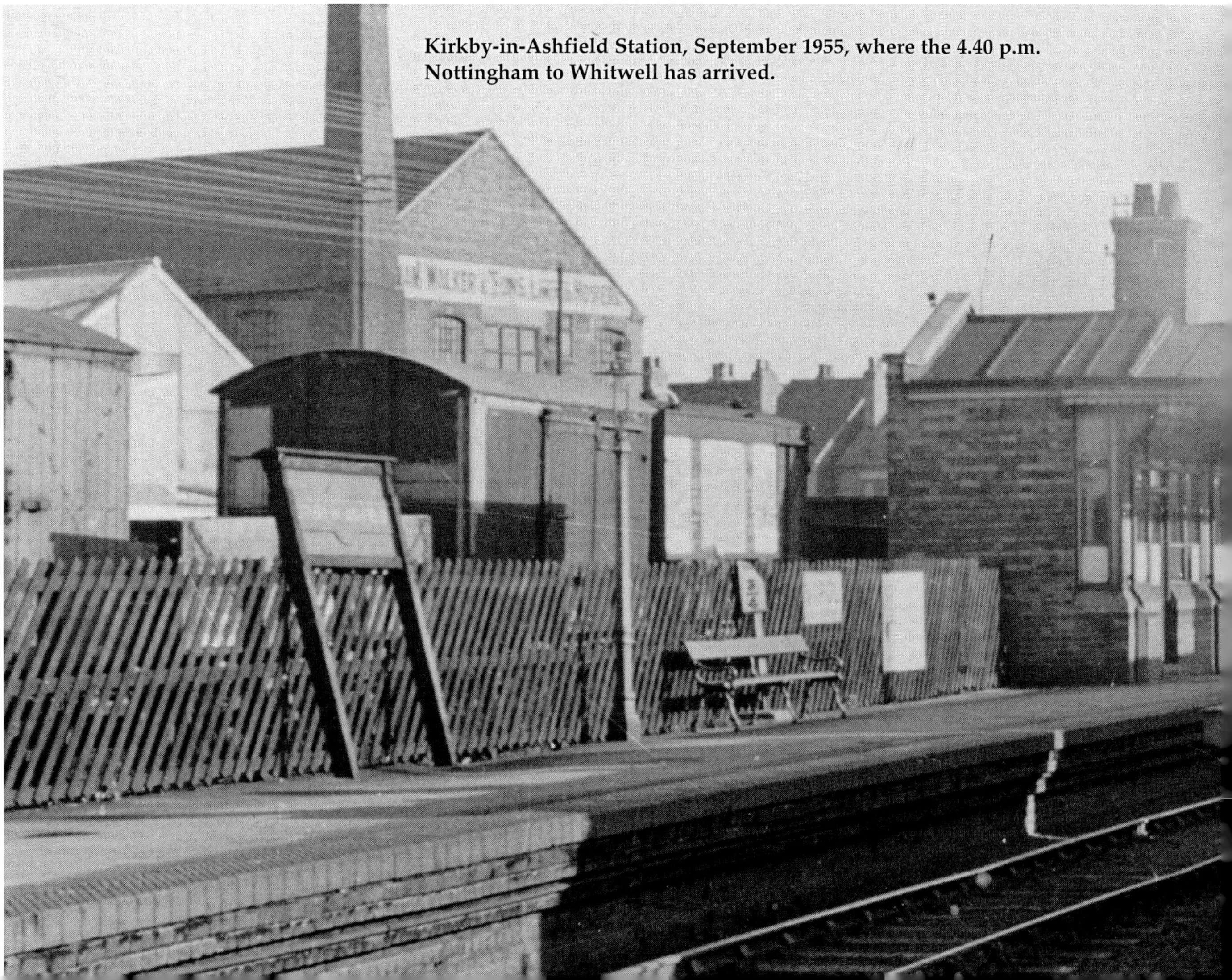

Kirkby-in-Ashfield Station, September 1955, where the 4.40 p.m. Nottingham to Whitwell has arrived.

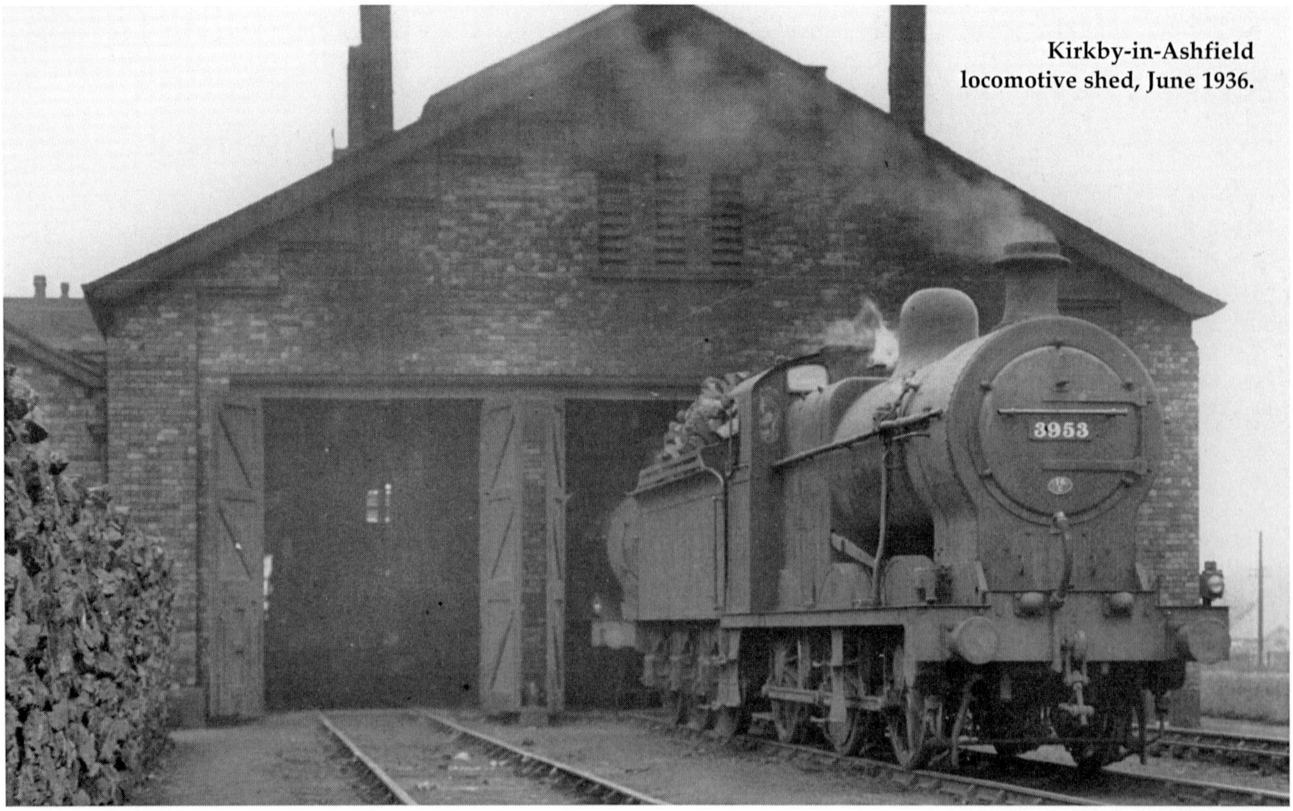


Kirkby-in-Ashfield
locomotive shed, June 1936.

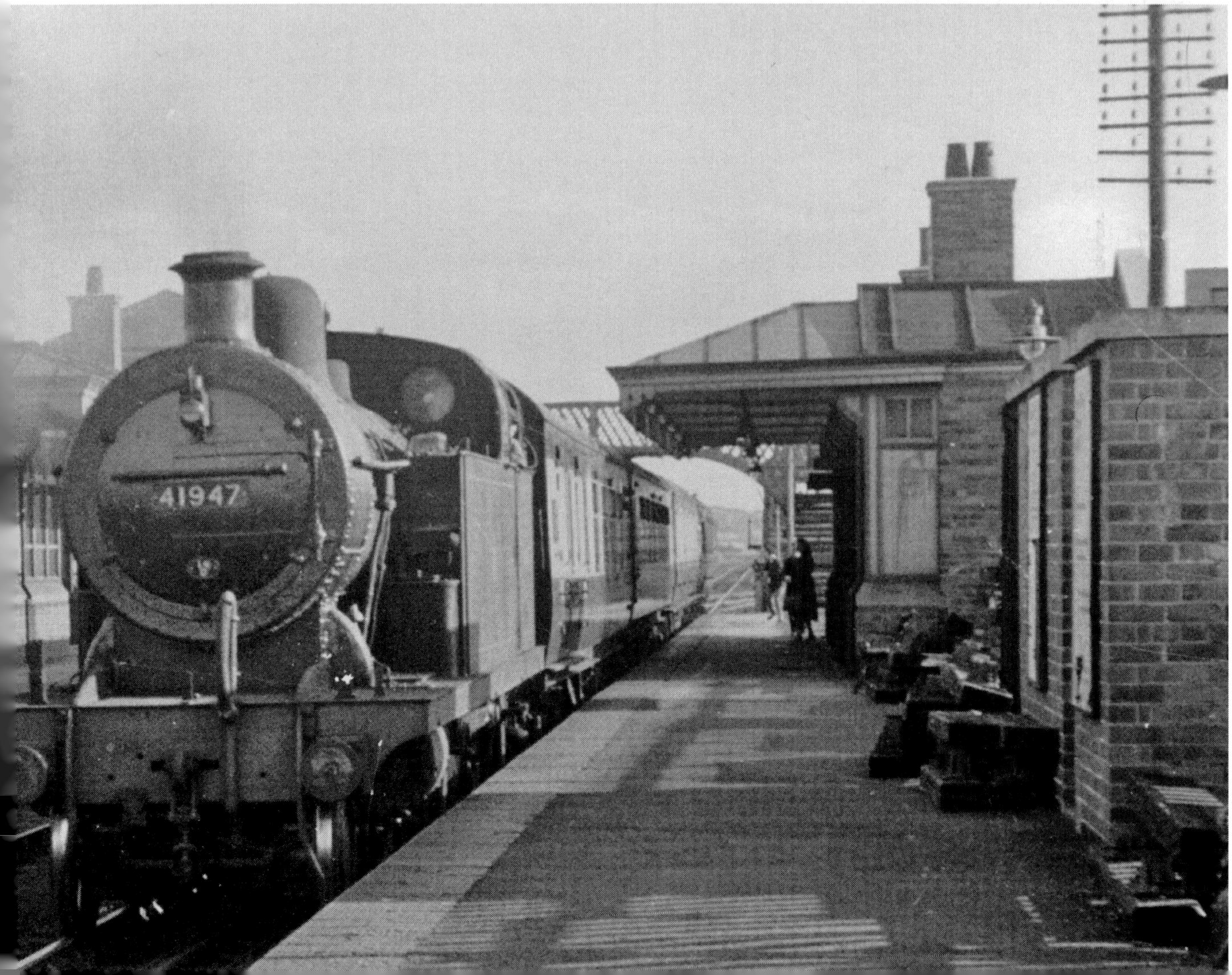

# Great Northern and London & North Western Joint Lines

## Harby – Bottesford – Newark *

*Passenger services withdrawn* see text
*Length* $15\frac{1}{2}$ miles
*Original owning company* Great Northern and London & North Western railways (south of Bottesford); Great Northern Railway (Bottesford – Newark)

| *Stations closed* | *Date of closure* |
| --- | --- |
| Cotham ** | 11 September 1939 |

* The closed station on this line that was in Leicestershire was Redmile.
** Closed between 2 April 1917 and 1 April 1919.

## Saxondale Junction – Melton Mowbray *

*Passenger services withdrawn* 7 December 1953
*Length* $15\frac{3}{4}$ miles
*Original owning company* Great Northern and London & North Western railways (jointly)

| *Stations closed* | *Date of closure* |
| --- | --- |
| Bingham Road | 2 July 1951 |
| Barnstone | 7 December 1953 |

* Closed stations on this line that were in Leicestershire were Harby & Stathern, Long Clawson & Hose, Scalford and Melton Mowbray.

Generally, it might be thought that the London & North Western and Great Northern railways were rivals and, in terms of their parts in the west and east coast main lines, this was so. But even the fiercest of rivals may make an alliance against a common adversary and this was the case in Leicestershire and Nottinghamshire when faced with the early dominance of the Midland Railway. The London & North Western wanted to gain access to the east midlands and did so by allying itself to the Great Northern over a long and straggling line running through some very sparsely populated uplands in Northamptonshire and Leicestershire from Northampton, through Market Harborough and Melton Mowbray to the Great Northern's Nottingham – Grantham line at Saxondale Junction. From there LNWR trains exercised running powers over the GN into Nottingham London Road Low Level Station, a splendid, though rather isolated, structure hard by the Midland's line to Lincoln: there was also an LNWR goods depot in Manvers Street, Nottingham.

The line opened in sections, that from Newark to Marefield Junction, south of John-o'-Gaunt in Leicestershire, being authorised in 1872 and the joint line two years later. The LNWR managed not only to gain access to Nottingham, but also Newark, from whence it exercised some running powers northwards over the East Coast Main Line. In truth it probably gained less than it hoped from all this effort, never making a major inroad into the Nottinghamshire coalfield and finding fairly sparse receipts from the thinly populated Leicestershire uplands. However, iron ore was quarried around Eastwell and Waltham-on-the-Wolds, at the end of a small network of mineral lines diverging from the 'main' joint line at Harby. Passenger traffic north of Bottesford ceased in the first weeks of the Second World War, followed by London Road Low Level Station in 1944, thereafter the few trains over the line being run from Victoria. Passenger traffic ceased completely in 1953 and goods in 1962.

A surprising amount of the line still exists, particularly in Leicestershire, the bridges, viaducts and stations remaining half a century after closure. London Road Low Level Station not only survives but has been converted to other uses and is a remaining railway landmark in the city.

Bingham Road Station, *c.* 1920.

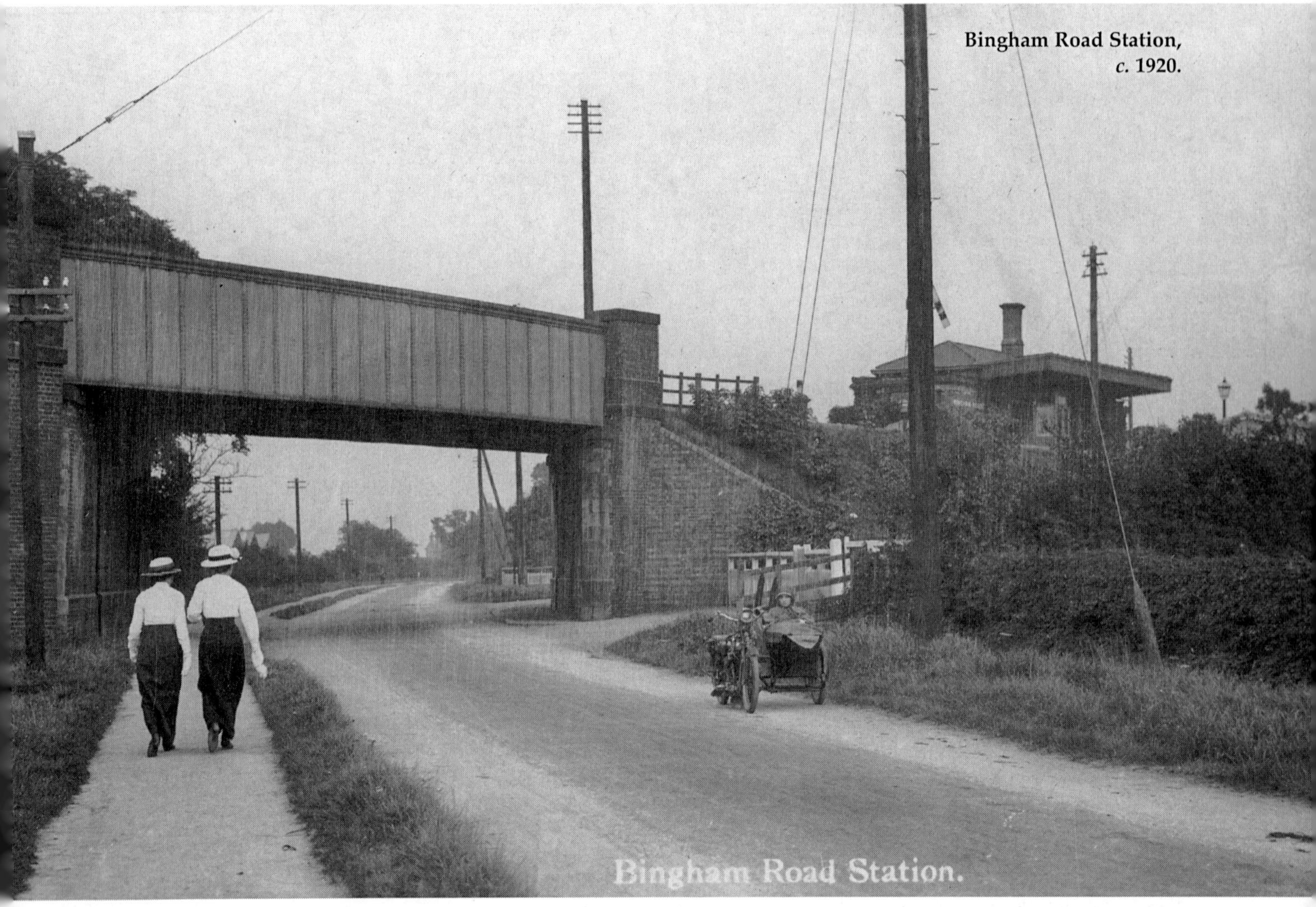


Barnstone Station.

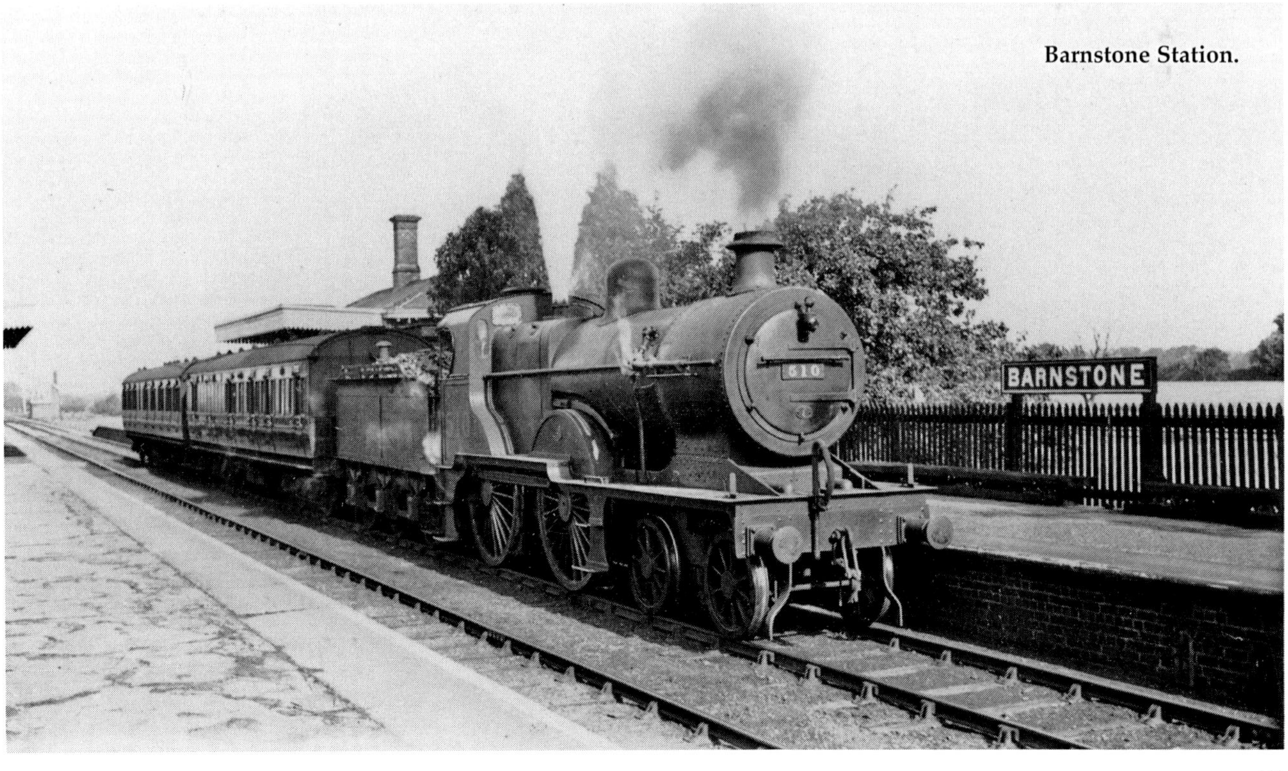

# Stations Closed on Lines Still Open to Passenger Services
## Gainsborough – Worksop

| | |
|---|---|
| *Original owning company* | Manchester, Sheffield & Lincolnshire Railway (Great Central after 1899) |

| *Stations closed* | *Date of closure* |
|---|---|
| Sturton | 2 February 1959 |
| Checker House | 14 September 1931 |

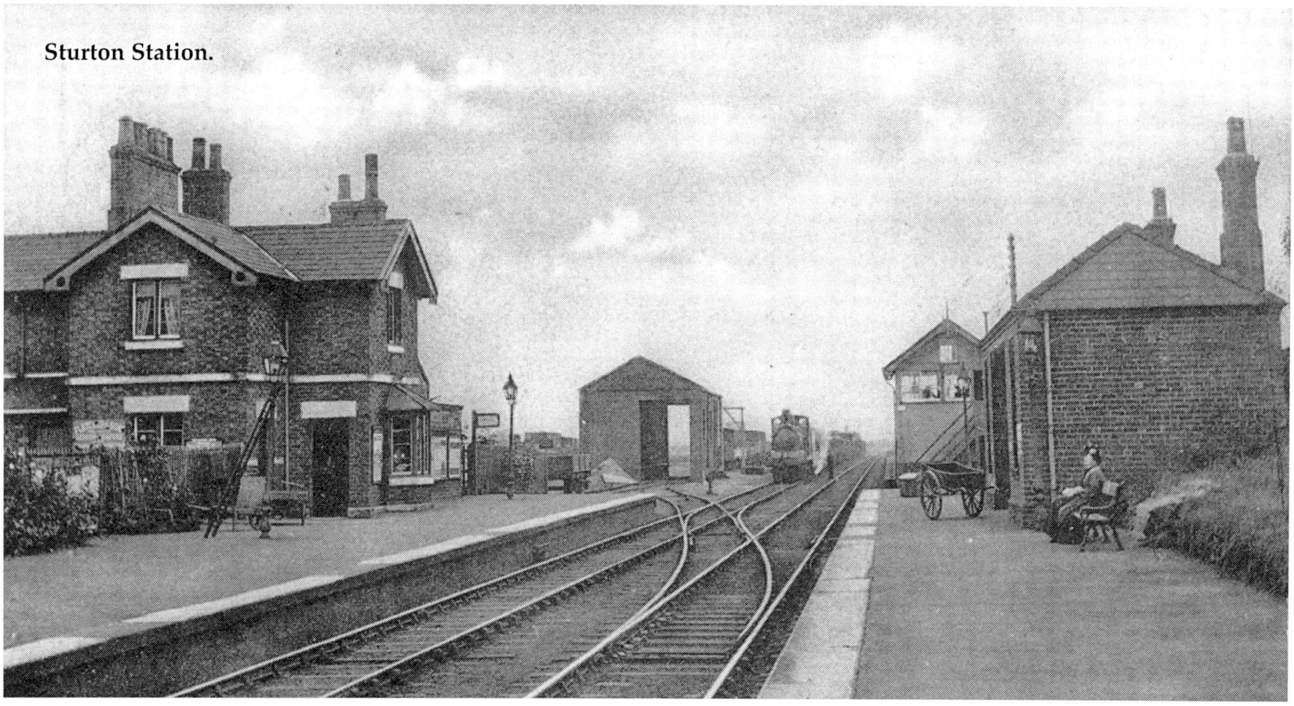

**Sturton Station.**

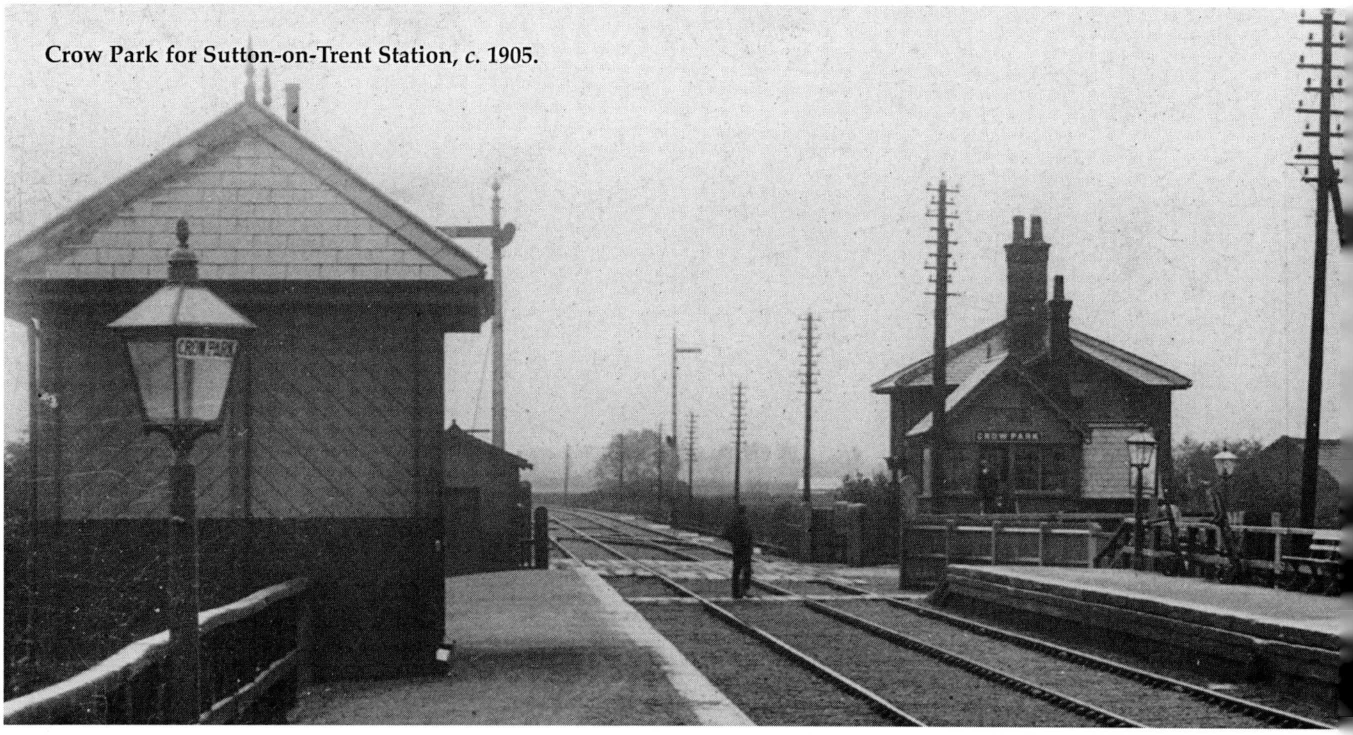


**Crow Park for Sutton-on-Trent Station, *c.* 1905.**

# Newark – Retford

| | |
|---|---|
| *Original owning company* | Great Northern Railway |
| *Stations closed* | *Date of closure* |
| Carlton-on-Trent * | 2 March 1953 |
| Crow Park for Sutton-on-Trent ** | 6 October 1958 |
| Dukeries Junction *** | 6 March 1950 |
| Tuxford North **** | 4 July 1955 |
| Barnby Moor & Sutton ***** | 7 November 1949 |
| Ranskill | 6 October 1958 |
| Scrooby | 14 September 1931 |

* Originally named Carlton until 1 March 1881.
** Originally named Crow Park until 1904.
*** The station was on two levels, the lower one on the East Coast line and the upper on the Lancashire, Derbyshire & East Coast line.
**** Originally named Tuxford until 1 July 1923.
***** Originally named Sutton and Barnby Moor until September 1850, then named Sutton until 16 November 1909.

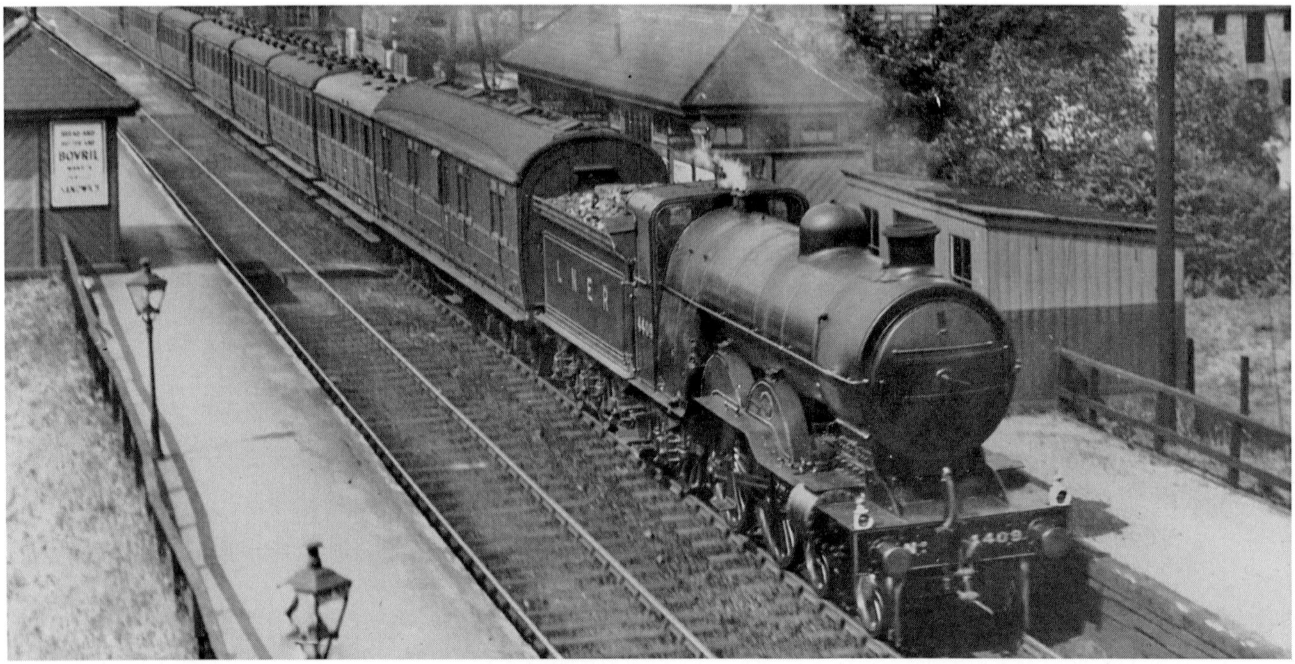


**Crow Park for Sutton-on-Trent Station, May 1935.**

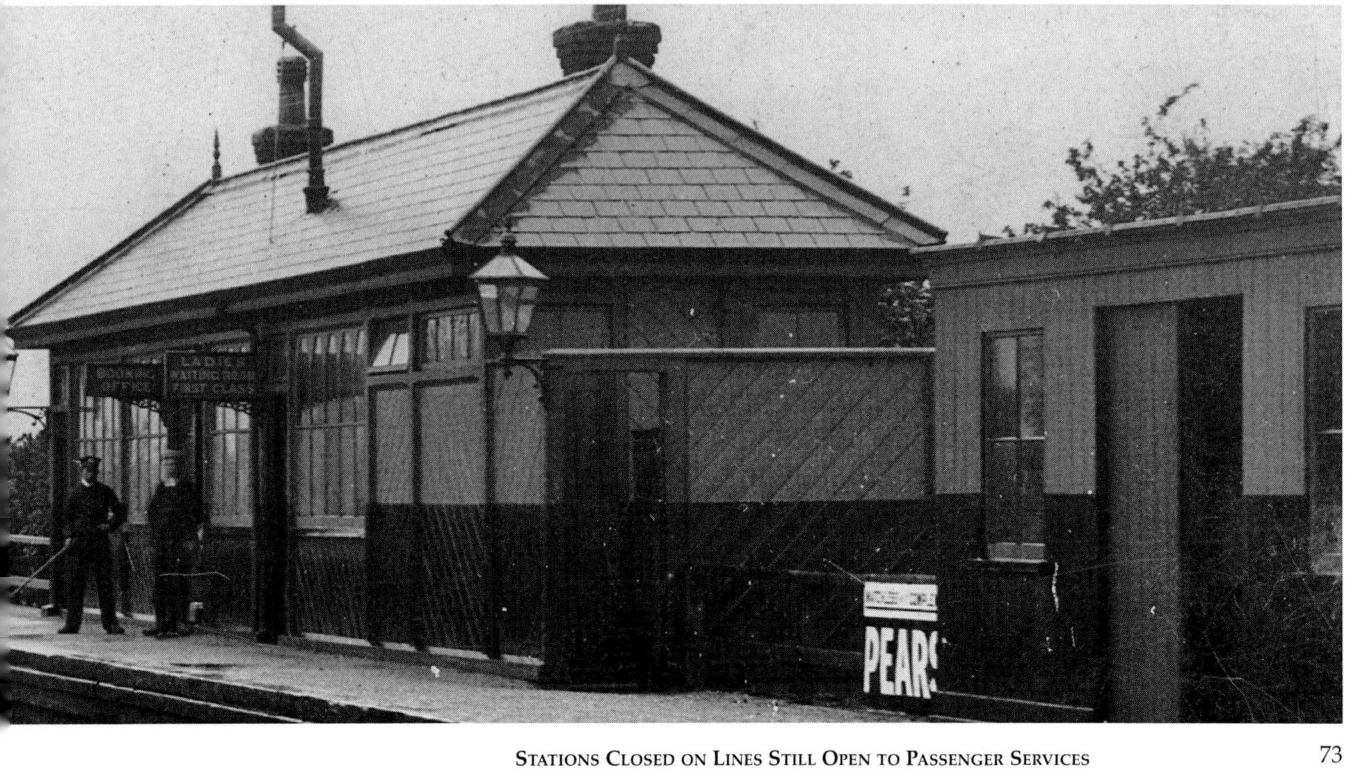

Dukeries Junction upper and lower stations, May 1946.

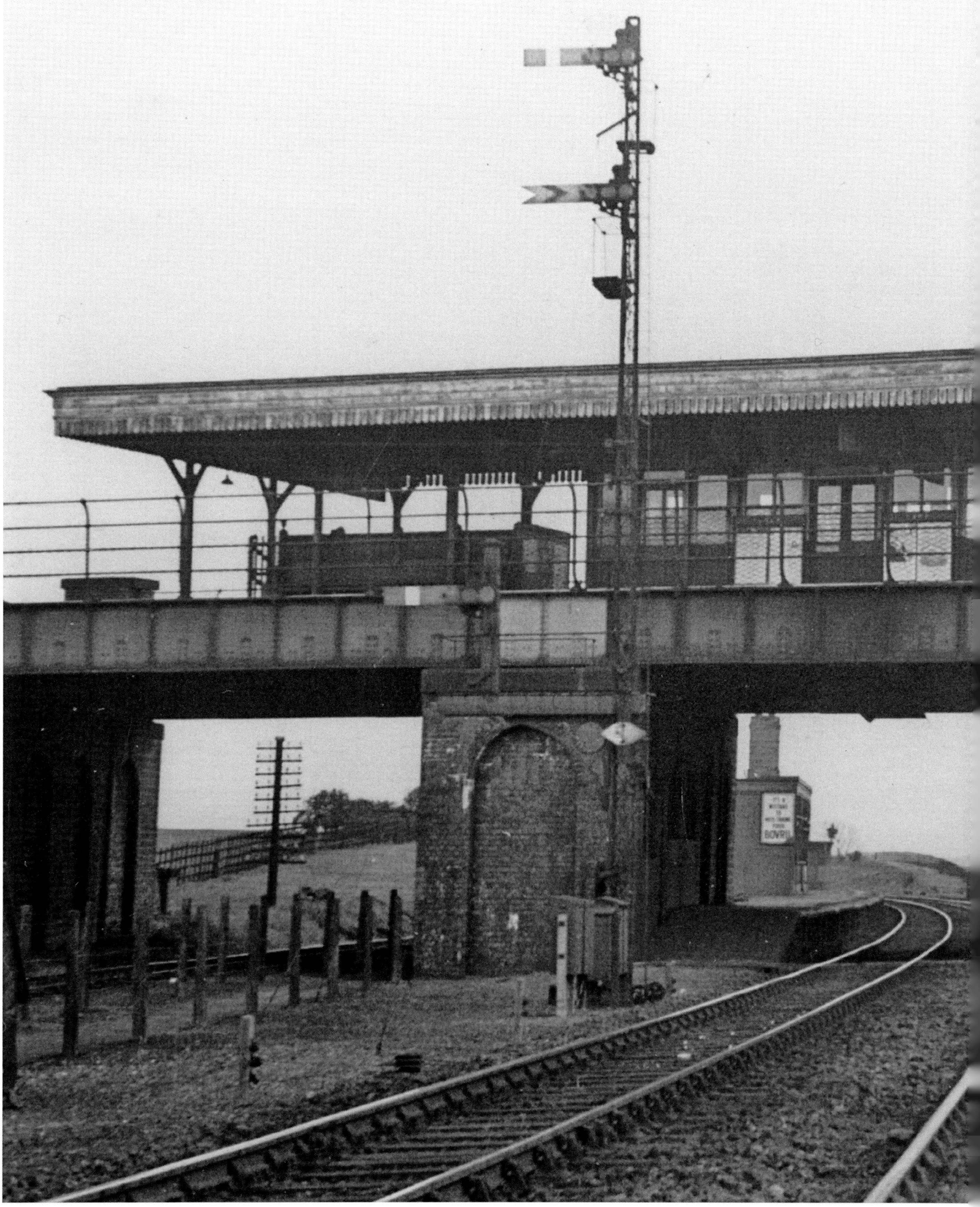

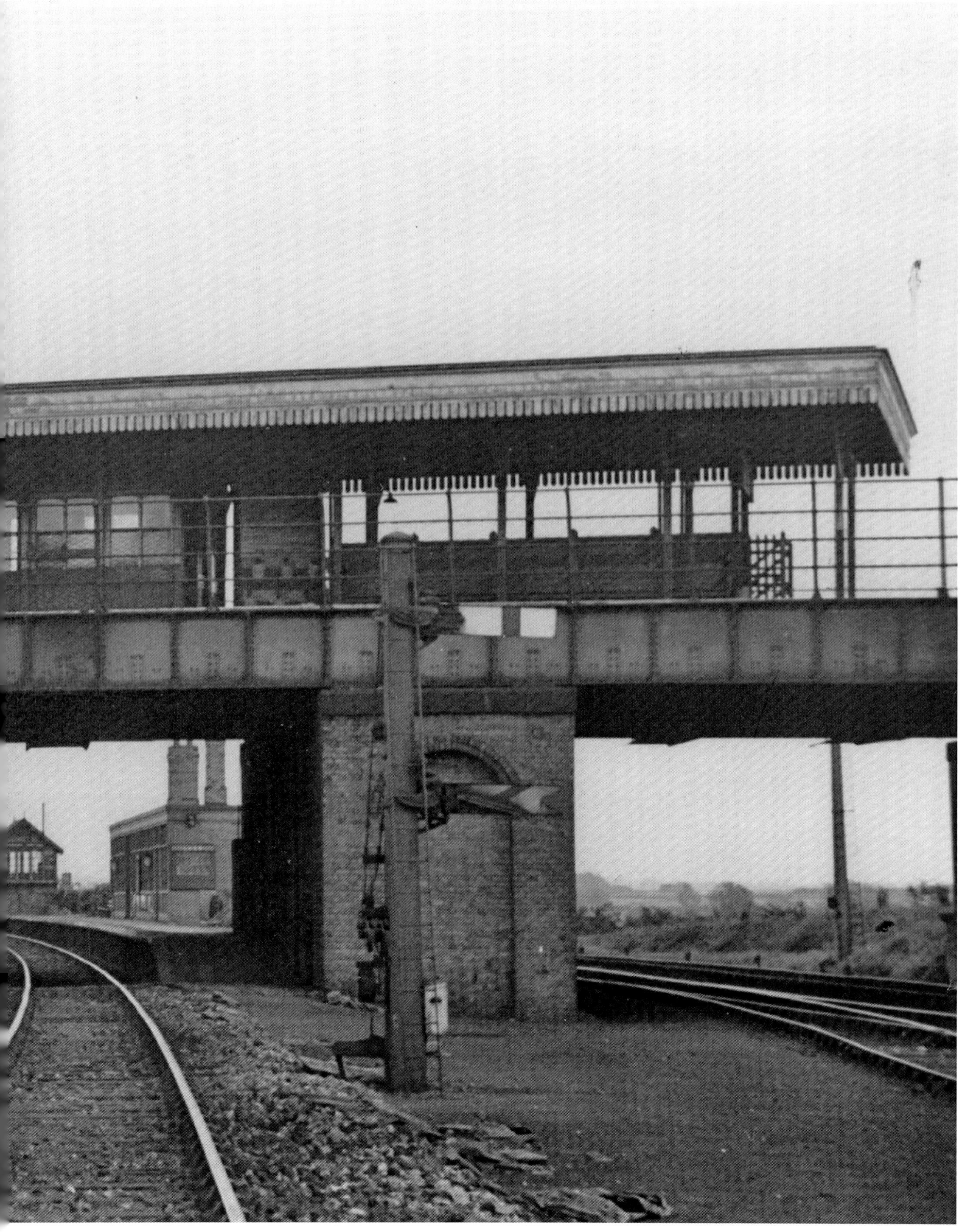

The lower level of Dukeries Junction Station on the Great Northern line, May 1946.

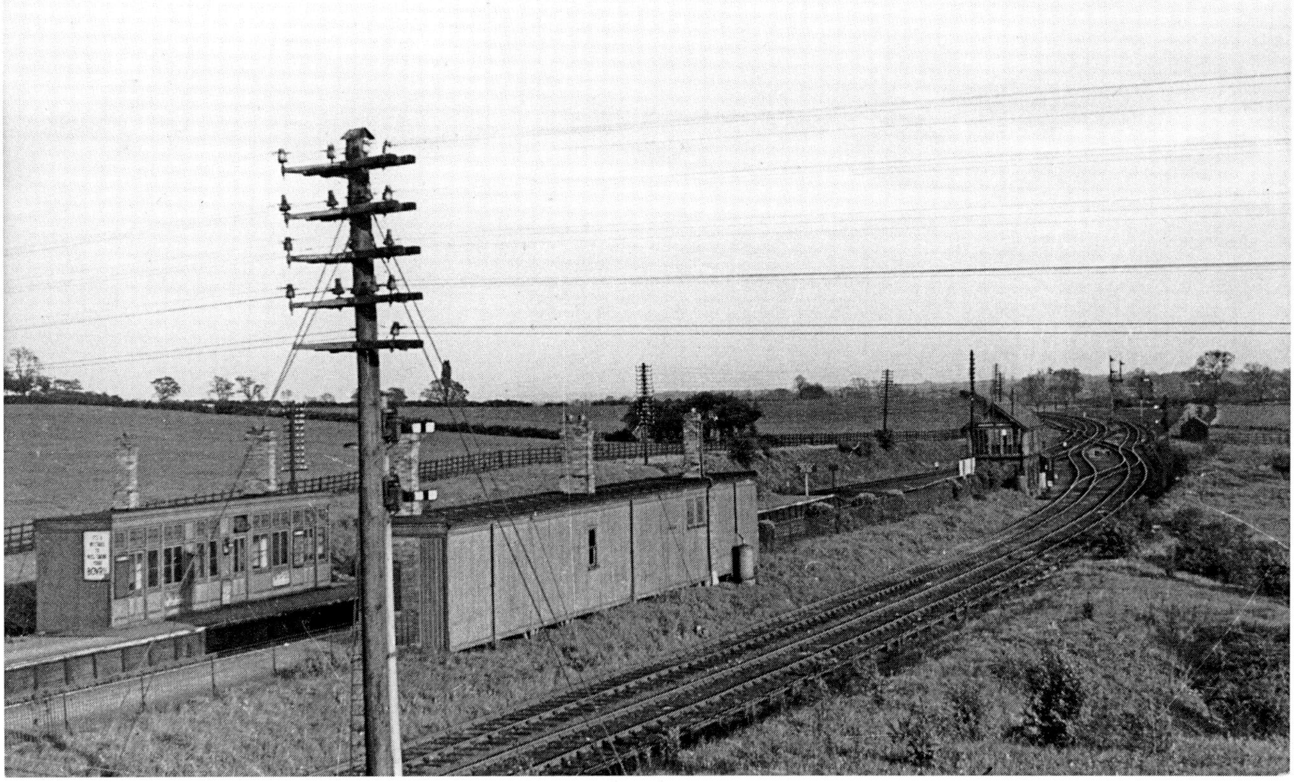

Tuxford North Station, *c.* 1900.

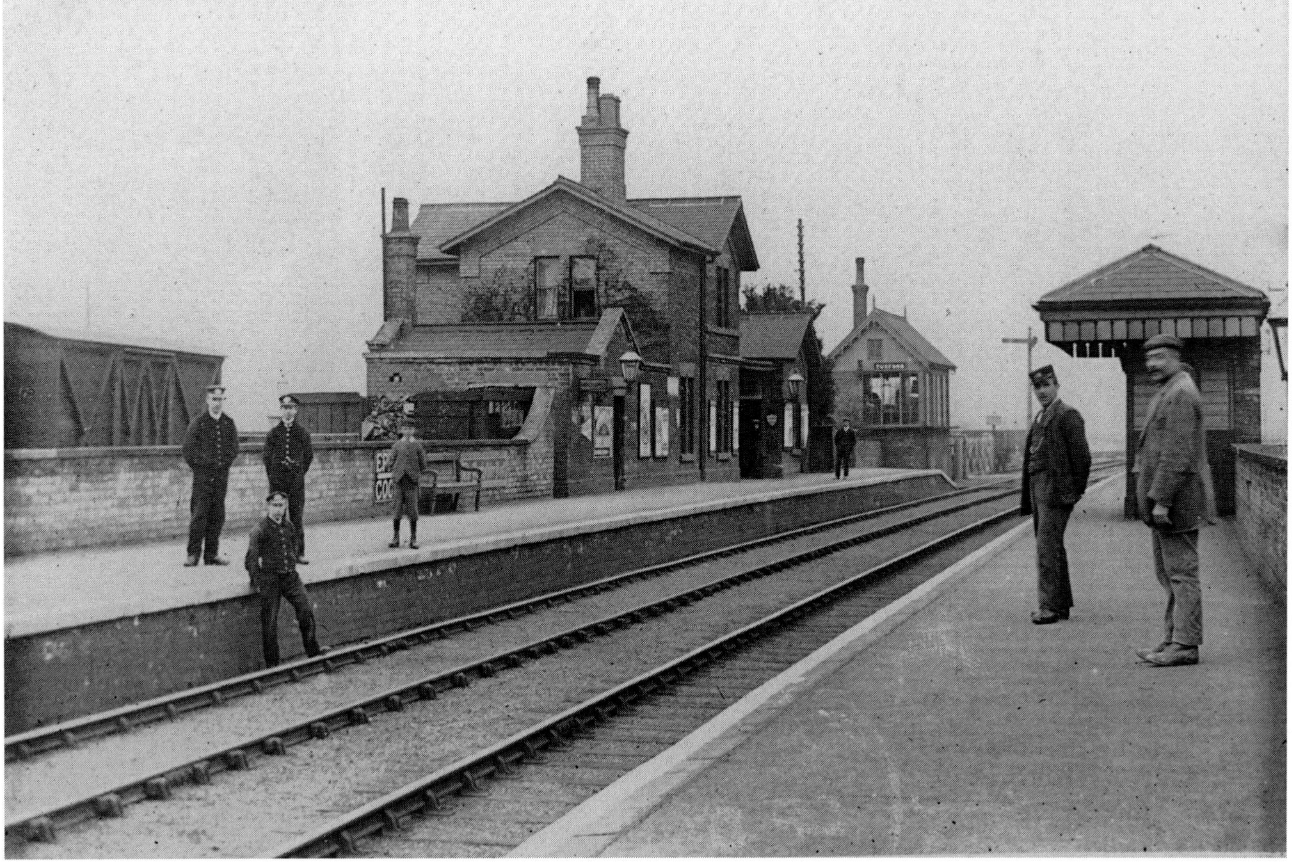

# Nottingham – Grantham

| *Original owning company* | Great Northern Railway |
| --- | --- |

| *Stations closed* | *Date of closure* |
| --- | --- |
| Nottingham London Road High Level * | 3 July 1967 |
| Nottingham London Road Low Level ** | 22 May 1944 |
| Nottingham Racecourse ** | 8 December 1959 |
| Sedgebrook *** | 2 July 1956 |

* Traffic subsequently diverted to use the Midland station.
** Originally named Nottingham London Road until 15 March 1899.
** Open for race traffic only.
*** Named Sedgbrook between April 1878 and January 1888.

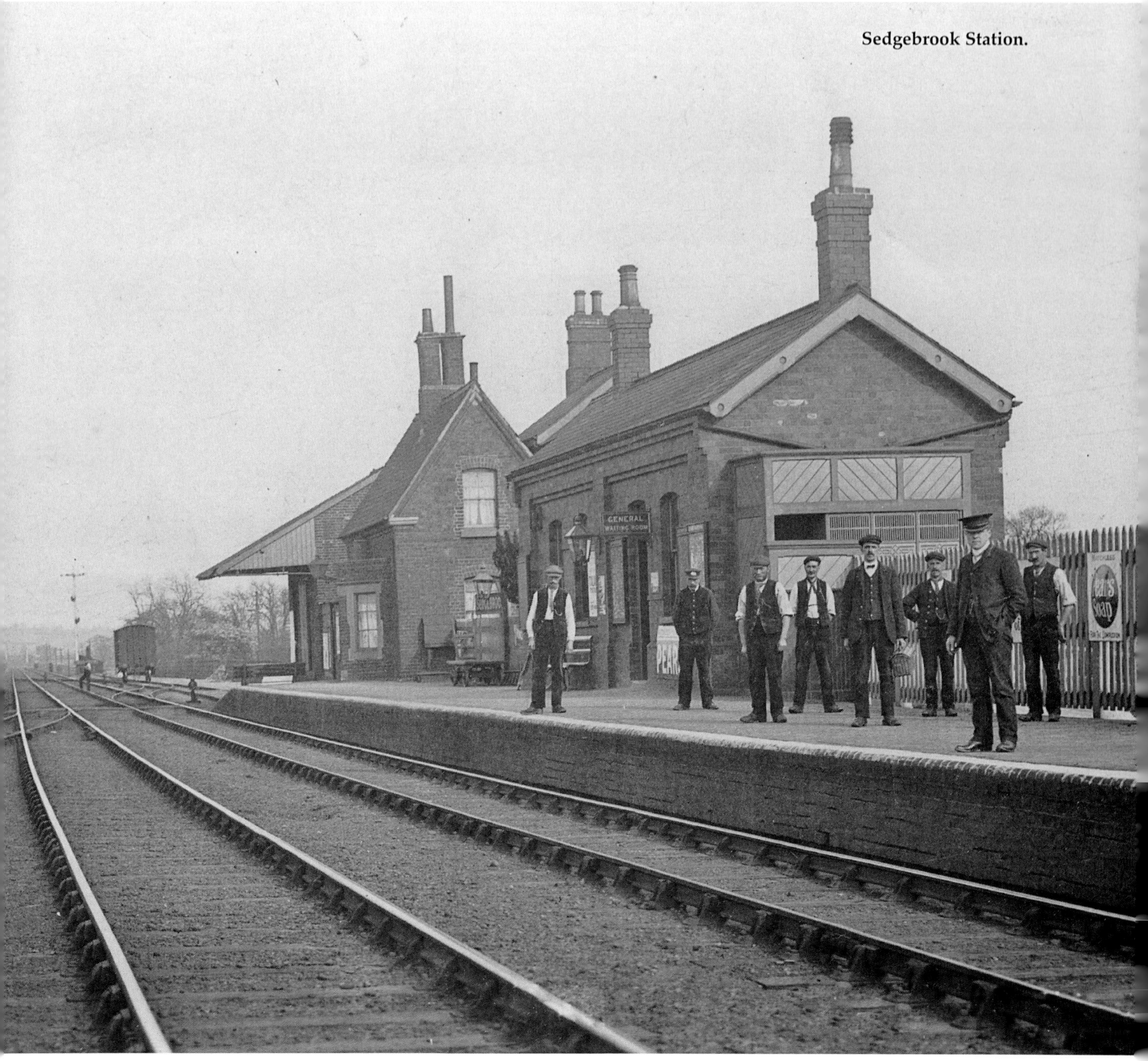


**Sedgebrook Station.**

# Nottingham – Chesterfield: Erewash Valley line

*Original owning company* Midland Railway

| *Stations closed* | *Date of closure* |
|---|---|
| Stapleford & Sandiacre * | 2 January 1967 |
| Trowell | 2 January 1967 |
| Ilkeston Junction & Cossall ** | 2 January 1967 |
| Pye Bridge *** | 2 January 1967 |

* Originally named Sandiacre & Stapleford until October 1884.
** Originally named Ilkeston until 1 July 1879, then named Ilkeston Junction until 1 December 1890.
*** Originally named Pye Bridge for Alfreton until 1 May 1862.

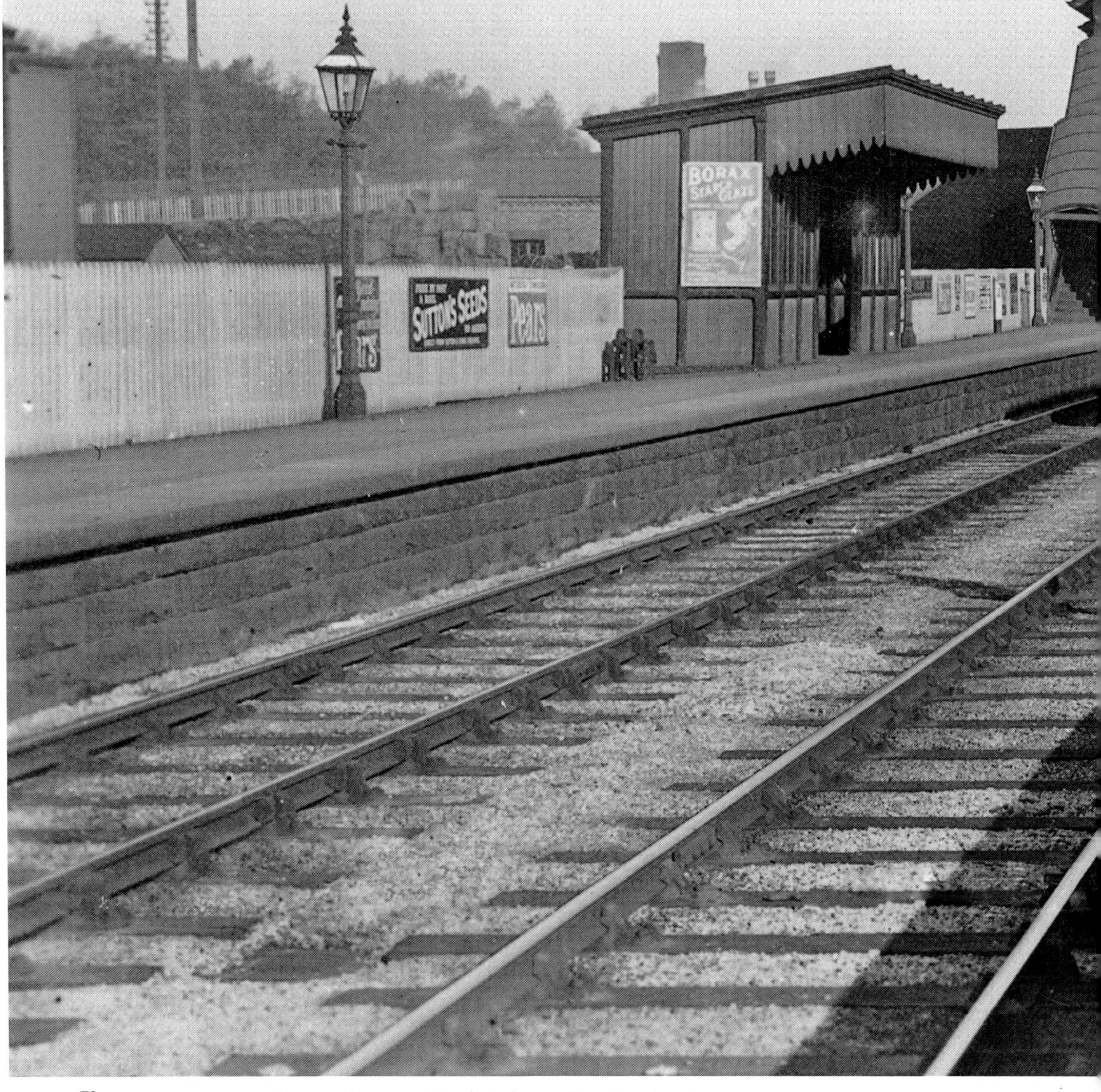

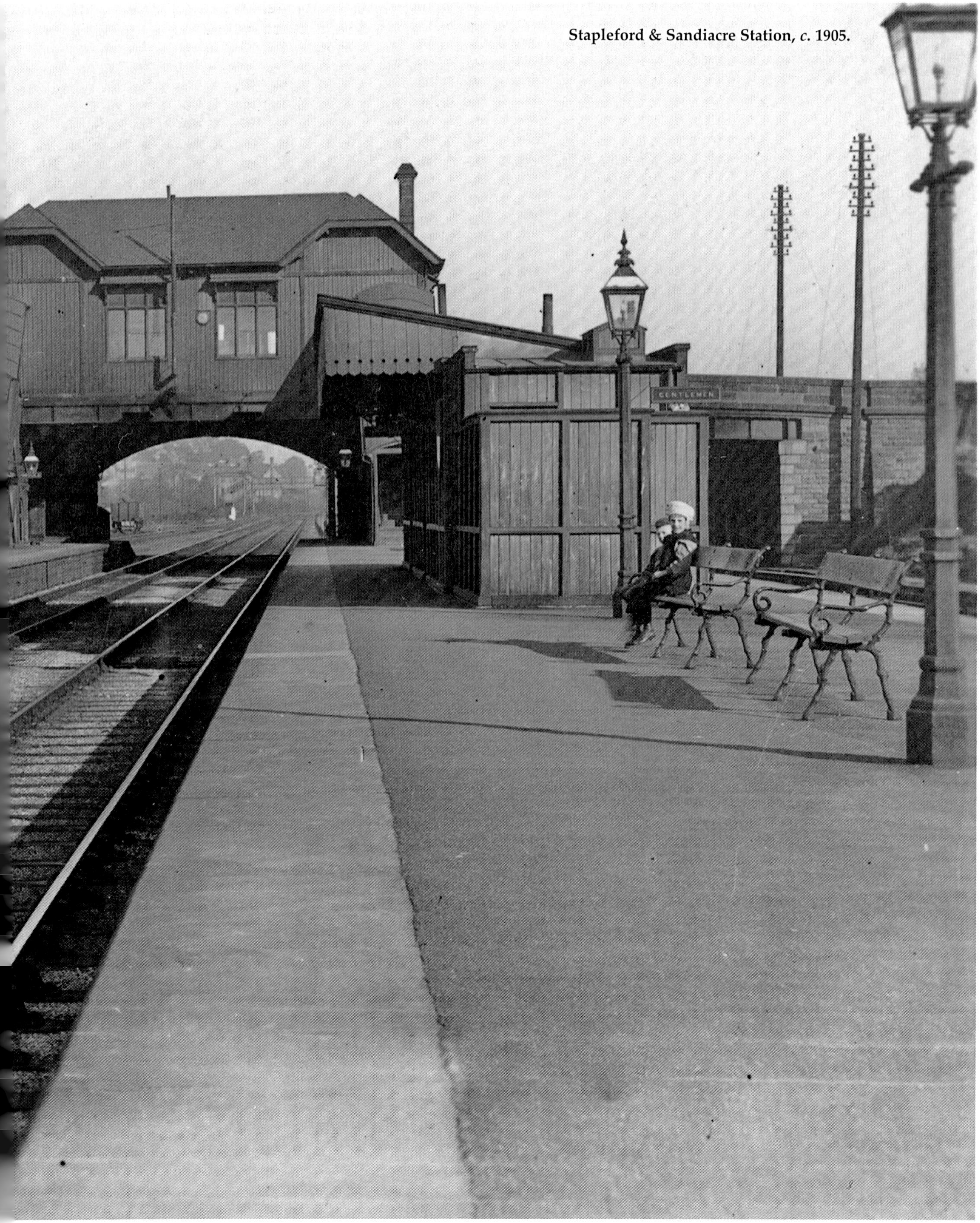

Stapleford & Sandiacre Station, *c.* 1905.

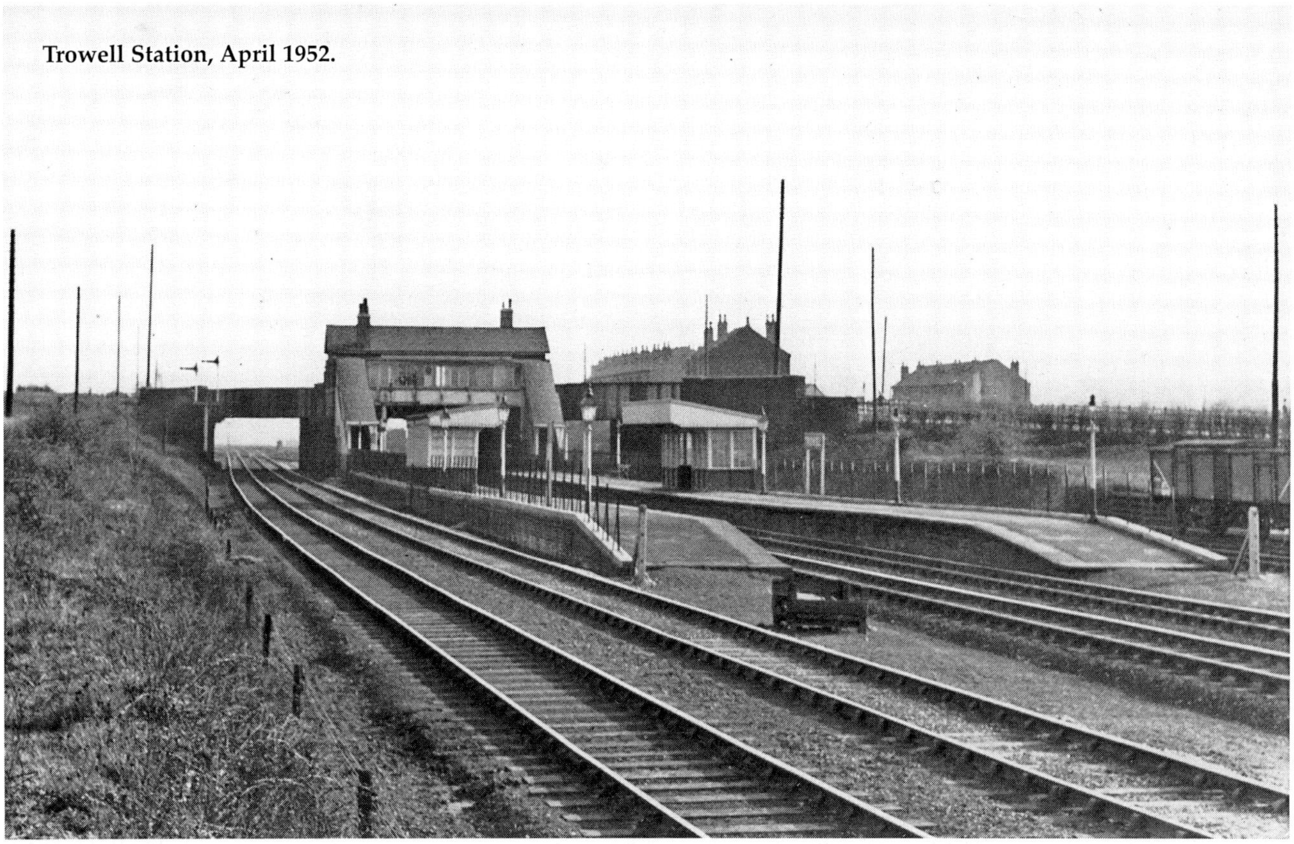
Trowell Station, April 1952.

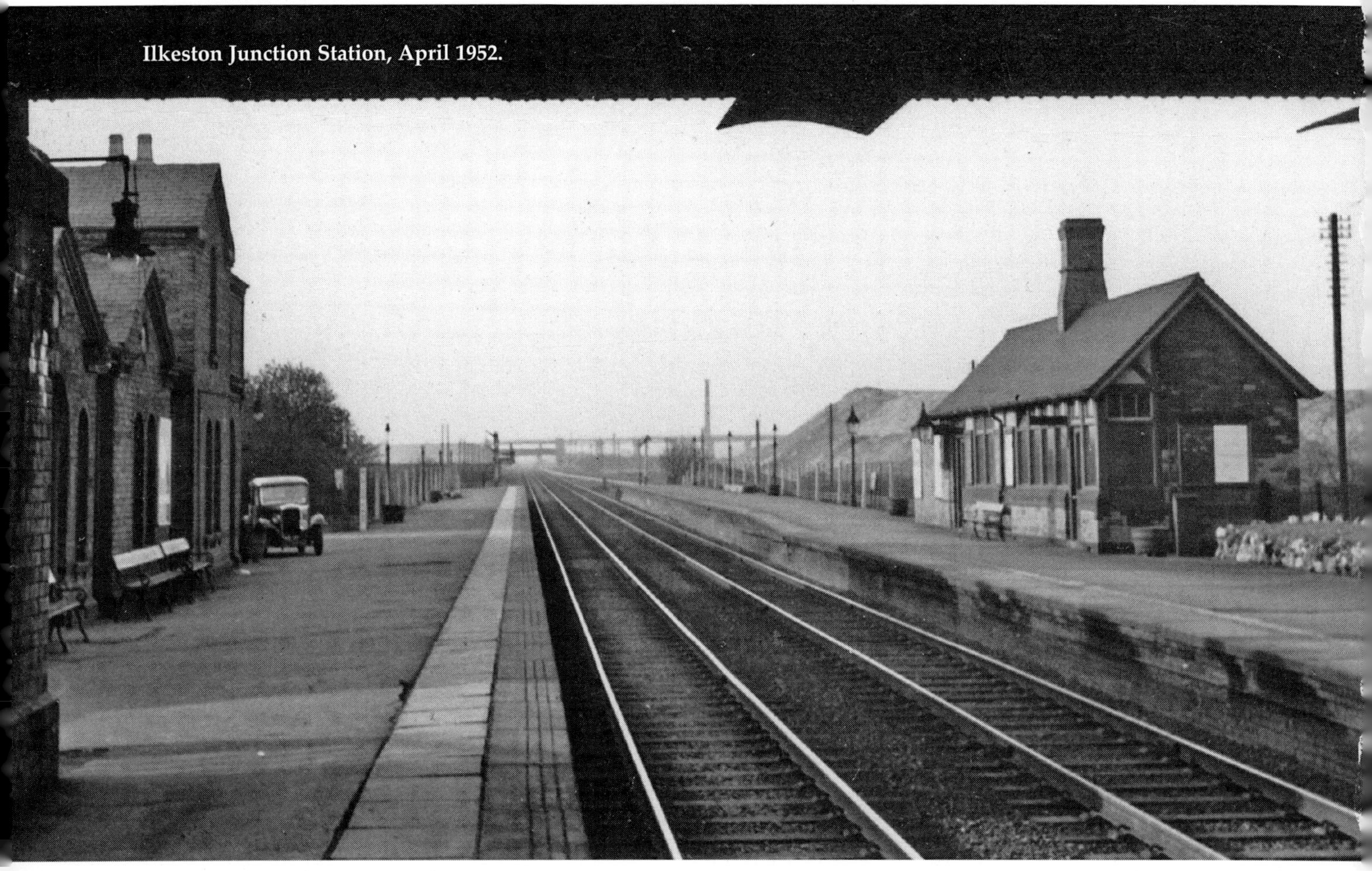
Ilkeston Junction Station, April 1952.